# MOUSEPADS, SHOE LEATHER, AND HOPE

## Lessons from the Howard Dean Campaign for the Future of Internet Politics

ZEPHYR TEACHOUT AND THOMAS STREETER ET AL.

Paradigm Publishers

Boulder • London

Copyright © 2008 by Paradigm Publishers

Published in the United States by Paradigm Publishers, 3360 Mitchell Lane Suite E, Boulder, Colorado 80301 USA.

Paradigm Publishers is the trade name of Birkenkamp & Company, LLC, Dean Birkenkamp, President and Publisher.

Library of Congress Cataloging-in-Publication Data

Mousepads, shoe leather, and hope: lessons from the Howard Dean campaign for the future of
    Internet politics / Zephyr Teachout and Thomas Streeter ... [et al.].
       p. cm. — (Media and power)
    Includes bibliographical references and index.
    ISBN 978-1-59451-484-5 (hc) — ISBN 978-1-59451-485-2 (pbk)  1. Internet in political
campaigns—United States.  2. Political campaigns—United States.  3. Internet—Political
aspects.  4.  Dean, Howard, 1948–  I. Teachout, Zephyr.
    JK2281.M68 2008
    324.7'3—dc22

                                                                        2007030211

Printed and bound in the United States of America on acid-free paper that meets the standards of the American National Standard for Permanence of Paper for Printed Library Materials.

Designed and Typeset by Straight Creek Bookmakers.

11   10   09   08   07      1   2   3   4   5

# Contents

### PART III: Reflections

# I
# Overviews

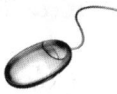

# 1

# Introduction

## *Redefining the Possible*

### *Thomas Streeter*

Technologies, as a rule, have an effect only in particular contexts. China had both moveable type and gunpowder by roughly A.D. 1050, but those technologies did not begin to have their transformative social effects until four centuries later, in the then-ragged and backward countries of Europe. Efforts to use the Internet for political purposes began at least as early as 1996, but it was not until the Dean campaign seven years later that its potential role in politics became undeniable and profound.

This book is a contribution to understanding the role of the Internet in the Dean campaign *in context*. The Internet clearly mattered in Howard Dean's bid to become the Democratic nominee for U.S. president in 2003 and 2004, but how and why it did so is an as-yet-unsettled question. Many claims have been made, of course. The Internet allowed the Dean campaign to temporarily circumvent the mainstream media, it has been said. Or it was the platform for an entirely new kind of grassroots politics, a kind that will eventually lead to "the overthrow of everything." Or it was merely a convenient way for the antiwar left to communicate. Or it was an echo chamber that artificially amplified the importance of an inexperienced candidate among a narrow and computer-obsessed slice of the American electorate, producing a bubble that popped on contact with the first real political contest in Iowa.

This book is intended to help take us beyond such conflicting, glib claims and provide a richer understanding. Some myths do not need a book to correct. A look at the public record will show that Howard Dean is not an extreme left-winger or an angry man or a politician who makes more gaffes than others; these, like the false claim during the 2000 campaign that Al Gore said he invented the Internet, are merely canards, seized upon by reporters struggling to find pegs upon which to hang their narratives during the ideological chaos of a national election conducted through a sound bite–dependent media.[1] (If one had to summarize Dean's speaking style, it might be best described as plainspoken and blunt, in a category with that of Senator

John McCain, though Dean has on many occasions given speeches of great rhetorical power, most famously his "What I want to know" speech of February 2003.) Some other common assumptions about the Dean campaign are dispelled in the pages that follow; some readers might be surprised to learn, for example, that roughly half of the campaign's record-setting fund-raising was offline, or that some of the more innovative ideas for the campaign were inspired by Republican efforts.

Readers who suspect that the Dean campaign was a trivial event might want to begin with our concluding chapter, which describes some of the most significant impacts of the campaign. But perhaps the most important impact is that the Dean campaign shattered the stranglehold of a decades-old system of belief about what is possible in American politics. It's not that the old beliefs are gone; merely that they are now contestable. As of this writing, thinking people of all stripes must admit that there remains a huge chasm of uncertainty around the question of whether a Dean or Dean-styled candidacy in the general election would have led to disaster or triumph. The old system of belief about how to get elected to national office still has many powerful proponents, and the debates and power struggles around this issue within the Democratic Party and elsewhere are fierce and complex. But the fact that this debate is happening at all is new. By that day in December 2003 when Al Gore, a practitioner of the old ways, signaled his conversion by endorsing Howard Dean, a wall in the taken-for-granted underlying assumptions of American politics was breached, and the range of what might be considered realistically possible was enlarged.

## Why Tell Stories?

When looking back at moments of dramatic turmoil and change, there is a temptation to try to package events according to the needs of the present, to boil things down into easily digestible bullet points. In so doing, we tend to exaggerate the intentionality of actions that were successful; obscure our mistakes, confusions, and ambivalences; and thereby risk oversimplifying and misunderstanding what really happened. The bullet-point understanding of the Dean campaign is already out there: The 2006 elections were crowded with techniques from the Dean campaign, from blogs to Meetups to personally signed fund-raising e-mails, and as of this writing the 2008 elections looked to be similarly crowded. Yet (with the exception of Ned Lamont's campaign in the Connecticut Democratic primary), few of these efforts had the same surprising, galvanizing effects as the original.

Whatever the Internet's role in the Dean campaign, it cannot be boiled down to a few slogans. The story is complicated; for all the differences among the contributors to this volume, on this we agree. A belief in the complexity of the problem is in a sense the organizing principle for this book. Clearly, the Dean campaign's most remarkable and unexpected features—the astonishing success in fund-raising from small donors, for example, or the intensity of the Dean supporters' emotional connection to the campaign—were the product of a complex confluence of factors, none of which alone can account for the campaign's successes.

To get at that complexity, we asked the authors of the following chapters, who were key participants in the campaign, to relate their experiences. Of course, not everyone with important stories to tell is included here; this is meant to be more of a representative cross section than a list of the most important actors. It is by no means complete. It is intended to start a conversation, not end it. We tried to represent a variety of perspectives: authors who were technical experts and technical neophytes, seasoned campaigners and newcomers, those who worked in headquarters, others who worked in the field, and some who worked in both.

This is a book of stories. Authors were asked to provide narratives of their experiences rather than analyses. But they are stories with a serious intellectual purpose, selected not for dramatic value but to illustrate a specific historical moment. Authors were asked to focus less on colorful details than on meaningful ones, and to provide a record of the changes in *perception,* changes in what was taken for granted and what was not, that occurred during the campaign. The goal has been to provide both the details of what happened when and an understanding of the shifting sets of assumptions and motivations that drove decision making, the Weberian *verstehen,* the "frames" through which participants made sense of events. This book, then, is about both the facts and how the facts felt. It is a record of how and when the experience of the campaign changed individuals' perception of what was possible in American politics.

Have we nonetheless, by using first-person narratives, risked promoting the stereotype of the Dean campaign's supporters as merely self-absorbed and out of touch with larger realities? Involvement in the Dean campaign was one of those uniquely intense personal experiences that, like sex or a profound religious conversion, are hard to describe and often look odd or pathetic to those not sharing in it. This common personal experience, for all its variations, was an objective fact of the campaign. And, we suspect, experiences like this are of a piece with deep social change, and will be a component of any successful effort to build a more democratic society in the future. It deserves its place in understanding what happened.

## A Brief History of the Dean Campaign

So what did happen? In order to provide a context for the chapters that follow, here I can provide a quick and broad outline of events.

### Background: Before the Campaign

Howard Dean entered politics with no particular interest in the Internet, a centrist Democrat associated with the likes of President Bill Clinton. Early in his tenure as governor of the state of Vermont, he supported "workfare," for example, and for reasons of practicality advocated a partial state health-care system for children instead of the statewide, universal single-payer system that some of his more progressive colleagues would have preferred to attempt. He gained some national attention as the president of the National Governor's Association in 1994 and 1995. This national attention in turn encouraged him to briefly consider, in 1997, running in the 2000 U.S. presidential election. He might, the thinking went, follow the path to the White House pioneered by Jimmy Carter and Bill Clinton, both of whom launched their successful campaigns from small-state governorships.

If Howard Dean was a centrist, however, in Vermont he was at the center of a broader, more variegated field than existed in most of the rest of the country. Vermont's political diversity is not all on the left. It has a strong Republican Party that has regularly elected candidates to statewide office, including, as of this writing, a Republican governor reelected twice over. But as a small state with a population of about 600,000 and a strong tradition of popular participation in politics, Vermont is less susceptible to a politics of sound bites and imagery than other parts of the country. So, for example, in the early days of the Bush administration, longtime Republican senator from Vermont James Jeffords declared himself an independent, withdrawing from the Republican Party to protest what he thought to be Bush's extremism and thereby turning control of the U.S. Senate over to the Democrats. And before that, Burlington mayor and democratic socialist Bernie Sanders was elected as an independent into Vermont's lone seat in the U.S. House of Representatives, becoming the first independent in the U.S. Congress in forty years; he went on to become the longest-serving independent in Congress in U.S. history, and after that became the U.S. Senate's first ever democratic socialist. Things happen in Vermont that are thought to be impossible elsewhere.

No accounting of the American political scene in recent years can ignore the broad effects on society, culture, and politics of the events of September 11, 2001. It is predictable that a society that feels itself under attack pulls together behind its leaders, and that this enables dramatic actions of both a good and a bad sort; consider the internment of Japanese Americans early in World War II and the historic racial integration of the military a few years later. Shortly after 9/11, Al Gore, George Bush's opponent in the bitterly contested 2000 election, publicly announced, "I support the actions President Bush is taking, without reservation." A similar sense of unity was felt and acted on in much of the society, including the media; in the ensuing months and years, that unity enabled a series of decisions and institutional changes in American society that would have been unthinkable in the time immediately before 9/11. Many of those decisions were, and to this day are, uncontroversial, such as the heavy screenings of airplane passengers at airports. But as the intensity of the shared feelings and the associated unity very gradually receded, many of those decisions began to look more controversial to more people. The Bush administration's decision to invade Iraq was just the centerpiece of a series of decisions whose public popularity seemed to start strong but to erode with time.

As a result, the period between roughly the summer of 2002 and November of 2004 represents a unique and dramatic episode in American history. A controversial war was prosecuted, wrongly declared over, and then unraveled both on the ground and in terms of its initial justification, becoming the most troubled U.S. military effort since Vietnam. The flagship institutions of American news, especially the *New York Times,* made a long series of decisions in both war and political coverage that proved misguided, accelerating an ongoing drop in external respect and initiating a period of internal hand-wringing and conflict over the structure and character of news gathering, conflict that of this writing had yet to subside. Films and documentaries with a sharp political edge, from *The Passion of the Christ* to *Fahrenheit 9/11*, attracted large audiences and proved commercially successful, upending long-standing rules of Hollywood and dramatically adding to the politically charged atmosphere of the culture.

As Howard Dean embarked on his campaign for the presidency, he had several quite divergent models of the possible to draw on: the pre-9/11 model that had defined most of his governorship and his previous interactions with national politics; the narrower immediate post-9/11 model of strong patriotic unity, a model that involved appealing to a growing but uncertain number of voters who held that things had gone terribly wrong in recent years; and the model of Vermont, where yet another set of rules prevailed. The political game is always unpredictable, but in the 2002–2003 period the uncertainty was not just about outcomes; the rules of the game itself were deeply uncertain. For someone with only minor national visibility, just what could be accomplished was exceedingly hard to say.

Long before Dean and his staff became associated with the Internet, he had developed a set of principles that he and his early staff and supporters thought might get him somewhere on the national stage. Some of these were of a piece with his previous political career, such as his mixture of social progressivism and fiscal conservatism, his emphasis on health care, and his tendency to speak bluntly and clearly; although he was associated with Bill Clinton's politics, Dean tended to stick to principle instead of engaging in Clintonian "triangulation" with the media and the polls. Some of these seemed to come upon him because of circumstance; much of his early financial support, for example, came from the gay community, who were encouraged by the fact that Dean signed Vermont's "civil union" law, the first law in the United States allowing something like gay marriage. And some seem to have come from straightforward reasoned conviction, such as his decision to oppose the Iraq War at a time when very few other centrist Democrats did so.

But neither Dean nor the phenomenon of his campaign is best understood in terms of a precise political ideology or a narrow set of issues. The Dean campaign was a pragmatic coalition; political purity was never a goal or expectation. The differing interests and motivations for the authors of the following chapters hint at the diversity of Dean supporters generally. For some, opposition to the war was a primary issue, but others were most concerned with other things, such as Dean's mix of fiscal conservatism and social liberalism, or his direct and plainspoken style. The common denominator seems to have been simply an urgent desire for a change in political direction, attraction to various aspects of his politics, and a sense that he could conceivably win.

## Discovering the Internet

In the fall of 2002, the Dean campaign was known as a serious but long-shot effort by a centrist Democrat with a strong interest in and record on health care. Dean predicted that "I'm going to be dead last in fundraising," and expected that he would have to rely on bottom-up, small-donor fund-raising simply because of a lack of other options.[2] The Internet was not a particular consideration at the time. Dean had expressed skepticism about the Bush administration plans for war in Iraq as early as August of that year,[3] but did not make an effort to directly associate himself with the public antiwar movement in the same manner as, say, Democratic congressman Dennis Kucinich.

On October 14, 2002, a little-known left-liberal website and e-mail list called Moveon.org sent out an e-mail on behalf of several candidates up for election that November, the most prominent of whom was Minnesota senator Paul Wellstone. Moveon.org originated during the effort to impeach President Clinton, asking the country to "move on" from the adultery discussion, and had continued using their e-mail list on behalf of left-liberal causes, eventually including opposition to the war in Iraq. Though few noticed at the time, Moveon.org had developed a practice of sending out e-mails with then-rare action-oriented links: Instead of just an electronic version of traditional political mailings, or links of the "click here for more information" variety, Moveon's links enabled the reader to *do* something, such as sign a petition, send a letter to a politician, or vote on a policy direction. (On September 5, 2001, Moveon.org sent out an e-mail under the subject heading "What do you think?" Clicking on the link took readers to a website where they could select from sets of issues and actions that they felt were most important, presumably to guide the organization's future efforts.[4]) Moveon.org had developed a unique style of e-mail composition that ensured that action links occurred early and frequently in the e-mail, so that readers would not have to read all the way to the bottom to get to the link. And most e-mails were followed up a few days later with a report on the success of the previous e-mails. Unlike most political discourse on the left (e.g., *The Nation*), the tone was generally very upbeat.

The Wellstone e-mail called for readers to send money to support a few candidates in tight races who had stuck to their principles and voted against the Iraq War resolution; the link in question allowed a person to easily donate money from a credit card with a few clicks. In addition to being action oriented, the e-mail was simultaneously impassioned—its header was "Reward the Heroes"—and highly tactical, with a focus on money and tight races in the days leading up to the November election. The next day, Moveon.org e-mailed its subscribers a typical follow-up e-mail: "Good news: in just 24 hours, ten thousand of us have given more than $400,000 for our four heroes in Congress." That alone was an impressive success. But two days later, a message from Moveon appeared that began, "Amazing. You blew away all our goals with an incredible $1,250,000 raised in three days, from more than 30,000 individual donations." Well over a million dollars raised in three days by a tiny unaffiliated organization was something new; this wasn't just a typical blizzard of e-mails to a congressperson, or a stern editorial in a tiny-circulation political magazine. This was real money, something any mainstream political operative would take note of—if they bothered to look.

Few did take notice, perhaps because the money did not lead directly to any electoral successes; Wellstone was tragically killed in a plane crash a few days later, and the Republicans subsequently gained enough seats in both the Senate and the House to completely dominate the federal government. During the next two months, the Dean campaign remained a tiny organization, and continued groping for a foothold in the national spotlight. But people inside the campaign began to notice a flood of e-mails coming in, e-mails expressing not only support but a desire to help, to *act*. Dean's assistant Kate O'Connor's personal e-mail inbox was flooded, as supporters searching for a contact on the campaign found her e-mail address. A few months later, Zephyr Teachout, a young lawyer recently hired as a deputy field director, noticed e-mails saying things like, "I'm an artist in New York and I'd love to help out"; "I'm a student in South Carolina and we'd like to *do* something"; "I saw Howard Dean on the news here in Pennsylvania and if there's anything I can *do*"; "I've written the campaign two times offering to help and I've heard nothing."[5] Meanwhile, an independent group of Internet-savvy enthusiasts set up a national listserv for Dean supporters—an e-mail discussion list—and began creating pro-Dean listservs in each state.[6]

Traditional campaign structure does not include procedures for dealing with directly e-mailed requests to help, particularly a year before an election. In January 2003, Jerome Armstrong, acting independently of the official campaign, posted a link on his political blog, MyDD, to the then-obscure website called Meetup.com; the "Meetup for Dean" graphic would soon become famous. People inside the Dean campaign, especially Joe Trippi (an experienced Democratic campaign consultant with a taste for technology who joined the campaign in January 2003), began to take note. After the MyDD posting, Trippi noticed that Kerry and Edwards had approximately 150 registrants each, whereas Dean had about 400—not particularly significant numbers for a national campaign, but at the time perhaps the only number in which Dean had a lead over the favorites.

In the ensuing months, a complex set of interacting factors came together: As online interest in the campaign started to build, Howard Dean turned his ear and his heart toward those in the United States who did not just disagree with certain policies, but were deeply troubled by the direction of the country post-9/11. Dean chose to give his campaign an insurgent tone, a choice marked with great effect by his February 21, 2003, "What I want to know ..." speech to the Democratic National Committee, in which he sharply criticized other Democrats for being excessively accommodating and then concluded, to wild applause, with a line borrowed from the late and much more systematically left-wing Paul Wellstone: "I'm Howard Dean, and I'm here to represent the democratic wing of the Democratic Party." The speech was instantly circulated on the Internet to listservs and blogs, and solidified Dean's unique status among the small but growing number of enthusiasts who learned about him from the Internet. During that same month, the campaign staff, noticing some of the online activity, began to think and talk seriously about using the Internet in new ways.

### Key Features of the Campaign: Media, Meetups, Decentralization, and Authenticity

As the following chapters reveal in detail, the integration of the campaign with its online following was gradual and in some ways haphazard. A key early moment was a March 5, 2003, Dean Meetup in the Essex Lounge in New York City (discussed in several of the chapters in this book). Trippi decided to use this Meetup to promote grassroots activity around the country, by promoting it nationally on the Internet and arranging for Dean to attend. The effort worked too well; less than half of the attendees could fit in the lounge. The event solidified the suspicion among those inside the campaign that Internet organizing—and Meetups in particular—represented a key and heretofore untapped resource. In the next month, against the backdrop of the U.S. invasion of Iraq and a polarized and bewildered electorate, staffers began to focus more on Meetups, blogs, the website, and online fund-raising.

The details of what happened inside the campaign in the next six months, during which Howard Dean rocketed from obscurity to break all campaign fund-raising records and change the tone of the national political discussion, are laid out in the chapters that follow. But several key features are worth mentioning at the outset. The first concerns the media: The Internet was not simply an end run around the media. The role of the Internet in the Dean campaign needs to be understood in terms of a complex dynamic *relationship with* traditional print and television journalism. It's true that, as more and more Americans began turning to the Internet for information, individuals who felt themselves to be outside the frame of what both the right and the left deride as "the mainstream media" could find alternative perspectives on the Internet. Dean, with his antiwar stance and other "unconventional" views, clearly benefited from the Internet's character as an alternative information source. So much is clear. At the same time, however, the Dean campaign was highly focused on and dependent on the mainstream media for its success (if also, some say, for its downfall).

Traditional news coverage of campaigns is frequently criticized for its obsessive focus on campaign tactics and strategy (at the expense of, say, coverage of issues and fact-checking candidates' claims).[7] Nowhere is this more obvious than in the seriousness with which reporters take what has become known as "the money primaries," the preelection fund-raising generally viewed as the first test of the "seriousness" of a candidate, particularly for national office. Whatever else played a role in Dean's popularity, without the extensive mainstream media coverage of his fund-raising successes he never would have been transformed from a minor long-shot candidate into a serious contender. As the numbers of Dean campaign contributors and contributions mushroomed logarithmically in the spring and summer of 2003, the mainstream media began to take note, gradually assigning more reporters to cover the campaign. Much of the campaign's symbolism—the famous red bat, the focus on FEC filing deadlines for setting fund-raising goals—was directed not just at supporters or Internet readers but at mainstream journalists, who would report on these fund-raising milestones with great interest. Internet efforts, then, were in at least some cases carefully attuned to *attracting* mainstream media coverage, not just circumventing it. As Dean's national media presence grew, therefore, potential supporters were as often as not learning about Dean from the mainstream media, and only then turning to the Internet to learn more or get involved. A complex, interactive relationship developed between the online efforts and mainstream media coverage.

The Internet then became not just a source of funds and support, but part of what journalism professor Jay Rosen aptly calls the "master narrative"[8] about the campaign in the traditional media: Early on, the Dean campaign as described by print journalists was "the Internet campaign." This was to a degree intentional. Every campaign looks for (and worries about) what hooks or frames reporters will use to describe the campaign to readers and viewers. In spite of the fact that Howard Dean himself barely knew how to use e-mail and many of the staffers (as subsequent chapters make clear) were not particularly interested in the Internet at the start of the campaign, once Internet use started to become significant, the Dean campaign, following the lead of Joe Trippi, seized on that fact and chose to encourage the idea that it was "the Internet campaign." The Internet thus came to play an important *metaphorical* role alongside its more concrete roles.

Another issue concerns the online/offline relationship. Sometimes the Internet is imagined as another space apart from the "real world," as a place that, for better or worse, people escape into—as cyberspace. The Dean campaign may have been an Internet campaign but it was not a cyberspace one. The experience of Dean supporters was much more about taking action in the real world and about connecting with others face-to-face. The most obvious expression of this was the use of Dean Meetups: The capacity to use the Internet to find and meet other Dean supporters face-to-face was absolutely crucial to the campaign's effect. And the face-to-face character of Meetups was not just about socializing for its own sake. As Michael Silberman points out in his chapter, the campaign discovered that the more a Meetup focused on action, on specific things people could *do* in support of the campaign, the more that Meetup would grow, the more people would be drawn in. Perhaps the Internet encourages activity, or perhaps the larger political context created a specific social need for activity to which the Internet merely provided access. But in either case, the Dean campaign tapped into an intense, widely experienced desire to *do something* on the political stage. The campaign became a genuine movement in a way that few if any Democratic campaigns had been for at least a generation, and it could not have done so without the Internet.

This raises a related issue: the grassroots, decentralized character of the campaign. The word *grassroots* is bandied about a great deal in politics, rarely with any precision. In the Dean campaign, however, the term clearly carried some weight, though in distinctive and complex ways. As the following chapters make clear, the campaign itself was no Quaker meeting, even after it began to define itself as decentralized and grassroots. In at least some cases, if control was decentralized it was simply because of unresolved power struggles and chaos. And those at the center of the Internet effort often found themselves relating to the hundreds of thousands of volunteers in the narrow attenuated medium of numbers: Considerable effort was devoted to instantaneous, real-time tracking of Meetup memberships and fund-raising contributions; staffers remember watching the numbers skyrocket as some of the most thrilling points of the campaign. But it is worth pointing out that climbing numbers on a laptop screen have more in common with television ratings than with rich, thoughtful, face-to-face interaction.

Nonetheless, there were many ways in which the Dean campaign genuinely decentralized control, particularly in association with the Internet. In that vast and complex realm of possibilities between the ideal types of completely bottom-up and completely top-down control, the Dean campaign shifted control toward the bottom, particularly in comparison with other campaigns (including John Kerry's subsequent campaign against George Bush). Small and large ideas filtered back to the central campaign organizers and to Dean himself. Often spontaneously, sometimes with gentle prodding from campaign staff, and even sometimes by accident, Dean enthusiasts created a remarkable number of their own organizations, campaign material, and campaign tactics, from flyers to television advertisements to websites that tracked and critically analyzed media coverage of Dean. These patterns became internalized to the campaign itself: The campaign staff began using a wheel-like chart to illustrate the power to be gained by allowing those on the periphery to connect directly to each other rather than going through the center. The fact that Howard Dean publicly asked his supporters (in an online poll) whether or not to forgo federal campaign financing is just the most obvious example of an ethos that to various degrees permeated the campaign. When he repeatedly told crowds, "You have the power to take America back," he said it with deep sincerity, and his campaign involved many shared experiences that reinforced that message.

Finally, there's a feature of the campaign that is essential but that the media ignored or at best only glanced at from a distance through jaded lenses: what one might call the campaign's generation of authenticity. The experience of authenticity, a modern experience of a deep emotional connection with something that seems to stand out as more "real" than its surroundings, is something that might be prompted by a breakthrough moment in a therapy session, or in the context of a religious conversion, or in a rock concert. Aldon Hynes, in his chapter, describes his initial experience of Howard Dean as an encounter with "the real thing," as a candidate who jumps out from the pack and comes across as markedly more honest and sincere, as less packaged or strategic than the norm. This experience was common, and it was not always just about Howard Dean the candidate; it was just as often about the community built up around him. One can glimpse some of the emotional attachment the campaign generated by reading discussions on the blogs: Mixed in with the general cheers, discussions of strategy, and so forth, there are regular posts that link events with the campaign to highly personal states, from the mundane ("tired ... need Seattle photos soon ... bed shortly thereafter") to the highly emotional ("OK—now I'm really crying. Oh my. I just can't describe my emotions right now. I'm completely overwhelmed").[9] Tens, perhaps hundreds, of thousands of individuals will remember their involvement in the Dean campaign as an emotionally intense and defining moment in their lives, in much the same way attendees at the Woodstock rock festival in 1968 remember that event, or the way others with different inclinations might remember the election of Ronald Reagan in 1980.

Clearly, Howard Dean is a remarkable individual who proceeded with more courage, intelligence, and integrity than many a major politician. He deserves an enormous amount of credit. But the creation of an authentic persona is not just about the person. Authenticity is a process, not a thing, and it is never universal, though it is sometimes imagined as such. Certainly not even all Democrats experienced Dean as "the real thing," and even Dean's Vermont supporters noticed some differences between their memory of Governor Dean and Democratic Presidential Candidate Dean. Generating authenticity in a political campaign is often attempted, and rarely succeeds. But authenticity is a frequent component of successful movements for social change; for those interested in political change, it is an extremely valuable phenomenon and worth paying attention to. The experience of the Dean campaign should put to rest once and for all the conceit that anything having to do with the Internet is inevitably inauthentic. But that still leaves open the question of how, why, and for whom the Internet played a role in helping to generate that experience. The following chapters, we hope, will help provide some insight into the phenomenon.

## Chapter Overview

Among the other works about the Dean campaign that have been published, Joe Trippi's *The Revolution Will Not Be Televised* is required reading.[10] The following chapters in the first instance build on these previous works, Trippi's book in particular, filling in gaps in the record, correcting some details, and adding a diversity of outlooks. But in doing so they also build a uniquely rich picture of what happened and what mattered in the campaign, and take things to another level. The next chapter, an interview with Howard Dean, provides his perspective, explaining how the Internet phenomenon convinced him that "this was about something much greater than a candidacy for president." We follow this with a chapter that inquires into the meaning of some of the key concepts at play in discussing the campaign: the question of the causal role of technology, the meaning of the term *grassroots,* and the productive character of decentralized networks. The concluding section of the book consists of reflections on the larger significance of the campaign: Sey and Castells put the campaign in the larger context of politics and the Internet worldwide, and Teachout and Streeter look at the enduring impact of the campaign on American electoral politics.

But the core of the book consists of stories and reflections from participants in the campaign. Jerome Armstrong provides some key details and insights into the historic convergence of efforts between a nascent blogosphere and the early stages of a struggling campaign, creating a synergy that surprised the world. Teachout provides a perspective on the campaign that is at once very much hers and yet is also representative: Like many, she came upon the Internet efforts almost reluctantly, and yet found them transformative. Mathew Gross, Bobby Clark, Michael Silberman, Kelly Nuxoll, and Nicco Mele fill in the picture of how that process developed within the campaign, together providing a rich picture of a remarkable confluence of political events and technologies. Some chapters provide important windows into what the campaign was like away from headquarters: Pam Paul tells the story from the point of view of Oklahoma City, Aldon Hynes from that of Connecticut, Josh Koenig from that of a New York–based online activist, and Amanda Michel, in the conclusion of her chapter, interestingly contrasts the differences between her experiences in Burlington and her experiences in Iowa leading up to the caucuses. Some of the differences among the chapters are less about geography and more about stages of life: The authors range in age from recent college graduates like Josh Koenig, a young, iconoclastic, politically concerned aspiring actor and online tool builder, to seasoned campaign professionals like Larry Biddle. There are some stories here that have received little previous notice, such as Amanda Michel's story of the youth effort—probably the most successful such effort since the McGovern campaign in 1972—and Larry Biddle's discussion of many of the unique aspects of the fund-raising effort, both on- and offline. Many of the chapters, most notably Zack Exley's, reflect on the long-term lessons of the campaign, though the general emphasis is on the concrete details, and not on sweeping generalizations.

Reading through all the chapters, however, common themes emerge. One theme is about the mix of technologies with the many intense, personal experiences of the campaign; throughout the book, for example, there is a remarkable amount of emphasis on the fine points of database structure, and yet there are also frequent mentions of random moments when the humanity of specific individuals broke through the relative anonymity of the lists. The picture is that of a rapidly evolving fluency with technology, not for its own sake but tightly focused on an urgent social and political purpose. Another theme is the constant tension between traditional campaign habits and the explosively growing grassroots efforts: In both Burlington and the field, the Internet effort cut across traditional lines of authority between established campaign structures and tasks in countless ways, particularly once the campaign fully embraced its grassroots character. At its best this tension was amazingly productive, but it also predictably led to some conflict and chaos. A related theme that crops up in many chapters involves questions of the control over "messaging": Who says what to whom in the name of the campaign and in what style? Clearly, the Dean campaign embraced a much more open approach to those questions than any other campaign did, and with great effect; the question of how to cultivate productive approaches to these questions remains an open one. Finally, a full read of these chapters provides a rich sense of the feel of the campaign, of a historic moment of change. This feel, we think, is as important as any of the details, and we hope that these diverse writings inspire for readers, as they have for us, both thought and action.

## Notes

1. Consider things that other politicians have said that might be easily construed as major gaffes but that were not, such as when Joe Lieberman told CNN that "Iraq did pose a threat to us" because "they had weapons of mass destruction"—on June 25, 2004, long after Bush's chief weapons inspector, David Kay, told Congress that "his group [of inspectors] found no evidence Iraq had stockpiled unconventional weapons before the U.S.-led invasion in March." For the truth behind the Al Gore "inventing the Internet" canard, see Richard Wiggins, "Al Gore and the Creation of the Internet," *First Monday* 5, no. 10 (October 2, 2000), available at http://firstmonday.org/issues/issue5_10/wiggins (accessed June 1, 2007).

2. Robert Dreyfuss, "The Darkest Horse: Vermont Governor Howard Dean Is a Fiscal Conservative Who's for Gay Civil Unions, Against the Bush Tax Cuts and Running for President as the Health-Care Candidate," *American Prospect* (July 15, 2002). The article continues: "'We're

going to rely heavily on people who can write checks for $25, $50, $100,' says Kate O'Connor, the governor's chief political aide. 'We're going to campaign from the bottom up. We're being realistic, knowing that for the $1,000 donors, Howard Dean isn't going to be their first pick.'"

3. "Dean Says Iraq War Would Be a Long One: Gov. Howard Dean Says a U.S. Attack on Iraq Could Lead to American Troops Being on the Ground in the Country for a Decade," *Rutland Herald,* August 21, 2002, B5:1.

4. E-mail from Moveon.org, September 5, 2001.

5. See chapter 5 in this volume.

6. Jerome Armstrong, a key figure in this development, discusses this at length in chapter 4 of this volume.

7. For a standard analysis of the "strategy and tactics" pattern of news coverage, see Michael Schudson, *The Sociology of News* (New York: W. W. Norton, 2003), pp. 51–54.

8. Jay Rosen, "PressThink Basics: The Master Narrative in Journalism," http://journalism.nyu.edu/pubzone/weblogs/pressthink/2003/09/08/basics_master.html (accessed March 3, 2007).

9. See the comments on Blog for America, August 25, 2003, "From the Road: A Sleepless Summer Update from Seattle, Washington," http://www.blogforamerica.com/view/1029#more (accessed June 1, 2007).

10. Joe Trippi, *The Revolution Will Not Be Televised: Democracy, the Internet, and the Overthrow of Everything* (New York: Regan Books, 2004).

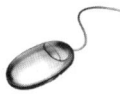

## 2

# How the Internet Taught Me
# That You Have the Power

## *Interview with Howard Dean*

*The following is an edited transcript of an interview with Howard Dean conducted by Thomas Streeter and Zephyr Teachout on January 25 and March 6, 2007.*

**When did you first notice the Internet's role in the campaign?**

The first time I was aware that the Internet was going to play a big role in the campaign was when my longtime employee Kate O'Connor started telling me about Meetup.com. As she explained, people were using Meetup.com—a for-profit company—to organize themselves in support of the campaign. At first there was a small group of supporters, but then suddenly our group became one of the biggest of any of the Meetup groups. We were number four on the Meetup list (ranked by group size), then we were number three, then we were number two. Then all of a sudden we took off. Soon we were so far ahead of every other group that Meetup became synonymous with the campaign.

At first, I had no idea what Meetup was, but of course I got caught up in the enthusiasm around how fast we were growing. That's when I first realized people were going to use the Internet as an organizational tool, and it's also when I realized that this was about something much greater than a candidacy for president.

By the end of the campaign we had a lot of Internet types—people working for the campaign with an amazing understanding of the new technologies. They were great artists and did incredible things—but there were clues about the power of the Internet before any of that.

**How did this early experience of spontaneous online activity affect your thinking?**

That's where "You have the power" came from. Individuals who clearly wanted something very different in the country were meeting up of their own accord to support a candidacy that had a very strong message about change, a campaign that was confronting wrong policy and wrongdoing.

I started saying "You have the power" because I started understanding that this was coming from people. This was not a top-down movement. People were self-organizing around a mission. It was an odyssey, a movement of people who had had enough, who were tired of the lies, who were tired of atrocious policies, and wanted somebody to stand up. I was at a fund-raiser recently and someone introduced me as "this is the guy who says what we think." That's not always a compliment, but in this case, that pretty much captured the campaign. I was saying what a lot of people were thinking. One of the most moving things someone could say to me on the campaign trail was "I thought I was alone before I heard you, and now I see all of these other people who agree with me."

**Do you remember your first encounters with Meetup-inspired supporters?**

I remember the Essex Street Lounge Meetup in New York City on March 5 very clearly. By this time we realized that there was potential in Meetup and Internet fund-raising. In February, I had gone to a Meetup, and there were about 60 people there—I don't even remember where it was. But there was a sense this "Internet thing" was starting and we were starting to raise some serious money. So we went to this Meetup on the Lower East Side. I thought there were going to be 60 people there, as there had been in February. Instead, there were something like 575 people, in a line literally out the door and around the corner and down the block—about three quarters of a block was filled with people who couldn't get in. It was one of the early awe-inspiring moments in the campaign when I realized that this was something much bigger than I had ever thought it was going to be.

**How important was online fund-raising for the campaign?**

Of course the fund-raising online is what got us attention. We raised a very respectable amount of money in the March quarter. The March fund-raising numbers put us in a very different place than the pundits thought we were going to be in.

But in June we had a record quarter. We outraised everybody else in the field—that's when all of the other candidates began to panic. To give you a sense of the shock, I saw a number on our website that was supposed to indicate how much we had raised and I thought it was too large. I remember calling Joe Trippi, my campaign manager, saying this can't possibly be right, you made a mistake here. But it *was* right. It was unbelievable.

We had a lot of fun with our fund-raising, although of course it was also very serious. In July, we had a great gag—I sat at my desk, ate a turkey sandwich, and had a picture taken of it at the exact same time Dick Cheney was raising $300,000 or something at a high-dollar, black-tie dinner in South Carolina. That may have been the first huge fund-raiser we had over the Net that wasn't tied to anything else, like the end of a quarter or an announcement. We announced that we were going to match Cheney: Cheney is going to have a posh lunch in South Carolina with his friends, and I'm going to have a turkey sandwich in front of the computer at my desk, and we are going to raise as much money as he does. We put it all on the Net, and we succeeded—we raised more than Cheney, and people just loved it.

That idea came off the blog. We had people whose job it was to read the blogs for feedback and ideas and we developed a feedback loop that allowed us to do these incredible events. The two-way conversation was key—you can't just talk, you also need to listen.

**What was the relation between online and offline fund-raising?**

While only half our money technically came from the Internet, a lot of the money that came in off the Internet was motivated by the grassroots and Net community that grew around the campaign. For example if I held a low-dollar fund-raiser, we would count somebody who sent us a check or put five bucks in the jar as somebody who didn't give on the Internet, but in fact they had given because of the Internet. It was the Internet that got them to the rally in the first place.

That said, we had a very, very good traditional fund-raising operation. Stephanie Schriock, the finance director of the campaign, was so good she ended up running John Tester's campaign for U.S. Senate in Montana and is now his chief of staff. In fund-raising, we knew what we were doing—though we did not start out exactly as a candidate with big dollars, we did start out with real competence and intelligence—and then the Internet clearly brought us to a new level.

**How involved were you with the Internet strategy of the campaign?**

I was involved but not with the nuts and bolts. My campaign manager, Joe Trippi, was responsible for managing the Internet team's innovations, and a lot of the day-to-day stuff was done by really smart, innovative twenty-five-year-olds. The young people who worked on our tech team were great artists—our tech operation was in stratospheres above everyone else. The people involved were driven by idealism, and would just kill themselves to do it right. There was a huge difference between our first website and where we were eight months later, and it was due to this constant artistry and dedication. The folks who were doing all of that stuff for us were incredibly young and incredibly innovative.

I can say what happened was very different than what we'd expected. We had intended to run this as a traditional campaign—an underdog campaign, but a traditional campaign. But then the Internet exploded and became this enormous, growing phenomenon, and with the growth also came growing pains. I had people who had been around me for a long time, and traditional campaign staffers, and then twenty-somethings who were completely comfortable with the Internet, and we had to fit it all together. Because we had a lot of people who were very tech savvy, we ended up with all kinds of bells and whistles and organizational tools, and fitting those into a traditional operation was not always easy.

I believe the first time I blogged was in the spring in Iowa ... and after that initial time I began to blog on a regular basis because it was clear that folks wanted to hear from me on the Net, not just hear from folks in the campaign headquarters. So we had a regular blog—once a week or every two weeks—I would go on to say something, do something, write something. But I never read other candidates' websites—I don't think many of the other candidates even had blogs, to be honest with you, until after the primary election was over.

**What do people miss when they talk about your use of the Internet?**

Most people even to this day don't fully understand what we learned about the Internet. Most politicians, and even the press, treat the Internet as a shorthand for an ATM.... The Internet is a community, a community of people who don't happen to live in the same vicinity geographically, but they are very much a community. They fight with each other. They care about each other.

For example, there was this woman named Kimmy—about thirty—she had an incredibly unfortunate story. She had been an early organizer of punks for the campaign, "Punx for Dean." Someone in her family died, and she was doing everything she could to deal with the tragedy, but also trying to find a place to live so she could stay involved in the campaign. A whole group of people from the campaign mobilized to help take care of her. First she got thrown out of her house because she ran out of rent, and somebody let her use her house. Someone else had a condo that they let her stay in, and other people helped in other ways. It was unbelievable—all of this stuff was going on inside the context of a presidential campaign. We were facilitating this incredible community that was developing, we were not just building a big list.

There was a huge virtual presence, which was not just generated by us, but generated by the community, and then they'd show up in person whenever I went somewhere. The grassroots and the netroots are really one and the same.

I think too many people fail to understand that about the Internet. And if you don't, you are going to find it tough to successfully use the Internet for campaigns. The Internet is about community building and the fund-raising has to be secondary.

**Do you need to take a populist position on issues in order to engage the grassroots?**

No, you don't need a populist position. A compelling message is different for every campaign. For us, the "what I want to know speech" in front of the Democratic National Committee was really important. I wanted to know why the Democratic leadership wasn't standing up for what they believe in, why they were going along with George Bush and the war and the deficits and so on. But the core message—the message that was so captivating—was that "you have the power to stand up for yourself, and if you recognize that you have the power you'll be able to exercise it." Of course there was powerful substance to it—like we shouldn't be in Iraq and so forth—but the real message was "You have the power."

**How important is the process of listening to people?**

One of the innovations of the campaign that I think was underappreciated—including by me at the time—and that I think may be the most important innovation, is the fact that our campaign was a two-way campaign. We converted a one-way campaign model into a two-way campaign. We would read the blogs, we would respond to the blogs, we had a bunch of people whose job it was to read the blogs and respond. And people felt like we cared about what they had to say. We had a two-way campaign.

We hadn't seen one of those for many decades. When television came in, and advertising on television began, campaigns became entirely one-way campaigns; that is, you gave money to the gurus in Washington and they spent it all on television ads and you talk at the people. There's a huge hunger in the next generation for two-way campaigns, where citizens' votes matter not just because they're going to elect someone who's going to do something different but because they actually help shape the campaign. And that *certainly* happened in our campaign.

I still have a coterie of folks who were grassroots supporters in the campaign, like Pam Paul, who e-mail me. I can't always answer but I always read them, and they influence my thinking. A few of them had a substantial impact on the 2006 congressional elections: On Election Day in 2006, I was sent information about problems with electronic voting machines all over the country. The DNC had lawyers in the field and we were able to send them there to help fix the problems. Sometimes we already knew about them, but half the time we didn't. That kind of rapid communication, that two-way discussion, was an innovation from the campaign that we pulled right into the DNC. There are a lot of people from across the country who continue to affect my thinking about how to democratize the Democratic Party and how to redemocratize the country.

Political parties have to evolve with the times; if we don't, we lose. Power is shifting away from centralized messaging and shifting towards voters who demand that politicians listen to them before they speak. Traditionally campaigns have relied too much on advertising and not enough on listening to people. Advertising and other forms of communicating with voters remain important, but if that's all you do, you simply can't win.

**What do you think you could have done better?**

We did not do the kind of organizing we really needed to do in Iowa. And we were unaware of that until very late in the game. The Internet is not why we lost Iowa.

One of the legitimate criticisms of the campaign is we should have done more off the Net with the grassroots. We probably should not have abandoned the traditional grassroots model quite as fast as we did.

I also think that we did not do the kind of organizing in minority communities the way we needed to do it, particularly among African Americans and Hispanics. We had an African Americans for Dean website, and we had a Hispanics for Dean website, and a Spanish website, but of course none of these really did the trick. I think the book has yet to be written on how to organize black and Latino grassroots networks using the Net.

**Some contemporary Republican strategists are bemoaning the fact that the Republicans are not using the Internet as effectively as Democrats. Do you think that there's some fundamental incompatibility between Republican Party politics and good Internet strategy?**

I do. Our tendency in the Democratic Party—amplified by the new generation, which is more and more Democratic—is decentralizing democratization. The Internet is fundamentally a democratizing tool, which is why Net neutrality is so important. If you start fettering it either commercially or politically, it destroys itself as a democratizing tool. The Republicans are inherently not interested in (small *d*) democratic organization; they tend toward top-down centralization and organization.

The Democrats tend towards true democracy. The truth is, we probably need to be a little bit more organized (you know the joke, "I'm not a member of an organized party, I'm a Democrat!"), but we do not need to be more centralized. Decentralization should not be mistaken for disorganization. The Republicans do a good job being organized, but they do a terrible job being decentralized, and so they have a hard time with the Internet. The Net is a tool that works best for people who believe in decentralization.

**Have you modeled your work on the Republican grassroots organizing of the past few decades?**

In general, I do not follow the Republican Party. However, I do think that the GOP used some very skillful organizing techniques, and we make no bones about copying some of those. They were very good at electing Republicans to library boards and school boards and county commission races and so forth—building a strong bench team. For a while, yes, I think they got better at grassroots organizing than we did, but grassroots organizing is a pretty old phenomenon. It's been going on for many many generations—it used to be the way the Democratic Party existed.

But television—and television consultants—got us away from direct contact with human beings. The Republicans, in general, in the 1980s and 1990s relearned more quickly how to connect directly with people. The Democrats (because we were in power and mistakenly thinking that what we were doing was working) did not get back into the grassroots. To that extent, absolutely, the Republicans were a model. The problem is, of course, that they engage in the kinds of things that are pretty destructive when they do their grassroots efforts—their hate radio is grassroots and effective, but it's not stuff that I would admire.

**We all like the idea of small *d* democracy, the idea that we should try to expand the involvement of ordinary folks in decision making. Do you think it also works better? Is it more effective?**

Yes, it absolutely works better. I was absolutely convinced by our campaign. Our campaign would not have gone anywhere without the original people who went to those Meetups. It was a completely grassroots phenomenon that had to do with their willingness to organize themselves—to see the power that they held and use it. I learned "you have the power" from watching thousands of people use the power that they in fact already had.

One of the things we have on our [DNC] website is phenomenal—it's called "Party Builder." It was originally conceived out of our campaign and it allows people to get together in their own communities and do things for the community and with the community. For example, you can look up everybody in your zip code/state/county who wants to do an environmental project cleaning up a river. You can also do it for whoever wants to campaign for such-and-such candidate. But the reason it's so important is because it makes the DNC not just a political party, but also a facilitator for people who want to exercise their democratic abilities. If you want to clean up a stream, if you want to do something for a food shelter, if you want to help buy school supplies, you can organize yourself through Party Builder. As the next generation comes along, I want them to see the Democratic National Committee as not just a political party, but as a facilitator to empower them in their own communities.

**How much did Vermont experience and political culture influence your attitudes in the campaign?**

The original reason I started running was that I wanted universal health care and I wanted a balanced budget. Bush was going in the opposite direction. These were policy issues in Vermont that mattered. The policy issues that I ran into as governor influenced me throughout the campaign: mental health issues, fiscal responsibility, land conservation, energy, all the things that you run across in Vermont.

But I also think that Vermont is very well run, and one of the reasons I think it is very well run is because ordinary Vermonters put a significant amount of time into their democracy. That certainly had an effect on my thinking. My directness and my support for decentralization were definitely affected by my time in Vermont politics, because it is one of the more decentralized states.

**Are there risks to opening up a campaign to outside input as you did?**

There are not nearly as many risks as politicians think there are. People always feel a terrible sense of risk when they cede control and cede power, but the fact of the matter is the power doesn't belong to them in the first place. One of the more Zen things I used to say in the campaign (although I'm not a real Zen person) is that you acquire more power by giving it away. When you recognize other people's power, it enhances your own. So I think there's a relatively small risk.

One risk is that people can mistake disorganization for decentralization. You have to have an intent and purpose and be willing to lead. If you're willing to apply some listening skills and some leadership skills, there is little risk to decentralizing a campaign.

You will always get people who go out and speak for you, whether that's authorized or not, but that happens even in very centralized campaigns. There are risks in every campaign, but I think the risks are very small for decentralizing and the risk of not doing it is far greater. If you really want to unlock the potential of people, you can't have centralized, top-down organization without any input from folks who are doing the work.

**What are some of the most important lessons and legacies from your campaign?**

To really use the Internet well, you have to build community, not just enable fund-raising. You need to listen, be willing to lead and willing to be decentralized.

Campaigns in the future are going to rely on three pillars. Television is still go-ing to be important—it's just not going to be nearly as important as it was, but still important. Grassroots organizing is important, and the Internet is important. They're all important. You can't win unless you do all three of them. You can't win without grassroots organizing, and I don't think you can win without the Net.

The most important lesson is that we didn't just use the Internet for fund-raising. It had been used—as many people have pointed out—in 2000 by Senator McCain, who had raised a lot of money after the New Hampshire primary. But we used it for something more—to facilitate millions of people to come together to support a whole campaign.

The value of our campaign in retrospect—since I didn't win—is that we enabled people to come together around a theme. We provided the theme and some of the tools—the public pioneered the rest of the tools—and the people showed us what they needed to come together. We enabled a feedback loop: They showed us where they wanted to be led and we led them.

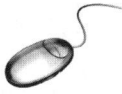

# 3

# Theories

## Technology, the Grassroots, and Network Generativity

### Thomas Streeter and Zephyr Teachout

#### Introduction: From Echo Chambers
#### to Interpretive Communities

In the ordinary course of life, many of the assumptions that undergird our sense of the world—the informal maps of meaning that we use to make sense of ourselves and others—are unseen. Like water to fish, these assumptive frameworks become so taken for granted to us that they become invisible. Yet there are moments in history when such assumptions suddenly erupt into view: An encounter with another religion, for example, can bring one to suddenly think about, and perhaps question, the fundamentals of one's own; an economic calamity can make one wonder about the underlying principles of the economy.[1] When a community comes up against alternative systems of meaning or sudden shifts in the social fabric, previously held "truths" are suddenly no longer truths but concepts, available for scrutiny and perhaps change. These can be moments of both disquieting vertigo and unusual hope; so much becomes uncertain, and so much becomes conceivable.

The Dean campaign, we believe, was such a moment. The chapters that follow are in a sense stories of life at a moment when old certainties dissolved and new possibilities opened up—stories of life inside a paradigm shift. Some of the certainties that fell by the wayside do not need elaboration, such as the once rock-solid belief that big money donors or appeals to the perceived political center are inevitable realities of any national campaign. But others deserve clarification. The Dean campaign's uniqueness is most often attributed to its use of technology and to its grassroots character. In this chapter, we explore some theoretical implications of these two claims. We inquire into the possible meanings of the words *technology* and *grassroots*, the assumptions they tend to carry along with them, and some of their strengths and limitations. And we suggest the idea of "network generativity" for capturing how the relationship between these two trends might best be understood.

But why and how do abstract theoretical questions of this sort matter? These days, discussions of the Internet and politics are often peppered with references to specific communities of belief: echo chambers,[2] inside the beltway, bubbles, the gang of 500,[3] and so forth. Too often, however, these phrases are used simply to imply a disconnect from reality, that those folks inside the bubble or beltway or right- or left-wing blogosphere have convinced themselves of one or another falsehood or irrelevance. This idea that particular groups of people have insulated themselves from the truth often underlies the deep and ongoing debate inside the Democratic Party over whether or not the Dean campaign was deluded or a harbinger of a more democratic (and Democratic) future. Each side tends to accuse the other of working inside an unrealistic bubble.

The problem is that such arguments are often nothing more than competing assertions about unknowables—what if the mainstream media had not attacked Dean as unelectable in the lead-up to Iowa? What if Al Gore had endorsed Dean two weeks before Iowa instead of two months after? What if Dean (or Kerry, for that matter) had been more (or less) sharp in criticizing the war in Iraq? Any thinking person has to grant that watertight answers to these questions are unobtainable.

The fact is that much of this is not about facts. Much of the discussion of political strategy and tactics in our day, for all its frequent claims about "practicalities" and "hard truths," is less about existing realities than about a set of efforts to *create* realities. The press corps' habit of designating candidates as "serious" or "not serious" in the early stages of a campaign is only the most obvious of these self-fulfilling patterns, where the description helps create that which it describes.[4] With varying degrees of self-consciousness, many of the recent assertions about what works and what doesn't in American politics are as much efforts to generate self-fulfilling political descriptions as they are efforts to describe them.

The argument here is not that all discussions of political strategy and tactics are really just smoke screens hiding someone's political agenda. The idea is that, in the face of so much uncertainty, it is inevitable that arguments carry at least some aspect of a normative vision. Those who argue that Democrats need to stake out centrist positions in order to win, not surprisingly, are more often than not people who are more comfortable with centrist political positions.

It is a sociological truism that social life is to a large degree constructed out of implicit or taken-for-granted systems of meaning or worldviews created and shared by groups of individuals—by what Stanley Fish dubbed interpretive communities.[5] We think this concept is usefully applied here. The debate about what to do with the Democratic Party is not only a debate about facts, but a debate about worldviews. What is at stake is not simply which interpretation is more accurate, but which worldview might be brought to success in the future.

The worldviews that undergird interpretive communities are as often implicit as explicit, and do not always fall out in a clean spectrum of left to right. People's strategic claims often emerge from what they assume about human nature and society, as opposed to what they explicitly advocate. For example, reporters, corporate managers, and politicians often share a managerial worldview that trusts experts, numbers, and functionaries; when trying to predict or understand political success, they tend to focus on things like money, technique, and the professional background of staffers. So when Dean confounded this group by being more successful than they would have predicted *on their own terms* (fund-raising), their impulse was to go off in search of techniques—the new technology of the Internet, "exploiting" the antiwar vote—that would explain it. Political managerialists, for example, often look with admiration at the efforts of their fellows in different, sometimes opposing, political camps.

By contrast, a certain kind of political activist of both the right and the left is often more concerned with passion, sincerity, or clearly formed ideology. For example, there's a mutual respect that anti-corporate leftists and libertarians sometimes accord one another, especially on the Internet; they share a distaste for inside-the-beltway emphases on technique and consensus building. So these groups are more likely to focus on things like Dean's sincerity ("he says what he means") or his willingness to break from the pack. Conservative direct-mail activist Richard Viguerie is an interesting example, not least because the larger world knows him mostly as a right-wing campaign technician. Yet his book with David Franke, *America's Right Turn*, depicts the Dean campaign as a case of liberals finally learning what conservatives learned thirty years ago: to speak their minds and circumvent the powers that be of the mainstream media using alternative venues.

Viguerie speaks of the Dean campaign with much more admiration than, say, Clinton campaign consultant James Carville or centrist pundit Joe Klein. (He includes, for example, a page of admiring quotations from Joe Trippi.[6]) What Viguerie shares with many liberal Internet activists, and what distinguishes both him and those activists from others in their own respective parties, is an implicit worldview that values autonomous individualism and that distrusts established power and an overemphasis on technique. (These are not the only worldviews that mattered to the Dean campaign, of course. As subsequent chapters show, many approached the campaign neither as managers nor as radical individualists, but in the spirit of a kind of community-focused collectivism, a belief in the political power and political wisdom of interdependent groups.)

"Echo chambers," in this sense, are an inevitable aspect of human social existence, not pathologies. Most often the existence of interpretive communities is used to explain cultural differences, such as why some people believe in shamans and others believe in psychiatrists. But interpretive communities need not mean that all truths are relative. The argument is simply that truths are in the first instance social accomplishments, achieved through shared languages and systems of meaning; it is through specific interpretive communities that we have learned that diseases are caused by microbes instead of witchcraft. And much of our world—money, nation-states, laws, for example—exists largely insofar as significant numbers of us are persuaded, through practices of interpretation, to believe that they exist. The success or failure of any given "echo chamber" often depends on whether or not it can persuade enough people with enough power that, by acting on the beliefs in question, they go on to make them true.

The mainstream media's habit of describing Dean as an angry, intemperate person rests alongside "compassionate conservatism," Iraqi weapons of mass destruction, "they will greet us with flowers," and other astonishing collective gaffes-with-consequences of post-9/11 America, gaffes that our society would do well to ponder at length. But these factual errors, we think, are not so much causes as symptoms of underlying systems of interpretation—systems rooted in a need to trust authority, systems that would not have evaporated in the face of a little more accurate reporting on CNN. And so we turn to some of the systems of interpretation that have been applied to the Dean campaign.

## Does the Internet Change Everything? Technological Determinism

There is no question that the Dean campaign could not have happened without the existence of the Internet as a widely accessible, decentralized, and, by 2002, familiar medium of communication. At the time, the technology was more omnipresent than it had ever been before and it was underutilized by both political operatives and conventional media, creating a context ideally suited for an insurgent campaign that was operating outside the common political wisdom, just as that wisdom was starting to founder on the Iraq War. In that particular context, the technology itself mattered.

But how should we interpret this? There is a temptation to use the lens of technological determinism, the idea that technology is an autonomous force capable of causing social change. *Wired* magazine—which has turned technological determinism into something like a lifestyle statement—published an article in January 2004 titled "How the Internet Invented Howard Dean," implying that the entire campaign was simply an effect of Internet technology.[7]

After a century of what seems to be ever-quickening waves of new technologies sweeping into citizens' lives, the idea that new technologies cause change might seem to be self-evident. But it is one thing to say that new technologies might make some difference in some circumstances, and another to treat new technologies as the *primary* cause of change—to essentially explain significant events like the Dean campaign primarily by reference to technology. What if the energy around the campaign had nothing to do with technology and everything to do with, as the conservative *Weekly Standard* suggested at the time, "group-think contempt for Bush"?[8] (Or what if, as some on the left argued at the time, it was all about Dean's stance on the war?) A line of reasoning that assumes the causal power of technology and proceeds from there makes it difficult to even address such questions.

Making fun of technological prognostication is not hard. The list of failed or disappointing technologically caused "revolutions" in human affairs is long and comic: Besides the paperless office and the 1990s stock bubble, there was, for example, the prediction in the 1920s that the airplane would end war, or the one in the 1960s that nuclear energy would make electricity too cheap to meter.[9] But even if one disavows the full-throated technological determinism that leads to such predictions, a tendency to make technology the central issue can nonetheless persist. The frequent description of the Dean campaign as an "Internet campaign," for example, can imply that the Internet was all that distinguished the campaign from other ones, and eclipse the importance of issues like the war or the grassroots character of the campaign.

It is important that the Dean campaign, at least on the inside, was *not* itself organized around a belief in technological determinism. As the following chapters make clear, the campaign focus was on human interconnection by any means: Traditional letter writing, canvassing, and of course varieties of face-to-face encounters from Meetups to house parties to Iowa's "perfect storm" were always central to the campaign. As Zephyr Teachout recounts in her chapter, at one point she took an old renovated Airstream bus on a city-by-city tour to meet Dean supporters face-to-face—an almost anti-Internet approach. Within the campaign, Internet technology was seen as a tool, as one tool among many, not as a cause, and certainly not as something whose effects could be taken for granted.

Broadly, we find it useful to think of the role of the Internet in the campaign not as a strictly technological issue, but as something more like architecture or urban design. The capacity to build with concrete, brick, and glass is one thing; the specific design of buildings and neighborhoods is another. The technological capacity to communicate via computers using websites, discussion lists, and e-mail was already more than a decade old by the time of the Dean campaign. Meetups, blogs, and so forth were a design innovation more than a technology, in a class with public parks or row houses. What was new in 2002 and 2003 was the adoption of new architectures for campaigning at a time of political crisis, and the social integration of these into political discourse and organization.

## Rhetorics of Technological Utopianism

Looking at the campaign through a technology-centered lens, however, was common enough during the campaign. This is partly because framing things through the lens of technology can be a useful rhetorical tactic. A technology-centered view, whatever its logical flaws, allows for the projection of a new discursive terrain.[10] Arguing that an entrenched institution is doomed to fall in the face of technological progress can be much more compelling than, say, arguing that the institution is simply wrong or in need of improvement. In the Progressive Era, Louis Brandeis found it effective to argue for antitrust action against the railroads because, he claimed, they were not run according to the latest scientific principles.[11] In the 1930s, New Deal reforms like the TVA were often touted as not just fair but modern, as of a piece with the march of progress. In the 1960s, Marshall McLuhan made technological determinism available to the counterculture: Peace, love, and altered consciousness were not just nice, they were (somehow) the wave of the future.

If Dean had been just, say, the advocate of national health care, or the more-to-the-left-but-still-mainstream candidate, or the fiscal conservative who was against the war, developing a following might have been extremely difficult. But as he was the "Internet candidate" his coalition could be broader, and individuals who otherwise might disagree on one or another political point could nonetheless find a reason to get involved. This is most obvious in the way that the Internet became a "news peg" for reporters to make sense of the campaign as it started to gain momentum; its newsworthiness, the thing that made it stand out from other candidacies, was that it was the Internet campaign. Yet the pattern goes deeper. Part of what made the campaign what it was, what attracted a slew of young Internet enthusiasts and created an iconoclastic sense of openness, an enthusiasm for experimentation, and a new sense of hope, was the way it became associated with the *vision* of new technology and a widespread fascination with the future.

Somewhat paradoxically, the Internet was a symbol as much as a technology, a metaphor as much as it was a means. It symbolized broad change and new possibility. The utopian hopes for democratic change associated with technological determinism were significant to the campaign's relative successes *independent* of the actual capacities of the technology.

Associating one's political cause with new technology is appealing in two ways. First, it eases the path for iconoclasm, for a kind of circumvention of standard political wisdoms. If a problem is defined as a relatively narrow human issue—say, Democratic Party fund-raising habits—then advocating change becomes a matter of arcane arguments and slow struggle. But if the problem is defined as keeping up with an inevitable technology-driven revolution, then calls for doing things differently have the force of the march of progress behind them, and those who express doubt risk putting themselves among the backward, among those who "don't get it." Relatedly, being the Internet candidate allowed Dean to take on other, substantive orthodoxies, implying by proxy that they too were old-fashioned. Coming from the Internet candidate, voting for No Child Left Behind was not simply immoral, it was anachronistic—the submerged story line being that the politics of the past and the politics of the future were different not just in technique, but in substance. Democratic orthodoxies that would have been difficult to challenge directly (and be taken seriously by the media) were then open to him to criticize, as the candidate of the future.

Second, technological determinism helps create an impression of political impartiality: The argument is not on behalf of this or that interest group or point on the political spectrum, but about something that—in theory—we should all agree on: being abreast of the times. (This helps explain some of the strange political bedfellows one encounters among Internet enthusiasts, such as libertarian and left bloggers who find solidarity in their sense that the Internet will overthrow entrenched interests.)

Did the image of the Dean campaign as Internet driven also have some negative effects? Could the technological aura of progress and inevitability that helped give the campaign credence and momentum have also lent itself to, say, the media's often glib and misleading treatment of the campaign (it was the Internet campaign, so there was no need to explore, say, the depth and richness of Dean's positions on foreign policy or taxation)? Even though the campaign was not at its core just about technology, could that aura have lent itself to the perhaps naive faith on the part of some of the campaign's online cheerleaders, or perhaps to the ineffectiveness of the on-the-ground efforts in Iowa? These are things that cannot be known for certain. But it remains the case that if symbols matter, they can also mislead. Even as a rhetorical strategy, wrapping oneself too tightly in the aura of new technology carries risks.

This leaves open the question of exactly how important the specific technologies used by the campaign were, and in what ways those technologies made a difference. Here, we think this is best treated as an empirical question, and refer readers to the chapters that follow.

## Visions of Democracy: Who and What Is the Grassroots?

In Joe Trippi's first post to the Dean campaign's official blog, he wrote, "We may not have as much money as other candidates, but we have more netroots support and grassroots support than all of them combined." He asked the "netroots" to donate money and asked everyone to go to Meetup.com to build a national organization of grassroots supporters.[12] At the time (March 15, 2003), a few thousand people had signed up for Howard Dean's Meetups, and between e-mail and direct-mail addresses, around 20,000 people were "signed up" to be contacted by his campaign. What did Joe Trippi mean when he said "We have more grassroots support than all of them combined?" It would not have meant much if it was simply a description of these still-paltry numbers.

Throughout the campaign, "the Dean grassroots" were lauded, encouraged, probed—but what are "the grassroots," and what effect does using this word have? The word *grassroots*—a central, persistent word within the Dean campaign, used both by those on the inside and those in the news media and the blogosphere—may be imprecise and generic, but it also contains a real power. *Netroots* and *grassroots* are both slippery terms—both allow such a variety of interpretations that they sometimes seem meaningless. McCain's use of the Internet for fund-raising in 2000 was said to have showed his "grassroots support," and massive online petitions are regularly called "grassroots efforts," while a small group of popular bloggers repeating the same story is often called a "netroots" pressure. Yet the word had a real meaning for many on the Dean campaign. When Trippi later called the campaign the "greatest grassroots campaign in modern history,"[13] the effect was different from, say, calling it "the greatest campaign in history" or "the greatest Internet campaign in history."

The word *grassroots* has a long and important history in U.S. politics dating to the Progressive Era, and carries a connotation of somehow being natural, and thus distinct from the imposed or hierarchical political relations of established political institutions. In many situations, including in its association with the Dean campaign, it is as much a statement of hope as of fact. It is not a direct statement of numbers—one can have more grassroots support and have less overall support. Nor is it a reference to voters of a specific socioeconomic status. It is a vision of organic or spontaneous collective political action from below. *Grassroots* signals a different relationship between the candidate or idea and those who support him or her—a candidate with strong grassroots support signals that the supporters are active instead of swooning—and pure adulation is incompatible with being part of a grassroots campaign if only because it indicates a fundamental passivity.

Furthermore, it stands in opposition to the idea of voters and supporters as consumers—most often expressed by those starting sentences along the lines of "voters don't want" or "voters are seeking," in which the word *consumer* could easily replace *voter*. In the voter/consumer model, voters have established preferences that they express by choosing a preexisting commodity or candidate. There is still a hint of this in the Rovian idea of the "base," which suggests a fixed set of ideals that can be appealed to, but a fundamentally passive mind and action. Appealing to "the grassroots" necessarily means appealing to people's own political capacity to lead and develop, not simply to their already fixed political preferences. The word *grassroots* also offers the expectation that the candidate is a reflection of those who support him or her, and not a fixed and final entity.

The word also signaled that this was not just a campaign of people at their keyboards, but was focused on the very old-fashioned idea of grassroots and face-to-face organizing. The companion term *netroots* actually had a relatively short life, used only early in the campaign, and was generally replaced by the term *grassroots* for the duration of the Dean campaign.[14]

The term *grassroots* carries with it the implication that ordinary society is not democratic enough. Those who use the term typically believe that political life is overly managed and exclusive. But in contrast with, say, libertarians or anarchic techno-utopians, who tend to see any form of collective governance as undesirable, the appeal to a grassroots is an appeal to some form of collective political action. It thus stands in opposition to both the managerial model and the techno-utopian/libertarian model of a good political society.

Grassroots can also imply authenticity:[15] an authentic involvement of people in a campaign and an associated commitment to a more open, distributed system of decision making. "Grassroots" action is often set up in opposition to mainstream media, or media-driven action. Grassroots support implies—and was often deeply experienced as—support that is derived from a set of authentic, individual experiences, instead of a media-created experience. The repeated use of the phrase "the greatest grassroots campaign in history" was a signal, a refrain that reinforced the burgeoning, open structure of the campaign in the phrasing. Authenticity, in this sense, was also deeply tied to community—one can be inauthentic in a broadcast setting, but it is very difficult to maintain an inauthentic personality over time with repeated contacts with a small set of people. The word *grassroots* communicated a sense of community and face-to-face interactions around social change and political action.

In a way, then, "the grassroots" was both the imagined community and the community that imagined the strategy for the rest of the country; it signaled that the campaign talked to its supporters because its supporters were the staff. The word, used officially, became a promise that each individual can have a more powerful relationship to politics.

As the chapters ahead reveal, how that was supposed to happen was never precisely defined. Exactly how to involve the supportive, active citizen was a matter of experimentation, debate, and sometimes just plain confusion. At what point do mass e-mails lose their authenticity and just become a kind of spam? Is the purpose of discussion lists and Meetups to extract ideas or just money? How autonomous can local groups be? Should e-mails use html so that they look polished or just plain ascii text so they come across as authentic? Is a bus full of Californians for Dean headed to Iowa the grassroots? Or is the grassroots the small political organizations scattered across Iowa? Is the undeniable grassroots character of the Dean campaign a peculiar product of the time, of the sense of crisis and the failure of the Democratic establishment prior to 2003, or is it something that can be sustained across many campaigns and situations?

The word *grassroots* is perhaps best understood as one of what Raymond Williams called "keywords," words like *democracy* and *culture*, for which "the problems of their meaning are inextricably bound up with the problems they are being used to discuss."[16] The word *grassroots* expresses a hope and opens up a question. It carves out a space for talking about people as political actors in a community, even if it does not explain exactly how that is supposed to happen. In the same way that a shared commitment to a text (a religious text or a constitutional text) can create a space to debate the meaning of that text, a shared commitment to "the grassroots" creates a space without specifically answering the question of the shape that grassroots can take.

## On the Generativity of Networks in Politics

The immense productivity of humanity during the last two or three centuries is dependent upon open networks of communication and the feedback loops of knowledge they occasion. Economist Joel Mokyr has argued that the industrial revolution was made possible in part by the development during the late Enlightenment Era of technologies and institutions that encouraged the relatively low cost and unrestricted sharing of information, emblematized in the rise of encyclopedias and scientific journals.[17] The traditional Chinese Mandarin culture, for all its brilliance, had limited effects on economic development because its communications were limited to a narrow elite. Sustainable economic progress, Mokyr argues, requires technological innovation, and technological innovation requires forms of communication that are widely circulated and open to criticism. In this view, the information revolution predates the Internet by centuries.

Yochai Benkler, in *The Wealth of Networks*, does not disagree. But he argues that computers and the Internet are enabling a new stage of the information revolution. The previous century or so of communication systems—from the first penny press newspapers to blockbuster-producing Hollywood studios—were dependent upon expensive, centralizing technologies like the steam-powered rotary press and special effects systems. Now, however, low barriers to entry have enabled a "networked information economy" characterized by "decentralized individual action—specifically, new and important cooperative and coordinated action carried out through radically distributed, nonmarket mechanisms that do not depend on proprietary strategies." This has led to an increasing importance of various nonprofit and nonproprietary forms of production, typified by peer-to-peer production of free and open-source software. For Benkler, this is not only of economic significance; the networked information economy improves the capacity of individuals to do more for and by themselves, to do more in loose commonality with others, and—significantly when thinking about politics—to do more in formal organizations that operate outside the market sphere.[18]

Jonathan Zittrain, in recent work, summarizes this new capacity under the heading "generativity."[19] What is distinctive about the Internet as a communications network is that any users who think they can improve the message-sending ability, or the operating system by which the Internet works, can do so. Zittrain argues that the capacity to transform this network while it was being built is what led to the development of hyperlinking, backtracking, and the great variety—and quality—of operating systems that exist. Zittrain worries that this generativity is threatened, however, by an opposing tendency, exemplified in relatively closed, centralized networks, such as CompuServe. Concerns about spam, viruses, and perhaps terrorism, he worries, might drive society to adopt a more closed information economy, a proprietary one in which we can play multi-user games on our Xbox 360s, but not easily make and distribute our own games, where we can surf the web on our iPhones, but not write or add software to those phones without gaining permission from—and paying—the corporations that control it. We will be able to buy operating systems, but not be able to improve upon operating systems that are working on our computer. Moreover, we will basically rent—not own—the tools we have on our own computers. Our computers' operating systems will be tethered to their makers—unlike a toaster, which we can use as intended to make toast, but also as the basis of a way, say, to mechanically distribute poker chips—we will only be able to use our operating systems in a limited way. Moreover, unlike a toaster seller, who would likely be arrested if he barged into one's home to upgrade a toaster at odd hours, our appliances will be regularly, invisibly updated by the sellers of the product. Not only will we not be allowed to improve our own experience, we will not own our own experience.

How relevant are these concerns to electoral politics? Does the Dean campaign represent a new form of "generativity" in politics, and is that generativity threatened by opposing tendencies? Indeed, one of the undersung accomplishments of the Dean campaign was its sheer creativity. Besides the well-known innovations like Meetups, house parties, e-mails, and general interactivity, there were other innovations, many of which are described in the chapters that follow: remixed political speeches like the Dean Dance Mix, a community-service flash-mob inspired by the desire to make a *Doonesbury* cartoon a reality, beach cleaning wearing Dean T-shirts, radio advertisements funded by independent supporters, Rapid Response Network, Punx for Dean, and a great variety of governance structures in the local groups. The point is not that each of these was hugely effective, but that the many innovations of the Dean campaign that *were* effective emerged from the same experimental and creative environment. In some sense of the word, the Dean campaign was definitely a highly generative environment, in which large numbers of citizens were able to do much more than simply select from a series of predetermined choices.

Yet politics cannot be reduced to computer networking. All politics—and the Dean campaign was no exception—depends on and will continue to depend on varieties of face-to-face communication, whether these are Meetups or churches or simple encounters with personal networks like coworkers and families. And Howard Dean was certainly not the first candidate to "come from nowhere" to surprise the political establishment; think of Bill Clinton or Jimmy Carter (or if one wants to go back that far, Abraham Lincoln or Andrew Jackson). The Dean campaign was on occasion referred to as an "open source campaign," yet to at least some extent this was a metaphor. When Dean made "You have the power" a theme of his campaign, he was making a political statement, not a technological one. Creativity, loose collaboration, and constant improvement may also be familiar to anyone who has done politics on a hyperlocal scale, in, say, city or town governments.

Yet the Dean campaign provided a model of what "generative politics" can look like on a national scale. National politics since the 1950s has developed a lot more like CompuServe than like the Internet. Most major political networks involved differentiated senders and receivers—those who made the messages and those who got them. Because of a culture that developed almost accidentally—and because of the central metaphor of the Internet itself, reinforcing this culture—the members of the Dean campaign network could, like a good coder, improve their own platform and communicate directly with any other member of the network about anything, without getting permission from the campaign. While Michael Silberman's stories about the monthly campaign conference calls with organizers around the country are inspiring, the fact that the organizers chatted in an ongoing, unmediated way through Dean-MeetupHosts and over 1,000 other listservs is more striking. If someone had an idea about how to reach out to minority neighborhoods in Atlanta, not only could they could start implementing the idea immediately, they could share lessons from what they were learning and talk directly to any other member of the network—typically, but not always, using the Internet to find another member—about their struggles.

Did this open, generative aspect of the Dean campaign flow automatically from its use of the Internet? Certainly not automatically, as most subsequent political campaigns that have adopted various aspects of the Internet demonstrate. The Kerry and Bush campaigns used the Internet extensively—raising more money and building bigger lists than Dean—but neither developed the same kind of open, generative community where people took ownership of their own ideas. In politics, the "technology" that constrains members from unmediated communication and platform improving is not a technology at all. It is culture. Likewise, the greatest enabling technology was not the technology per se; it was a culture in which people were encouraged to have a meaningful conversation about strategy, media, politics, and power without a single representative of the campaign in the room, and to act on those conversations. Meetup was not only a technology that enabled those meetings; it was a technology that signaled openness to those meetings—even those that weren't held through Meetup.

Although tools like Meetup, e-mail, and Deanspace can enable open activities, they are no guarantee of a generative culture. Although nearly every 2008 candidate is using a blog and some kind of social networking tool, there is a vast difference in the degree to which they are inspiring creative input. A generative culture is fragile, and most often occasions a lot of resistance; culture can close down a network as quickly as it can open one up. Zittrain's fear about the Internet is that the frustration from things like spam and viruses will kill the Internet's generativity—we, the people, will beg for the spam and viruses to be shut down, and we will give up our freedom in the process. In politics, the reason candidates frequently give for not wanting to give up too much control is that it will hurt them. Someone will say something stupid, the campaign will go off message, explanations will have to be given to the press, and things will unravel. It will be the "scream" many times over.

People are accustomed to a sender-receiver culture; without something dramatic, like an acute sense of crisis or an acute sense of new possibilities (the Dean campaign had both), few are going to be eager to change that. In most national political campaigns, all communications between state directors will gravitate toward being mediated, and even though the national group is constantly asking for creativity, the people they ask for creativity are in an inner circle—and it is generally understood that there are clear limits to the kinds of information that less central groups should talk about. Local supporters are supposed to be tethered to the central campaign; whatever generativity exists is just on loan.

The Internet was always both means and metaphor for the Dean campaign, creating a confusing blend of possibilities—and also a confusing blend of limitations. Although political generativity is possible without the Internet, it is hard to imagine on a national level, in a country with a population of 300 million. So it seems reasonable to say that future, nationwide forms of political generativity will be fundamentally dependent on—though not caused by—the openness of the Internet and its descendants. Furthermore, the technically limited future that Zittrain fears is finally a function of culture, not technology—the limitations arise from the fact that we can only suffer so much chaos. But in politics, the difference is that the cry for control of political generativity tends to come not from those users who experience it—not from the citizens, millions of whom are not particularly active, and untroubled by a little uncertainty—but from people who would act as our representatives.

## The Future of a Citizen Identity

Jürgen Habermas's notion of a democratic public sphere is as likable as it is difficult to operationalize. Perhaps in the American context, part of the problem is the translation of Habermas's *Öffentlichkeit*—literally, "openness"—by use of an essentially spatial term ("sphere"), as if achieving open democratic dialogue and generativity were mostly about creating specific spaces apart from the rest of life. This location-based emphasis is echoed in the standard historical examples of effective public spheres: the eighteenth-century London coffeehouse, the Parisian salon, the colonial American tavern. Yet what is perhaps missed in the translation here is the way in which significant historical moments of political openness and generativity happen, not because there is some sort of escape into a different space, not so much *in spite of* the constraints of their time, but *because of* the specific, contingent textures of life at a given time, the specific mix of opportunities and constraints that shape different historical moments. *Öffentlichkeit* is something that bubbles up out of everyday life, not something that needs protection from it.

"Openness" is a better description of the Internet's function in the Dean campaign than is "public sphere." The campaign was no philosophy seminar. It was not apart from the media, or apart from the play of power and passions that shape American life. It was alternately chaotic, playful, pragmatic, and driven by a sense of crisis. Most of all, it was deeply improvisational, and characterized more by a flow of new and changing ideas and individuals than by any kind of carefully structured, tightly balanced debate. The Internet did enable some very significant kinds of openness to new kinds of political activity and association, to new individuals, and to new ideas. But perhaps the most significant thing about it was simply that at the time it was a new, underutilized flexible tool. The Internet did not cause the campaign to be creative. Rather, because the contributors to the campaign were innovative, it used the Internet.

  Effective democracy needs something more than rules and formal institutions. It needs energy and passion, for without them, it is likely to decline in the face of apathetic cynicism, or be overridden by energies and passions associated with, say, ethnic identity or nationalist feeling. Considering this problem, Habermas has called for a new "constitutional patriotism," for a new kind of citizen identity that bears some of the energy of national identity but is directed toward the principles and practices of democracy rather than toward the interests of a particular nation-state.[20] The Dean campaign suggests one possible vision for energizing citizens not just around a candidate but around a creative process of democracy making. Being involved with the Dean campaign meant being involved in a series of relatively self-conscious experiments in forming connections among citizens for the sake of broad democratic (small *d*) change. Some of these experiments worked better than others, some took place in the full glare of mass media and others completely offscreen, and many of them may have worked because of the specific historical context. But perhaps the most important legacy of the campaign is the way it points to the possibility of a generative, open process of citizen activism on a national level, and suggests at least one way that such a process might manifest itself.

## Notes

1. The response is not always the abandonment of the original system: A theology or a new economic theory can be brought in to defend the no-longer-obvious truths. But if it's worth defending, then it is something that can be questioned, and its defenders are no longer "all reasonable people," but a specific group.

2. "Echo chamber" was used to refer to conservative efforts, but has since been used to refer to self-delusions on the left, for example, http://dir.salon.com/story/tech/col/leon/2004/11/03/echo_chamber/index.html (accessed June 1, 2007).

3. http://en.wikipedia.org/wiki/Gang_of_500 (accessed June 1, 2007).

4. See Michael Schudson, *The Sociology of News* (New York: W. W. Norton, 2003), pp. 17–18. As a classic example of this kind of coverage, see Howard Fineman, "Living Politics: Who's for Real in Democrats' Race," *Newsweek* (September 18, 2002; online only).

5. The phrase *interpretive community* was made famous by Stanley Fish in *Is There a Text in This Class? The Authority of Interpretive Communities* (Cambridge, MA: Harvard University Press, 1980). The general idea that meanings are collectively created and stabilized in symbol use by interacting communities, however, has a much wider currency in anthropology and

sociology, going back, on this side of the Atlantic, to the works of C. S. Peirce, G. H. Mead, and the symbolic interactionist school and, on the other side, to Husserl, Alfred Schutz, and the tradition of phenomenological sociology.

6. Viguerie portrays his famous efforts to use direct mail to help bring conservatives to power in the United States as a rebellion against the powers-that-be of the dominant liberal media, not as a technique. Richard Viguerie and David Franke, *America's Right Turn: How Conservatives Used New and Alternative Media to Take Power* (Chicago and Los Angeles: Bonus Books, 2004), p. 312.

7. Gary Wolf, "How the Internet Invented Howard Dean," *Wired* 12, no. 1, January 2004; http://www.wired.com/wired/archive/12.01/dean.html (accessed June 1, 2007). Wolf actually takes a somewhat more nuanced stance than the title implies, arguing that Dean was having an impact because "he listens to the technology," that Dean succeeded because he was sensitive to the Internet and the disaffected political voices that populated it. Yet the article's emphasis still draws the causal arrow largely from the Internet to the campaign.

8. David Skinner, "Howard's Web: The Dean Camp's Internet Impresario," *Weekly Standard,* http://press.Meetup.com/archives/000593.html (accessed June 1, 2007).

9. For the airplane bringing peace, see Joseph J. Corn, *The Winged Gospel: America's Romance with Aviation* (Baltimore: Johns Hopkins University Press, 2002).

10. Thomas Streeter, "The Cable Fable Revisited: Discourse, Policy, and the Making of Cable Television," *Critical Studies in Mass Communication* (June 1987): 174–200.

11. Thomas K. McCraw, *Prophets of Regulation: Charles Francis Adams, Louis D. Brandeis, James M. Landis, Alfred E. Kahn* (Cambridge, MA: Harvard University Press, 1984), p. 92.

12. http://www.blogforamerica.com/view/2 (accessed June 1, 2007).

13. Jonathan Raban, "The Flip-Flop Candidate," *Guardian,* January 17, 2004, http://books.guardian.co.uk/review/story/0,12084,1124901,00.html (accessed June 1, 2007).

14. A review of Blog for America posts shows that *grassroots* was the term of choice for most of the campaign. A Lexis-Nexis review of news articles from 2003 shows frequent references to the Dean grassroots, and fewer than five references to the netroots.

15. The existence of the word *Astroturf* to describe top-down commenting on blogs and listservs is proof that people distinguish between authentic and inauthentic grassroots, that authenticity is part of the term's meaning.

16. Raymond Williams, *Keywords: A Vocabulary of Culture and Society* (New York: Oxford University Press, 1985), p. 15.

17. Joel Mokyr, *The Gifts of Athena: Historical Origins of the Knowledge Economy* (Princeton, NJ: Princeton University Press, 2002).

18. Yochai Benkler, *The Wealth of Networks: How Social Production Transforms Markets and Freedom* (New Haven, CT: Yale University Press, 2006), pp. 3–8.

19. Jonathan Zittrain, *The Future of the Internet and How to Stop It* (New Haven, CT: Yale University Press, 2008). See also Jonathan Zittrain, "The Generative Internet," *Harvard Law Review* 119 (May 2006): 1974.

20. Jürgen Habermas, *The New Conservatism: Cultural Criticism and the Historians' Debate,* ed. and trans. Shierry Weber Nicholsen (Cambridge: Massachusetts Institute of Technology Press, 1989), especially "Historical Consciousness and Post-Traditional Identity: The Federal Republic's Orientation to the West," 249–267. Clarissa Rile Hayward offers an astute overview and critique of the issue in "Democracy's Identity Problem: Is 'Constitutional Patriotism' the Answer?" Occasional Paper 27 of the School of Social Science, Institute for Advanced Study, November 2006.

# II
# Stories of the Campaign

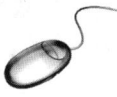

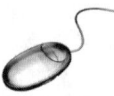

# 4

# How a Blogger and the Dean
# Campaign Discovered Each Other

## *Jerome Armstrong*

*Jerome Armstrong founded the political blog MyDD and is a key figure in the creation of what some call "the liberal blogosphere" or "netroots" as a political force. He started blogging in support of Howard Dean's candidacy in April 2002, and in the fall of 2002 he joined the volunteer-run Dean Nation blog. In the months that followed the campaign kickoff in January 2003, he worked with the campaign directors to integrate the decentralized online movement with the campaign, and he persuaded Joe Trippi to use Meetup.com for organizing. Within the campaign, from May 2003 to February 2004 at the Burlington, Vermont, headquarters, he directed Internet advertising, helped coordinate blogger outreach, and built and administered Dean's ForumForAmerica.com community website (built with Markos Moulitsas; Murshed Zaheed ran the community), among other campaign tasks, but in this chapter he focuses on the early months, providing details of how the nascent netroots and the Dean campaign discovered each other. This was an essential and unique event—essential, because this serendipitous alliance transformed the campaign and charted new political waters, and unique, because having a campaign so open to outside influence was unprecedented. It is important to remember that at the time (and in many cases still to this day) the events Armstrong describes here—the spontaneous creation of pro-Dean blogs and websites, for example, or the free offering of strategic advice—would have been considered irrelevant or even annoying to the vast majority of professional political campaigners. Armstrong and his online compatriots managed to bring a mixture of political urgency, an improvisatory spirit imported from the Internet, and thoughtful optimism to the effort.*

## The Birth of MyDD and the Online
## Progressive Community 2000–2002

I first learned about Howard Dean before he was even a candidate. In the fall of 2001 then-governor Dean traveled throughout the states to seek support for his potential presidential run. I was in graduate school at Portland State University, and lived in Seaside, Oregon. I spent a good deal of time following politics online.

In the fall and winter of 2000, I'd become enthralled with participating in the political board forums of Salon.com as the presidential election heated up and then simmered on for a couple of months in Florida. It was my political junkie moment. The U.S. Supreme Court's 5–4 decision to elect George W. Bush president sparked the opposition movement among progressives, and it began online. As the nation watched the events in Florida unfold, mostly on television, I, along with a few thousand other folks, followed the events through information gathered over the Internet and shared in places like Salon.com's Table Talk forums.

At the time, Republicans were more organized in using the Internet to influence political coverage. For instance, in December 2000, it was a conservative member on FreeRepublic.com that Photoshopped a "Gore Lieberman" campaign sign to say "Sore Loserman." Another member of the community website, this time in Florida, took action and printed out stickers and yard signs with the slogan and handed them out to on-the-ground Republican activists; the conservative activists then paraded with them before the television cameras, as the Republican talking heads parroted the name calling.

The Republicans had been effectively using the Internet since the mid-1990s, when they had pushed the coverage of the Monica Lewinsky sex scandal, through FreeRepublic.com, DrudgeReport.com, and Lucianne.com, working with conservative talk radio, into the mainstream press; nothing similar was done by progressives and Democrats in response. But even more painful than watching conservatives mobilize over the Internet in greater numbers than progressives in 2000 was seeing the leadership of the Democratic Party take the defeat while making barely a peep of resistance. I felt outrage and disgust at the Republicans' contempt for the democratic process, and ready to help kick some spine into the Democratic Party.

Beginning in May 2001, when Salon.com went to a subscription model for posting privileges, I (along with writers such as Duncan Black of Atrios) moved from writing on message boards to blogging. I started off by writing political exposés on MyDD.com, covering campaigns, and predicting election outcomes. The first tagline I had for MyDD was from a quote by Jello Biafra, "Don't hate the media, become the media." I had long ago given up on television and newspaper, so all of my news sources were online, and though I had no idea as to whether anything I ever wrote would make a difference, I was participating within an ad hoc community of websites that were linking progressive readers to each other.

I couldn't even believe I had readers, but I did, numbering a few dozen and then a few hundred daily by the end of 2001. BuzzFlash.com often posted links to the pages, including one I created in early 2002, at Howard_Dean_For_President.MyDD.com.

## Why Dean?

Why Dean? The appeal of Howard Dean to the early progressive activists on the Internet was his straightforward manner of speaking, which especially translated well in the black-and-white world of Internet print format. His statements of contrast and opposition against Bush were enough to make me stand up and be counted as his supporter from very early in the presidential cycle.

On April 4, 2002, introducing the first Howard Dean for President web page, at a time when Bush was very popular and not at all being attacked by Democrats, I blogged:

> Bush polls what words people like to hear, and uses poll-tested words while pushing his rightwing agenda of unpopular policies—a little bit stealth and a lot of bit sneaky.
>
> There is a political opening here for attacking Bush. This *spin speaking* should be a rather straightforward task for the Democrats to dismantle for the voters to see. The only problem is that most of them are using the same tactics, so they'll poll on what words to counter the poll words with. A tit-for-tat we saw a lot of in 2000 with Gore versus Bush, nearly radically bested by the authentic candidacy of the moderate, plainspoken McCain. The Democrats need a voice like McCain's, who doesn't need to look at polls to know what to say, because their policies are already in line with the people, and can shoot from the hip while criticizing Bush.
>
> The voice may belong to VT Gov. Howard Dean. Here is an informal webpage with some clippings from articles online I've gathered: Howard Dean for President 2004.[1]
>
> In regards to this issue, when I look out across the likely Democratic field for President in 2004—Gore, Gephardt, Kerry, Edwards, and Dean—it's the latter who stands out in comparison with Bush. Maybe things will change from now till then as the candidates shape up, but Bush's poll-tested spin-speaking is an issue of credibility just waiting to be exploited by an authentic Democrat.[2]

The "Howard Dean for President in 2004" page was a simple collection of quotes spoken by Dean, pulled from over a dozen different sources, letting Howard be Howard, simply speaking on the issues. A sample includes:

> "I'm not interested in countering Bush," Dean said in an interview with The Associated Press. "I'm interested in laying out a vision for people, a practical vision based on experience."
>
> "I oppose virtually every position he has taken," Dean said of Bush. "I fundamentally believe the president's policies are very bad for this country." And "I think Democrats are interested in somebody who speaks their mind very frankly and is not afraid to take on conventional wisdom such as rolling back the tax cuts," Dean said.
>
> "I am deeply disturbed that in this country today we appear to be returning to the borrow-and-spend politics of the '80s," said Dean.
>
> "I think the president is absolutely wrong on his domestic agenda," Dean said. "This country is the last industrial country in the world that doesn't have universal health care, and we really ought to have it."
>
> "I'm driven by what I believe in. I believe that my vision of America is accepted by a great many more people than his vision of America is," Dean said of Bush.

In early 2002, I'd relaunched MyDD.com on a Gray Matter platform that included comments. All of a sudden, with the posting format changed to include immediate feedback from the readers, an interaction that formed an online community began to happen. I was used to posting about whatever I wanted, but the comments had a way of driving an expectation of coverage, and the blog became more and more politically focused, especially on Howard Dean.

I wasn't under the illusion that Dean would win. I'd backed long-shot presidential candidates like Jerry Brown, Bruce Babbitt, and Gary Hart in previous elections, and wasn't shy about going with the dark horse. I felt that the words being spoken by Howard Dean reflected the sentiment of the times. Having that voice of opposition to Bush was all that mattered. And I knew I wasn't alone. By the spring of 2002, others who liked Howard Dean found their way to the MyDD blog, commenting in support. Even though Dean was still unknown to the public, and we might have only numbered a few thousand, we were all together on one web space, interacting with each other in the comments, writing and reading the notes of others that supported Howard Dean.

## Contacting the Campaign

I took the next step, offline, in June 2002. Howard Dean was the keynote speaker for the King County Democratic Party in Seattle, Washington. I would meet Howard Dean. I drove up to Seattle in the morning and checked into the Seattle Youth Hostel. Changing for the event into a suit and tie that I hadn't worn in a few years, I had to ask a fellow hosteller from Britain to help knot my tie. I thought briefly, as I was walking up past Pikes Market to the Hilton hotel, about bailing on this crazy idea of just showing up to meet Howard Dean.

Beyond voting, I'd always shunned politics as too incremental and full of compromise for my transformational taste. But George Bush, to the Democratic Party's credit, had a knack for changing that dynamic; not only for myself, but also for millions of others that are awakening to being politically active in the first post-2001 decade. Howard Dean was running for president to defeat Bush, and I was his brother in arms for the battle.

I walked into the Hilton about an hour before the speaking event, paid my $50, and asked, "Where is Howard Dean?" The answer, "Take the elevator up to the top floor," pointed me in the direction. A few moments later, I was in front of Dean. Not realizing there was a reception before the event, I hadn't really thought much about what I would say. I blurted out the question, "Are you going to run for president?" Dean answered, "I intend to" without hesitation. A week or so later, in a post on MyDD titled "On Meeting Governor Howard Dean in His Questful Candidacy for President," I blogged: "I liked the answer—no skirting. A couple of others that were listening in were surprised, asking him if he'd already announced his candidacy (*he will in January*)." I was expecting some sort of hem or haw. Dean's straightforward candor engaged me.

I'd had no interaction with him or his staff previously, and no idea if he even knew about his online support from thousands of others on MyDD and other places where

Democrats were gathering around to chat on different blogs and community websites. We first chatted about Joe Trippi, competing in Iowa, and how the press likened Dean's potential appeal to that of McCain and then about the online support for Dean. I'd printed out about a dozen of the "Howard Dean for President" website pages to hand out, and explained the positive response it had created.

People that heard him speak someplace in person, I explained, or saw a news clip about him someplace on the Internet, or a clip on the television, would go to a search engine like Google, type in Howard Dean, and MyDD would come up as the top-ranked site. They would come to the Dean page on MyDD to learn more, and join in the discussion on the MyDD blog.

I continued on with what had become a pitch, that a community was forming over the Internet to support Dean for President and that this needed to happen with guidance from within his campaign whenever it got up and running. Howard responded by reflecting on what he recognized as problematic for him at the time. Without having national headquarters or campaign staff, he would go to a city, find receptive individuals, and have no means to keep in touch with them once he traveled on to the next place. Right on, I thought. Dean, who admitted he had little experience with the Internet (and it was probably the first time he'd ever heard of a blog), understood that the Internet could be used to organize. He got it.

I was satisfied by his affirmation of the effort, handed a copy of the web page to Dean's Vermont bodyguard for Dean to take back with him to his staff, and then listened to his speech and the receptive approval of the county Democrats. Afterward, I drove back to Portland, Oregon, to continue finishing up a graduate degree. I had a two-year-old son, and was applying to school in Hawaii for a doctoral degree. Increasingly, though, I was becoming a blogger first and foremost.

I followed up on meeting Dean by blogging[3] in early July, "Right now it's a question of whether or not he breaks through the current paradigm that has him stuck in the low single digits." A few days later, I blogged, "In a CNN/Gallup/USA Today poll on July 12th, Dean only polls 1 percent, actually down from 2 percent in their last poll, and now behind Al Sharpton!" If you were only paying attention to the national Gallup polling, Dean wasn't gaining any traction, but he also had nowhere to go but up. I continued to mull over how Dean could break out, and then later in the month, on July 31, 2002, I blogged about the online strategy that Dean could use:

> We've seen the articles that compared Dean with Jimmy Carter and John McCain, here comes the one on my mind, "Howard Dean: The Bruce Babbitt of Campaign 2004" [from CNN's Inside Buzz]. Right, OK, I know Bruce Babbitt, Bruce Babbitt was a friend of mine, and Howard Dean, you are no Bruce Babbitt … I hope. Seriously, Dean's in the exact same position in terms of the polls as where Babbitt was in 1988. The lineup is a bit different this time around, and Dean's a better candidate and speaker than is Babbitt, but in terms of *ideas rather than endorsements, organization, or money*, CNN is right on the money.
>
> Here's what Dean could do to transform his weakness into his strength. Exploit the internet. His current website is sparse, not updated, and not very interesting. What he needs to develop is a website that gravitates the online discussion of 2004 toward him.

A practical, user-friendly site that sticks content to the user and sparks online debate. What I have in mind is a professional-looking campaign news-weblog that posts all the Dean and related press headlines with the ability for users to comment, with moderators in place to keep the discussion from being freeped.[4]

Jerry Brown was nearly able to upset Bill Clinton through using a 1-800 number for fundraising and setting up a national grassroots organization. The money and organization is right here on the net for Dean to get, it's just a matter of him putting a few things in place to set it rolling in that direction. McCain pulled in millions overnight from online contributions after his NH win, Dean could bring in even more than McCain. There is not another 2004 candidate that is more authentic and forthright than is Dean, which is what wins amongst internet pundits and commentators.[5]

Already, even though Dean was stuck at 1 percent in national polls, something entirely different was happening within the blogging community. I performed a poll on August 1, 2002, on MyDD, and Dean was in second place to Al Gore, with 390 users voting:[6]

Gore (159) 41 percent
Dean (135) 35 percent
Kerry (48) 12 percent
Edwards (39) 10 percent
Gephardt (9) 2 percent

I blogged on August 8 to the community of Dean supporters, "Taken at face value, this MyDD user poll is a good indicator for Dean that he is a viable candidate, and in the thick of the race for the Democratic nomination for President.... Let's admit that we have a lean for Dean. However, he's obviously no Babbitt. Could it be that we are seeing signs amongst *early adopters* when informed of his candidacy, positions, and persona?"[7]

Other bloggers, including Greg Greene ("I'm still a John Kerry man. But Dean looks more and more credible by the day") and Jason Rylander ("Dean's message is a breath of fresh air. Could it be that Democrats finally have a candidate who says what he means and means what he says?"), began blogging favorably about Dean. Jules Witcover's profile[8] of Dean, "In the Footsteps of Carter," and early coverage by progressive magazines in the summer of 2002, including pieces in the *New Republic* ("Invisible Man")[9] and in the *American Prospect* ("The Darkest Horse"),[10] broadened awareness about Howard Dean among the bloggers.

There was a linkage between mainstream coverage of Howard Dean in television interviews and the spike in traffic that it would create on the MyDD pages supporting Dean for President, as people wanted to learn more about Dean. A number of other political blogs linked to the page, and then ABC's influential "The Note" drew in a couple of thousand visitors (huge for the time), noting the election countdown on the page. In the middle of July, Howard Dean had ventured onto *Meet the Press*, and hundreds of new visitors arrived on the website. I didn't have a ton of website coding or graphic expertise, and people who didn't see the prominent disclaimer and link to Dean's PAC website and mistook it for the actual campaign site would e-mail in advice or criticisms, e-mailing to me things like:[11]

> "The message is good. The display is gray. Brighten it up! How about a picture of Gov. Dean on the website?"
>
> "I am a fan of Howard Dean. I wish him well. In that spirit, I'd like to point out that the site is missing some apostrophes. It should be 'Dean on the nation's Economy' (nation-apostrophe-s), 'Dean on the nation's Values,' and 'Dean on the nation's Health.' I might also suggest capitalizing 'nation' if 'Economy,' 'Values,' and 'Health' are capitalized. By the way, please take this in spirit offered; I'm the last person to take delight in errors in others' writing since I make so many myself."
>
> "I have long supported the idea of Gov. Dean as a Presidential candidate, and now that he's openly expressed his interest, I would like to turn that idea into action. So I went to this website for information. But the website is just plain awful! Count this as my first contribution to what I sincerely hope will be a successful run against Bush: Retool your website immediately. It's a major, big-time turnoff."

The "Howard Dean for President" web page on MyDD, with the link to the site's blog, provided supporters with an opportunity to become engaged with other like-minded supporters. That was happening throughout 2002, first on MyDD and then on other websites and blogs too.

One of those blogs was the Dean Nation blog (DeanNation.blogspot.com), which was started on August 31, 2002, by Aziz Poonawalla, a Ph.D. student in medical physics in Houston, who wrote the blog in his spare time; within a few days of its launch, fellow Texan Anna Brosovic (Annatopia), who worked as an IT professional in Dallas, Texas, and I joined as Dean Nation bloggers, making it the unofficial Dean campaign blog.

I joined the effort because I felt it was time for a blog that was all about Howard Dean, and if the campaign didn't yet have the staff infrastructure to build one, we'd do it ourselves. Over the following year, now-prominent bloggers such as Matt Yglesias, Ezra Klein, Matt Singer, and others would also contribute to the Dean Nation blog, making it in some ways a "farm team" of sorts for future liberal bloggers. For those of us on the Dean Nation blog in those early months, before a central campaign or an official blog was launched, we took it on ourselves to evangelize about Howard Dean over the Internet.

In September 2002, Dean became the holdout among the Democratic presidential hopefuls backing President Bush's aggressive Iraq policy, saying in a telephone interview with the *San Francisco Chronicle*, "The president has to do two things[12] to get the country's long-term support for the invasion of Iraq. He has done neither yet." To us, this was one more example of Howard Dean being right in his opposition to Bush.

On November 7, 2002, following the loss by Democrats in the midterm elections, Aziz blogged on Dean Nation:

> BTW, there was a huge spike in visitors to the Dean Blog on Wednesday (after the complete election results were finally in). The average visits are about 50 a day, the previous

spike was 150, and Wednesday saw 250 unique visitors. The referral logs show a large number of Google queries about Dean's position on Iraq and the Bush tax cuts. Clearly, it isn't just bloggers but also web surfers in general who are putting 2 and 2 together.

On December 18, 2002, I first blogged using the term *netroots* to describe the phenomenon that was happening online for Dean, blogging: "OK, so Dean is still polling 1–4 percent nationally, so what. Look at the netroots. Democrats.com has a weekly straw poll. Over the four weeks it's been done, with Gore included, Dean has finished a cumulative second."

## Official Collaboration Begins

The official campaign started coming together in late 2002. Previously a lurker on MyDD, Joe Trippi started posting comments on MyDD in December 2002. In January, he became a consultant for the campaign. Joe Trippi and I started e-mailing back and forth about an online strategy for Dean, leading to many long-distance phone calls. I also started e-mailing back and forth with Brian Young, who lived in Vermont, about an online strategy for the campaign. In January 2003, Markos Moulitsas of DailyKos. com and I started working together, having done political blogging alongside each other in 2002. Markos understood website designing and had updated MyDD in the fall that year with Movable Type, and we formed a consulting partnership. Markos flew up to Portland, Oregon, the first week of January 2003, and we formalized the online strategy proposal I'd been working on with Joe Trippi to use for Howard Dean's campaign.

Via conference calls over the weekend, the three of us discussed what we believed could be brought inside the campaign from the ongoing decentralized effort—the gist of "the revolution" being to launch an official national campaign blog, where the online community, fund-raising, and organizing efforts could be centralized, and a more localized fifty-state blog network of Howard Dean communities would follow. Trippi was gung ho about the whole thing, and was trying to solidify the integration of an online effort inside the campaign.

After Al Gore dropped out, as 2003 was beginning, you could feel the energy growing for Dean on the Internet. Firsthand stories would spread throughout the blogs, such as "Sunday Afternoon at the Three Tomatoes with Howard Dean" by Roy Morrison (Forward.com) on January 3, 2003, in New Hampshire:

> The smallish room is packed. Then Dean starts to speak. I've heard my share of forgettable stump speeches with lots of rhetoric, feel-good lines, winks and little substance. But Dean, as he gets going, has a lot to say.... Dean evokes Harry Truman. "We have to have a party that believes in our message." Dean says what he thinks.... He's much more concerned about how federal money is spent and balancing the budget than about tax cuts for the rich. And, of course, as a doctor, he has an effective outline for bringing health insurance to all Americans, modeled after an expansion of Vermont's success. On his controversial support for gay civil unions, Dean says, "Never deny human rights because it is politically

inconvenient." A standup guy. Suddenly there's a warm feeling in the room. He's saying things of real substance that make sense. Not just what people want to hear. Dean's obviously a very smart man. That couldn't hurt. It feels like this guy has a real chance.... My friend Jan, who's been known to shake things up, is organizing a house party for Howard in my town of Warner. There's a buzz: "Have you heard about Howard Dean?"

The mainstream media was beginning to notice the buzz for Dean. The Pragmatic Progressive (pragmaticprogressive.blogspot.com) blogged on January 7, 2003:

Dean is creating a real buzz in the state [New Hampshire] where underdogs who deserve to be top dogs and straight talkers are pointed out for all of America to see. There is a growing sentiment amongst pundits like Howard Fineman and Pat Cadell ... that Howard Dean will be the guy you see explode. Says Cadell on Hardball on MSNBC, 1/7/02, "He's the only guy out of the half dozen or so candidates that doesn't speak Washington speak."

A prime example of this, which was blogged on MyDD, was Dean's being quoted in the *Boston Herald* about the other democratic presidential candidates: "Now they're trying to say, 'We tried to constrain the president,' Dean told reporters in the leadoff primary state. 'Nonsense. They all voted to give the president a blank check.'"

On January 15, 2003, an American Research Group (ARG) poll came out of New Hampshire showing Kerry at 27 percent and Dean in second at 15 percent, the first real sign that Dean had grassroots strength and name recognition in one of the early states. The earlier thought that Dean might break out now seemed inevitable. However, the online portions of the campaign were still unorganized in their outreach and integration efforts.

The importance of Joe Trippi's being able to bring the execution of an Internet strategy inside the campaign cannot be understated. The momentum for Howard Dean had grown week by week over the Internet. The website Democrats.com had been doing a weekly online presidential preference poll of its community, and after Al Gore dropped out in December, John Kerry led for a couple of weeks, but beginning in January 2003, Dean led in the Democrats.com straw vote poll for the Democratic nominee, outpolling John Kerry by a nearly two-to-one margin by January 23.

It was right at this time that Meetup for Dean, the most successful grassroots organizing effort within presidential politics ever done over the Internet, was beginning. The first week of January 2003, I had been on a conference call with Joe Trippi, in which he had made the problem of Dean's current campaign clear. "John Kerry," Trippi said, "has 20,000 supporters nationwide, and for each one of those he can reach out and ask for $20 or $200 at any time, and they deliver. Dean has a shoebox of business cards."

"Yea, yea, yea, yea," Trippi would say in response to my enthusiasm for the campaign's starting a blog, "I get it. What I want to know is how Dean is going to use the Internet to match the national base that John Kerry has spent the last twenty years building. How are we going to do that?" I admitted that I didn't know the answer, but confidently said I would get back to him with a solution.

A week later, a Meetup official, William Finkel, reached out to the members of the unofficial Dean blog to see if we would be interested in starting up the effort, writing in an e-mail:

> I think that our service can be a great asset to Governor Dean's campaign, in that we can allow for grassroots organizers to meet with other local supporters to coordinate and plan. We are currently in 477 U.S. cities with over 100,000 members (in just 6 months), allowing us to have meetings in many cities where your supporters do not have an established structure. You can see what the page for this Meetup looks like at http://dean2004.meetup.com.

Asking if we should pursue it, Aziz forwarded the e-mail from Finkel to Anna and me. The concept of people gathering at the same time in different places once a month, based on their support of Howard Dean, was brand new, and none of the other candidates (even though Finkel had tried) would embrace the effort. I replied to Finkel about the idea, and he was persistent enough, so it seemed good enough to us for giving it a shot with the blogs.

I went to Meetup.com, becoming the third person to sign up for Dean. On January 15, I put the soon-to-be-famous "Meetup for Dean" graphic on the MyDD.com blog, saying, "Here's a link to grassroots support of Dean breaking out on the net: Join the Dean campaign!" The Meetup for Dean numbers reached nearly 200 by the end of the day, passing all the other '04 contenders. I knew this was the answer to Trippi's request.

Aziz blogged on Dean Nation, also on January 15:

> Despite clear leadership from the campaign to the grassroots level, the netroots are self-organizing. For example, Meetup.com has a Meetup page devoted to Howard Dean, which will be enormously useful to Dean supporters who want to organize.... It's really up to the campaign whether it wants to give an official blessing to these kinds of netroot efforts or not—but they will likely happen regardless. Still, with some explicit outreach, the campaign can reap far greater rewards.

While Aziz blogged the entry noting that the campaign would reap benefits from embracing the decentralized online effort backing Dean, I was making the same argument to Trippi about the campaign's embracing Meetup to serve as the vehicle. For the next two weeks, I would correspond with Finkel and call Trippi up at all times of the day and night, updating him on the Meetup numbers until he became obsessed himself with trying to get the campaign to put the Meetup graphic on the official website. By the end of the month, Trippi succeeded in getting the campaign to officially adopt the use of Meetup. Finkel and I pushed for Trippi to get an official e-mail from Dean on Meetup. Sue Allen, Dean's gubernatorial communications director, drafted a "Dean in 2004 Meetup" e-mail on Dean's behalf.

The January 28 e-mail went out to all of the 478 attendees who signed up for the first Meetup. I posted it on MyDD, further validating the activist effort and spurring on more sign-ups:

I want to thank Meetup.com for creating a platform for people to organize around the issues we all care about. I hope to attend Meetups of my supporters as I travel the nation, and my campaign will provide suggested issues that need to be discussed, as well as ask for organizational help to build our campaign at future Meetups.

One issue that I think is appropriate for the February 5th Meetup is the pending war with Iraq. I hope that those who attend will look at positions of all the Democratic candidates for President on the war, and square it with the vote they cast on the Iraqi Resolution that gave President Bush a blank check to prosecute the war when he decides to do so. I opposed the Iraqi Resolution and believe the President must make his case to the American people before sending our armed forces in harm's way.

Please visit my website at www.deanforamerica.com and I hope to see you at a future Meetup!

Thank You

Howard Dean

The partnership of Meetup with the Dean campaign, and especially this e-mail from Governor Howard Dean, began the interaction of the campaign and the online community. It was a strong validation of the effort we were making online to promote his candidacy.

## Takeoff

The months of February and March 2003 were pivotal in launching the Dean campaign. Dean was showing poll strength in the key state of New Hampshire, and nearing a majority on the Internet polls.[13] Meetup and fund-raising, alongside Dean's unequivocal opposition to the invasion of Iraq, were the developments in February and March that served to raise the excitement for Dean. The level of interaction and integration between the growing decentralized movement and the official campaign that started up at this time could have been due to the luck of timing, but no matter; it symbolized how to bring a movement into a campaign.

For the first Meetup, on February 5, 2003, there were 501 people signed up for Dean, 227 for Edwards, and 295 for Kerry. We had eleven Meetups throughout the nation, including one in Portland, Oregon, that I attended. I brought along three "Howard Dean for President" stickers that I'd ordered online from Café Press, and blogged afterward on Dean Nation: "Portland's Meetup for Dean was well attended, with 5 persons confirmed on the Meetup site, and 9 showing up for the Dean event! A good group of experienced campaign workers. The host of the event had contacted the Dean campaign, and, with another volunteer having a VCR/TV, two videos were shown: Dean on Meet the Press, and a Dean bio/campaign clip."

David Nir attended the February Dean Meetup in New York City, and e-mailed this report, which I also blogged on Dean Nation: "We had a very good turnout (around 15 people) at the NYC Dean Meetup last night. (The meeting lasted about an hour.) A broad range of people from Manhattan, Brooklyn & Queens showed up, and everyone seemed enthusiastic about doing work on behalf of the candidate. Since we currently lack any guidance from the campaign, we discussed ideas that we could work on ourselves."

Both places formed Yahoo! groups, and planned for leaflet or literature handouts to get "more people involved with the campaign." There was a strong pragmatic focus for each state, with the Portland, Oregon, group deciding that "working with Vancouver, WA, Dean supporters, for their early primary" was an important focus, and in New York, to "prepare for petitioning for Dean to get on the ballot (NY has the toughest ballot-access laws in the nation)."

After the first Meetup, William Finkel, "the man behind Meetup" as Anna would call him on Dean Nation, sent out an e-mail to all those signed up for Meetup for Dean, saying: "I wanted to let you know about last night's Meetups and their huge success. From the polls I've been receiving; it seems that the New York, Boston, Minneapolis, and Baltimore Meetups have essentially declared themselves as field offices for the campaign. THIS IS AWESOME!!! TRULY, TRULY GRASSROOTS!"

The online excitement grew after the first Meetup. On February 20, it was announced on Dean Nation by Anna that Dean would attend a Meetup in New York City: "Dr. Dean is scheduled to attend the March 5th Meetup in New York! The New York Meetup is the second-largest group after Washington DC, with 92 supporters, so this will be a very exciting opportunity for Dean to see for himself just how strong his netroots are."

In the lead-up to the March 2003 Meetup that Dean would attend in New York, Finkel wrote in another e-mail, in late February: "I think the fact and manner in which Dean has embraced Meetup reflects his commitment to grassroots, community and technology. All the candidates are aware of our service, but Governor Dean, personally, understands what we can do. What we can do is exemplified by what our chapters have done: create self-organized, autonomous field units that will be prepared to support the governor, however he needs, whenever he needs them."

There was the feeling on the blogs that we were participating in something unique with the potential to transform the presidential contest. One particular moment that I recall as symbolic of the campaign's early outreach to the movement was when Dean came to the Dean Nation blog and commented on one of the threads, on March 9, 2003.

Howard Dean, I later learned, was often sent links to what the bloggers were saying about him, and he'd check his e-mail and would be able to click through and read the blog posts and the comments. Following the very successful Meetup in New York City that Dean attended in early March, he came to the unofficial blog and posted a comment under the "Meetup Report" thread that activists around the nation used to tell about their Meetups. Dean wrote:

> Thanks to all of you for your energy and your help. Raising money in small dollar amounts (all matchable from the FEDS) and getting the name and record out now is exactly what we need to be doing. I can't tell you how helpful this is. Many many thanks. Howard Dean
>     P.S. And a special thanks to all of you who went to the New York Meetup last week. It truly was incredible. I'll try to get to another one in April. Howard Dean[14]

A quick check of the IP address matched it up to Dean's Burlington, Vermont, residence and confirmed its authenticity. Meetup was becoming a huge success, and, as Dean mentioned, in March 2003 online fund-raising became the next big thing for the campaign.

The concept of raising funds for candidates over the Internet was still a novelty in early 2003. Fund-raising wasn't discussed much on the blogs or in the Meetups of February, but by March it had become a major focus of the campaign, with a grassroots effort. While Dean was making solid progress offline, it was over the Internet that Dean found his insurgent strength.

In mid-March 2003, Anna blogged on Dean Nation, writing about the addition of a penny to online contributions to note that it was coming from online supporters of Dean: "This idea started out of the New York Meetup.... There are now almost 5,000 members signed up at Meetup.com for Howard Dean.... We can demonstrate the power of grassroots internet activism by adding a penny for the internet. Go over to www.deanforamerica.com and make a $10.01 contribution today.... Take the Million Dollar Meetup Challenge for Dean!"

It made the rather mundane and anonymous task of contributing somewhat of an innovation and highlighted online fund-raising—becoming the sort of thing that made its way into press coverage. Process stories around Dean's Internet organizing through Meetup and record-breaking fund-raising efforts would continue throughout the year. By the end of March, Dean had raised over $2.6 million, with over $750,000 being raised over the Internet, and over 10,000 persons had signed up for Meetup, setting the path for 2003.

March 2003 was Howard Dean's breaking-out moment in more ways than just Meetup and fund-raising. The twin "What I Want to Know" speeches that he gave at the DNC's winter meeting in Washington, D.C., in February and at the state Democratic Convention in California in March have gained historical importance.

I went down to California and joined with Markos Moulitsas in Berkeley to attend the California Democratic Convention in Sacramento. We'd reached out to the California Democratic Party to seek out press credentials, and were granted them to cover the event as press by blogging. It was a first, and with no wireless set up for our blogging the conference on location, we had to blog reports afterward in the evening.

The event began on Friday, but Howard Dean would not speak until Saturday afternoon, after Kerry, Edwards, Kucinich, Sharpton, and Lieberman. We arrived on Friday, and I attended a "technology caucus" and got into a discussion with a couple of other attendees about presidential preferences. One after the other, attendees signaled that Dean was their favorite. I was dumbfounded, as Dean still only registered as an asterisk in the national polls in March 2003; but here among the activist California delegates, Dean was in the top tier. I knew Dean had support online in our blogs, but this meant that everything that we were doing over the Internet really mattered in the sense that it was in sync with influential Democratic Party workers.

The attendees at the California convention were the grassroots support of the Democratic Party, and the awareness of Dean was palpable. As the hours moved toward listening to Dean later on Saturday, people chatted in the back of the hall throughout the speeches from the other candidates. I wondered aloud to Markos, as we sat in the press rafter in the center of the hall amid about 400 attendees, who chatted during the speeches by the others, whether Dean would be able to quiet the hall.

Because it was just a few days before Bush would signal the invasion of Iraq, tension was in the air as Dean took his turn at the podium. Earlier in the day, John Edwards and Joe Lieberman had been booed and hissed for voicing their support for invading Iraq. I blogged[15] on March 17, 2003:

> At the convention, I commented to DailyKos about the candidate speeches, that if one hadn't known the poll numbers prior to the candidates speaking at the convention, then watched them all, one would surmise that Dean was the frontrunner, given the delegate participation. Dean had probably 5x as many sign-wavers as Kerry and the others. As one Dean organizer in CA, Joe Ross, commented, "the delegates came here interested in Dean wanting to hear more, and after hearing him speak, they are loving him."

It only took one line by Dean to galvanize the attention of the audience. Everyone stood, clapping and hollering within a few moments into the speech; people abandoned chairs and rushed toward the stage to listen closer. Lee Fink, via "The Hauser Report" blog,[16] wrote about the event on March 18:

> Finally, let me comment on Howard Dean. Dean spoke Saturday. He was supposed to go at about 11, but it was noon before he took the stage, and the delegates were interested in leaving. Edwards had already spoken, and he should have been the highlight (at least according to the buzz). Dean, an MD, had signs that said "the Doctor is in," and "Dean for America." ... Dean came to the podium and the first words were "What I want to know is why in the world so many Democrats are supporting the President's unilateralist intervention in Iraq." ... Dean then named names. He said he would support Kerry or Edwards (the two that had spoken before him—I don't think he meant to exclude others), but "I don't think we can win by voting for the war in Washington and coming to California and saying we oppose it." ... Dean's speech then hit a peak that I have never personally seen (although attendees of national conventions may have). Dean had the place sold as he yelled over the absolutely raucous cheers "I want America back. I don't want to be divided any more. I want my country back."
>
> And then the line that sent the house through the roof: "I'm tired of listening to the fundamentalist preachers!"
>
> It was absolutely unprecedented. Kevin Shelley, the California Secretary of State who followed Dean, shouldn't have even bothered. He joked himself that they drew straws and the one with the short straw had to go after Howard Dean.
>
> Dean's booth got mobbed. A friend of mine jumped behind to help out the volunteer handing out buttons, signs, and signing people up, and got about 100 people in 20 minutes. The table was absolutely barren, and they were left passing out Vermont Cheese (in the biggest dairy producing state in the country), and it got taken.
>
> Dean was the talk of the convention. The coolest response (as in "cold," not "hip") I got from anyone was "well, I came in liking Kerry, but Dean was pretty good." When Art Torres, the party chair came into the bar at half past midnight to start drinking with the Young Democrats that were there, even he acknowledged that Dean was the one

everyone had talked about. No straw poll was taken, but Dean would have won going away.

And as for me—I'm sold.

In a state of awe, Markos and I shook our heads in amazement with Karl Frisch in the pressroom afterward. Karl, a day later, loaded a transcript and video of the speech onto the California Democratic Party website, which was relayed to many thousands across the nation through our blogs. Earlier that week, the Dean campaign had officially launched the "Howard Dean 2004 Call to Action Weblog" begun by Mathew Gross, who had moved on from being a blogger on MyDD.com to becoming the official blogger for the Dean campaign. Gross blogged alongside Zephyr Teachout and Joe Trippi, and his blog signaled the first official online campaign presence in the blogosphere.

The events I participated in during the month of March 2003—attending another Portland, Oregon, Meetup with nearly forty attendees, going to Dean's website to contribute and adding a penny with other online activists, and experiencing Dean's motivating speech with hundreds of others—all coalesced to end my thinking that this was just an online phenomenon by disenfranchised activists. It also confirmed that the growing movement of opposition to Bush was now a part of the Dean campaign.

Increasingly, Dean's message was framed within the movement that came into the campaign. Trippi, in a blog post on Dean Nation titled "Taking Back Our Country—Planting the Seed of Change—Growing to Victory" on Sunday, April 13, 2003, reflected on the same appeal of Howard Dean that I had first noted—a message of Dean's that "it's time to take a stand and take our country back":

> "You may not agree with him on every issue, and he will make his share of mistakes during this long campaign (everyone does), but Howard Dean says what needs to be said, challenges what needs to be challenged, stands up forcefully to those that attempt to divide us, and has a vision powered by the simple fact that as Americans we are all in this together." And about the campaign: "As Governor Dean has said 'the pundits like to talk about the invisible primary, but there is another primary that is only invisible to those who are blind to seeing it.' Our goal is to build a netroots and grassroots campaign that is so strong in numbers—so powerful in collective action that no one will turn a blind eye to it again. And if we do that together—we will not only win this election—we will prove that we really do have the power to take our country back.

Dean's message had brought the oppositional momentum of the online movement into the official campaign in the spring of 2003. And with it, the initiative for the online operation of Dean's campaign shifted to within the campaign.

Dean Nation continued to operate as the unofficial blog, and took on new activities such as Dean Defense Force, a coordinated rapid-response volunteer effort, initially led by Matt Singer, that sprung up to reject the Democratic Leadership Committee's (DLC's) letter that bashed Howard Dean as unelectable. Joe Trippi continued to do blog outreach from inside the official campaign, blogging on July 5 on the unofficial Dean Nation blog a post titled "THANK YOU—It Started Here as Much as Anywhere

Else," and blogging, "While the press and other campaigns try to figure out what has happened and what it all means—we at Burlington HQ know that it was this blog and a few others that have from the very beginning sustained the campaign."

By the end of March 2003, even the establishment in Washington realized that something was happening with the Dean campaign through its use of the Internet, something that was on its way to catapulting the campaign to top-tier status.

In May 2003, I joined the official campaign. I abandoned grad school[17] and dragged my wife and three-year-old son to Burlington, Vermont, to come on board the campaign and work alongside Joe Trippi. Fully obsessed and committed to the cause, I settled into being one of many staffers in the campaign headquarters working to elect Howard Dean as president, for America.

## Notes

1. http://web.archive.org/web/20020802030319/howard-dean-for-president.mydd. com/2004.html (accessed June 1, 2007).

2. http://web.archive.org/web/20020811114954/www.mydd.com/archives/00000003. html (accessed June 1, 2007).

3. http://web.archive.org/web/20020802084806/www.mydd.com/archives/00000205. htm (accessed June 1, 2007).

4. *Freeped* is a term that is used to refer to the self-identified "freepers" on FreeRepublic. com who go out and troll on liberal blogs.

5. http://web.archive.org/web/20020827115858/www.mydd.com/archives/00000234. htm (accessed June 1, 2007).

6. http://web.archive.org/web/20030818030730/vote.sparklit.com/poll.spark/663748 (accessed June 1, 2007).

7. http://web.archive.org/web/20021119175108/www.mydd.com/archives/00000255. htm (accessed June 1, 2007).

8. http://web.archive.org/web/20021112005521/www.mydd.com/archives/00000116. htm (accessed June 1, 2007).

9. Jonathan Cohn, "Invisible Man: Will the Democrats Notice Howard Dean?" *New Republic* (July 1, 2002).

10. Robert Dreyfuss, "The Darkest Horse," *American Prospect* (July 15, 2002).

11. http://web.archive.org/web/20020802082826/www.mydd.com/archives/00000204. htm (accessed June 1, 2007).

12. "Dean said President Bush needs to make the case that Iraq has weapons of mass destruction, such as atomic or biological weapons, and that he has the means to use them. He also needs to explain to the American public that a war against Iraq is going to require a long commitment in that country—up to a decade." http://www.casi.org.uk/discuss/2002/msg01590. html (accessed June 1, 2007).

13. On February 2, the *New York Times Magazine* featured Howard Dean in its "Seven Questions" column, and included an online poll asking, "If the Democratic primary were held today, which candidate would get your vote?" Howard Dean, at 19 percent, trailed the front-runner, John Kerry, at 26 percent.

14. E-mail, March 9, 2003.

15. http://web.archive.org/web/20030320112038/http://www.mydd.com (accessed June 1, 2007).

16. http://web.archive.org/web/20030320112038/http://www.mydd.com (accessed June 1, 2007).

17. When the campaign ended in March 2004, I returned to finish dual M.A.s at Portland State University, for a cathartic withdrawal, for a while, from presidential politics.

# 5

# Something Much Bigger Than a Candidate

## *Zephyr Teachout*

*Zephyr Teachout, the director of online organizing for Howard Dean's campaign, tells the story of a campaign's transformation from a small, awkward operation to an enormous grassroots movement, under the leadership of Joe Trippi. Besides providing an evocative and detailed look at the tone of the campaign and the tools developed, she highlights many of the structural uncertainties that the campaign faced, and how those uncertainties were sometimes chaotic, sometimes productive, and sometimes a little of both.*

### Cortés

It was early February 2003. I sat at a table across from consultant Joe Trippi and proudly showed him a proposal for managing the volunteers in the seventeen states for which I was responsible as a new deputy field director. I started talking him through a plan involving three volunteer groupings in each state, communication charts built like Amway or Tupperware. Trippi looked at my charts blankly for a moment and then started staring over my shoulder and shaking his head. "You are approaching this all wrong," he said.

Then he told me the story of Cortés.

When Cortés came to conquer and pillage Mexico, Trippi said, his men landed on the shore and made an initial assessment. They found thousands of warriors lying in wait, and reported to Cortés that attack was impossible and they would surely be slaughtered. He listened and took their counsel—we'll camp on the beach for the night, he said, and leave in the morning.

That night, while his men slept, Cortés ordered one of his aides to take a small rowboat out to the ships and burn them.

In the morning the men woke and saw they had no escape. So they fought with the fury of people who have nothing to lose.

This, he said, is the Cortés campaign.

## Tom Sawyer

It was the coldest winter in a decade in Burlington, and Lake Champlain froze all the way across. When I wanted to think I borrowed data volunteer Luke Peterson's big dog and let him drag me around the slippery cove by the shore. The office was thick with confusion—campaigns, I was quickly learning, are more unstructured and ad hoc than almost any other organization.

I joined the campaign in December 2002, when I was thirty-one years old, having worked as a post-conviction death penalty defense lawyer and run a North Carolina nonprofit that trains death penalty trial lawyers. I'd also worked for Dean before when he ran for governor in 1994, and when I heard he was running for president I decided to move home to Vermont to join the campaign. Unlike many, it was not an act of inspiration—I knew what his speeches were like (straightforward, but wooden and technical), I thought he'd make a fine president, I thought governors were more likely to win the presidency than senators, and I'd been looking for an excuse to come back home. He had been a good governor and I was a good Vermonter; I thought I might get a job doing research on agricultural policy, and possibly impact national policy if he won the election.

I started by volunteering for the research shop, bringing some ideas from the death penalty nonprofit. When I was cofounding the death penalty nonprofit, I'd explained the idea to a friend of mine: There are people who want trial training, and there are indigent clients who need help; we wanted to connect the two. "Yes!" he said, and with his finger sketched two circles on the wall of the Indian restaurant we were eating at—an empty chamber next to a chamber bursting with water, with nothing between them— "you're building the pipes!" he said. "The pressure will be let out somewhere so you're building the pipes!" This image stayed in my head throughout various jobs—the key is to find the valves and to allow the pressure that is already built up to release. I thought about this as I was faced with the task of researching Dean's policy positions over the previous eleven years—I divided up the research that needed to be done and passed it out to volunteers who had offered to help research. After three weeks campaign manager Rick Ridder offered me a job as a deputy field director, responsible for organizing seventeen states, most of which were late in the primary calendar.

Within a week I was overwhelmed with e-mail. My inbox was full of requests, all asking to help. "I'm an artist in New York and I'd love to help out"; "I'm a student in South Carolina and we'd like to do something"; "I saw Howard Dean on the news here in Pennsylvania and if there's anything I can do"; "I've written the campaign two times offering to help and I've heard nothing." I also had a big folder of printed-out e-mails with similar subjects. My answering machine regularly ran out of tape to hold the voice messages.

After a week of sending the equivalent of rejection letters to these offers, I started to realize that my inbox, far from being a problem, represented thousands, maybe millions, of unused hours of people's time. If we could figure out an architecture—like aqueducts, perhaps, a water system, the series of valves—a scalable system that could handle thousands of e-mails, a powerful organization might be built from these offers.

I started borrowing Luke's dog more frequently, pacing on the ice and daydreaming about organizational models.

The first move was to imitate Tom Sawyer, to give away parts of my job to anyone who came through my inbox. "I am going to make myself irrelevant," I told Trippi. "I'm giving away my job." He gave me an amused look, letting me know he thought I was already irrelevant. "Nobody understands what you are talking about," he said, in what became his favored refrain, and turned back to his computer screen. "I'm glad that you're enjoying yourself."

The second move was to give the Tom Sawyer delegation some order—I developed a simple flowchart starting with a state coordinator responsible for answering and sorting e-mail, and pipes between the coordinator and three branches, representing counties, constituencies, and colleges, with pipes to local iterations of each of these groups. I set out to fill my organizational chart with volunteers, as if I were hiring people. The volunteer leaders would not be responsible for reporting to each other or following each others' directions—the regional leaders "below" the state leader would not be not working for the state leader. Instead, the tree was like a phone tree, a method for communication. This is the flowchart I had shown Trippi when he told me the Cortés story.

The test case was Oregon. I queried the database for Oregon residents (we had about 400 at the time) and sent out an e-mail titled "Organize Oregon for Dean!" asking for a five-to-ten-hours-per-week volunteer commitment. I received about fifteen coherent responses, and two incoherent ones. I wrote back or called to ask for more details, and sometimes for references and resumes.

The responses tended to be straightforward and open: "I'm a mechanical engineer living in Eugene, I can work 8 hours a week, and I have been involved in a few local organizations, but never as a leader. I'd be happy to organize Eugene if you give me some suggestions."

My two coworkers in the field department (Maria Handley and Aaron Holmes) were much more swamped with setting up official meetings—their states were more important—but they also experimented with the same model. We built upon opportunity, not from the top. We allowed for quick growth—a node could explode before the central structure was in place. A woman became the county coordinator for some tiny county in eastern Oregon long before there was a central state coordinator. Each volunteer received a crude list of things he or she could do to organize—grow lists, attend public events, identify local support, write op-eds—and was added to our master state charts.

Many people didn't fit the regional model, but everyone who offered to help was given a five-to-ten-hours-per-week option. If someone sent me an e-mail saying he wanted to help Dean and was a disabled rights activist, I asked him to start a "Disabled Rights Activists for Dean" Yahoo! listserv[1] and to start compiling lists of contacts. "Lawyers for Dean" developed from two separate e-mails from eager lawyers, and later grew into a very useful consulting service for activists.

We called it hiring people for free. By mid-February, I'd hired over fifteen very good people for free in several states; by the third week of February I had a state coordinator in fourteen states and over thirty people committed to five to ten hours per week. If someone called the Dean campaign from Savannah, she was given "state coordinator" Tim Cairl's number in Atlanta instead of mine. Tim was then responsible for incorporating her volunteer time and ideas. Each e-mail to georgia@DeanForAmerica.com came to me and to Tim Cairl, so that I could take a few minutes each day to skim incoming e-mail for remarkable ones, but I also trusted that Tim would ask me if he wasn't sure how to handle something.

It seemed like every day, a new force would sprout—not in the formal aqueduct manner I'd imagined, but something more forceful, spontaneous, and strong, a thousand little springs bursting from the computer screen. The volunteers did not fit a type, but were independently interesting, exasperating, and often funny—profoundly pragmatic people who wanted to be a productive part of the campaign—a videographer from Brooklyn, a stylish divorcée in New Mexico, a building contractor in Oregon. A retired Scottish adman from Connecticut became a biweekly caller, giving useful suggestions about language and form in a beautiful brogue. "This needs to be a movement," he said, "so it needs music. There's never been a movement without music."

Toward the end of February, the campaign as a whole was receiving so much unreturned e-mail that the governor was hearing complaints from people he met and donors he called. Trippi held a meeting with the field staff to find out what we were going to do about it. Despite some early efforts to have weekly field meetings, real meetings were rare and organized on only a few moments' notice. We sat in the dank conference room kitchen, on a few chairs and an old couch. "What the hell is going on?" Trippi sighed. "Why the hell can't we return e-mail!" He said he'd never been on a campaign that people hadn't returned every single phone call or e-mail. Every e-mail had to be returned, starting now.

The others in the department explained that we were simply overloaded—if we needed to arrange meetings with key political people, talk to key political people, and answer the ten to twenty daily phone calls, we couldn't spend time answering e-mails. I had been waiting for this meeting. I brought out my pile of notes to explain what I'd been doing and describe how we could apply it to the entire campaign, how the e-mail problem could be solved, how volunteers could build their own structures. The acting field director listened, and then asked me to clarify—unpaid people were making choices about how to answer e-mail that was coming to the Dean campaign headquarters? "Yes," I said. "But they are all committed, and they know more about what can be done in their states." "No," she said. "You can't do that. We can't have people we don't know anything about answering the governor's e-mails." I explained that I did know something about them; I had some of their resumes and their references. "They could say anything," she said. "Why would they want to say anything?" I asked. "No," she said, "you think the governor is hearing complaints now; what about when a funder gets a reply from some guy in Arkansas who isn't even part of the campaign?"

Having become dependent upon these organizers and correspondents, I couldn't actually comprehend the other option—polite rebuffs to the thousands of people pleading to help, telling them to "tell their friends" and give money until we had staff to work with them. Stop the energy of the thousand bursting springs? Before I could come back with a full response, the discussion went off in other directions—bringing in interns, improving our autoresponder. I'd like to say that I clearly understood the risks and the benefits, but I didn't—I was careening on an instinct so deep I didn't recognize it as anything but logic: We had to build a structure that used this power being offered us. I decided her response had been a suggestion, not an order—that if Trippi really wanted me to stop he'd have told me himself.

During this time, I found a handful of Dean supporters—a lawyer in Ohio, a veteran in New Hampshire, a man in Oregon—who had met online in the fall and created a national listserv, the "National Dean Network."[2] They had made it their task to find organizers in each state to start their own listservs. I increasingly found my state e-mail answerers from suggestions in this group, and became dependent upon them, with almost daily e-mails and weekly phone calls with some members of it—making suggestions and collaborating, arguing, and giving them what information I could about what was happening at the Burlington headquarters.

Throughout the month of February, it started to feel like these people—not my coworkers at headquarters, who were planning the governor's trips and meetings with important political leaders—were my colleagues.[3]

## The March Meetup

I kept Joe Trippi updated on our growing unpaid staff—numbers, stories of new co-ordinators. One day in late February I mentioned that I was repeatedly running into volunteer coordinators involved with Meetup, and he became very interested. I quickly learned that getting Meetup on the official website had been a difficult obsession of his, and he interrogated me, eager to hear what effect this new tool was having.

I told Trippi that I had approached an existing New York for Dean Yahoo! listserv, only to learn that they had already built a small existing structure, having met each other through Meetup. They had formed a New York for Dean committee, and were flyering for Dean at the antiwar rallies. The three committee members for New York and I arranged a conference call. I sent them the model organizing chart and delegated the project of organizing the city to them, with David Nir as my main contact. Their first job, Trippi said, was to make sure that hundreds of people came to a New York City Meetup on March 5, because Howard Dean was going to be there. They were already planning on it.

Trippi's big ideas always had several moving parts—we watched him like a brilliant impressionist painter, or a director. Often they didn't work, but often they did. The March Meetup idea worked beautifully. In Trippi's vision, Dean's trip to the March Meetup would be a signal to all Dean supporters that the campaign embraced the Meetup tool, and would inspire Dean supporters around the country to start going to Meetups. Trippi fought against scheduling ("it will be too crowded and collapse like the Rhode Island nightclub!"), finance hesitations ("we could fit in another fund-raiser instead"), and others concerned to have this two-hour-long time set aside for Dean's visit.

I wrote every person in the database within my jurisdiction—including Oregonians, Mississippians, and Arizonans, as well as closer supporters—exhorting anyone who knew anyone in New York to ask them to go. I collected a database of Dean-related Yahoo! groups and blogs. We sent this e-mail to the New York for Dean Yahoo! list:

> This is an unbelievable phenomenon. It is going to stop being an unbelievable phenom the instant Kerry, Edwards, etc. see what happened and get their millions task-forcing on this UNLESS this gets tons of press and is so big that 6,000 people suddenly jump on line to Meetup for Dean. This is something you guys have made happen, so far, and since that's true—MAKE IT HAPPEN! Make this unbearably big! Bring five of your reluctant friends—this could be the moment that moves Dean's campaign past its first high into a more continuous high! People could write books about this! So: (1) show up! Show up early and when you get there call your friends who aren't there and make them come, (2) do whatever online organizing you all do to get other people to come, (3) get the press there—we'll worry about big press, but if you happen to have good contacts in the press, use them—we want cameras, radio, print, and online news groups—whatever else you have to do to make this historic.

New York for Dean was working at a high, intoxicated pitch—they flyered extensively, made hundreds of phone calls, and used e-mails to get their friends there. They put out the word to enroll the press, and the *New York Times,* the *Village Voice,* and two local TV stations showed up at the event—despite having initially rebuffed our official press secretaries' efforts to get them there.

The March Meetup landed on a bitter wind-thick night, and I had a terrible cold. I flew down, rashly paying my own way because I didn't want to miss this moment, and arrived there an hour and a half before the governor. The restaurant was full. New York for Dean people wore name tags and were signing people in as they entered, greeting press, and passing out informational flyers. The language of history making was mumbled in the line outside and in the small clutches that were pressed together inside. People identified me as a staffer and grabbed me to give me checks and ask what they could do to help. I walked down the line outside of shivering, foot-stomping supporters talking about the war, about Dean, about themselves. One New York for Dean volunteer walked up and down the line like a subway cop, clicking a counter to measure the size of the crowd.

By the time the governor arrived over 550 people were waiting. I stood outside during his speech, which echoed down incoherently into the streets from high windows in the lounge—the line stood cheering, looking up toward the windows.

That Thursday, the *New York Times* Circuit section ran a story about the Meetup and the Meetup numbers started climbing, both through word of mouth and press. "I want you to run the Internet," Trippi said. I refused. I told him I didn't know anything about the Internet. "I don't want people who know things," he said, "because then they will do what has already been done and they won't listen to anyone else."

When I was leaving the office I stopped by his desk. He gave me a Post-it note: "You're doing the Internet." I shook my head, but after that he started expecting me to write and send e-mails and change the website. He eventually sent Tamara Pogue, the new field director, into my office. "Trippi wants you to stop doing all field stuff now and just do the Internet," she said. I moved my desk into the Internet closet two weeks before the United States invaded Iraq.

## The Cave

The Internet team that winter included one IT specialist (Dave Kochbeck), one environmental writer and blogger (Matt Gross), one high school student (Marc Chadwick), one short-term database developer (Luke Peterson), and two lawyers (Bobby Clark and me). Kenn Herman, the database guru, and Nicco Mele, the webmaster, joined us at the end of April, and after that our staff doubled every few months. But those early months were an odd time, both dark and hopeful, when we worked from an equipment closet we called "the cave" and etched fantasies of what the Internet could do for politics into each other's minds. We had no web designer; Jim Brayton, a volunteer, taught me basic html to make content changes.

We had a database system that was built for fund-raising, and no direct ability to send our own e-mail. When we drafted an e-mail it could take between two and six days to send it. Without room to think, without roles, without e-mail capacity, without web design skills, and with a workable database a month away, we found a small space to think in, and these became almost violently creative days—like dreaming awake, with no capacity to act. The cave was a petri dish, fetid and fertile, with ideas being thrown into the air and toyed with, and we worked and dreamed far beyond our technical limits.

Bobby Clark, the first Internet director of the campaign, had the kinetic energy of a grasshopper, his hands and mind always moving. Dave Kochbeck, the IT person, was tall with a wide face and a slow walk, and an instant-message buddy list of a few hundred people. Although the same age as Bobby and I, he exuded an avuncular air, tossing off ideas and aphorisms with a sure sway of the head.

"You are winning whatever game you are playing," he always said.

"Bobby is winning the game of having so much he has to do he can't finish it," he said, "and you are winning the game of being yelled at by Trippi."

Joe Trippi would storm into the Internet cave, demanding an immediate change, and ignore any pleas of impossibility. I spent two nights learning how to work the database so I could answer his daily question, "How many people have signed up online from where?" and after I boasted my ability to him, he turned to me and asked me why the Meetup contract wasn't signed yet. The night after our second successful Meetup and the shocking first-quarter fund-raising, he withered Matt Gross and me with disgust as he showed us an online poll we had lost. We worked with the exuberance and recklessness—and fear—of a group of people living at the edge of a cliff. Or, as Trippi would yell, "at the top of a ten-story building and only cement below us and no one to catch us but the people." Our charge was to get everything done and be inventive and do anything—including press releases, speeches, fund-raising, and organizing—that Joe Trippi wanted done quickly. Our roles were uncertain and constantly changing, as Trippi would turn to one, then another, then another of us. Although later that led to some fairly deep stresses, in the early days we were playful enough—and not in the public eye—that there was some room for freedom and a powerful culture of innovation.

The ideas for many of the tools and tactics that we later developed came out of those three fertile months in the cave. The phone banking system we developed in late fall came from a lunch conversation with campaign manager Rick Ridder. The open source policy platform we launched in September came initially from our schemes to get Slashdotted (linked to from the immensely popular technology website Slashdot) to raise our traffic. The instant-message get-out-the-vote effort used during the Moveon primary came from Dave Kochbeck's familiarity with a website called Zoo.com. Personalized posters—what we called Posters for America—came from studying an antiwar website, Patriots for Peace, and inviting them to build a poster system for us. Get Local, as I explain below, came from everywhere and everyone. Bobby Clark started sketching out plans for grassroots bundling, what became Teamraiser. Handwritten letters from Meetup attendees in Iowa and New Hampshire came from Eli Pariser. I first heard Trippi's idea for recruiting 5,000 volunteers to canvas Iowa in April. Trippi made us read *Small Pieces Loosely Joined*, *SmartMobs*, and *How to Run Internet Campaigns*, and called us into the kitchen/conference room to find out what we were thinking and to teach us how Gary Hart had won Iowa, and how we could do one better by adding the Internet to Gary Hart's concentric circle organizing. The very fact that we were reading books about South Korean protests and Hart's political education changed the way that we thought—while it wasn't clear what we were going to do, it was clear that our responsibility involved breaking up old models. We were not simply supposed to innovate for the sake of innovation; we were supposed to somehow change political culture.

Our own culture quickly evolved to one of fairly powerful dependence on (and corresponding respect for) autonomous organizers. Right after the March Meetup we needed flyers for International Women's Day, so we asked the New York for Dean people to make some. We started getting requests to vet dozens of flyers for various antiwar marches, and our policy/communications team didn't have time to vet them, so on the recommendation of our lawyer we started telling people that we would not review materials at all, because a serious review would create a logjam. We would point to good posters, but we wouldn't vet them—supporters were responsible for creating them and making judgments about style and form.[4] My crude html skills were not adequate to making a website with featured posters, so until Nicco Mele arrived we directed people to submit and use posters from a site set up by New York for Dean.

Matt Gross launched a blog on our site on March 15, using blogspot. It had no comments, no design, no calendar features, and no chat room. We became dependent upon the volunteer-run Dean Nation blog for interaction, regularly cross-posting important blog posts and reading the comments there to get feedback and ideas.

The best ideas were from others—when an anonymous March Meetup attendee challenged the Dean grassroots to raise $500,000 before the end of the March FEC filing deadline, Trippi immediately seized on the challenge and included the anonymous supporter's language in every online communication. When a Massachusetts Dean group suggested that people add a penny to each donation to show that it came from the Internet, he seized on the "penny for the net" idea and added that. The signs of magic—the March Meetup, a dance mix made by remixing Dean's "What I Want to Know" speech with Caribbean rap, a tax day flyer imagined by Seattle activists and created by New York supporters communicating through a central e-mail list—drove us and inspired us, but we also believed Dean had a chance of winning and we needed all the help we could get. We would sit with our fingers on the keyboards like small shovels, digging away at this vast untapped and powerful field.

Many ideas fizzled or failed. We planned to redo the homepage modeled on a blog with threaded, rated comments (Kiro5hin), we planned an online scavenger hunt, we planned a map of instant-message traffic, we planned dozens of projects that I've since forgotten. We also implemented many ideas that just didn't work. For five months, Trippi was almost as obsessed with text-messaging as he had been with Meetup, but our text-messaging "Wireless for Dean" groups never became anything more than a system for a few thousand people to get notices before Dean appeared on TV.[5] Trippi persuaded Dean to invest in a service that created "Dean TV"—our own online TV channel that people could subscribe to—which became a niche obsession but never played a significant role in either building community or sharing Dean's message.

Perhaps the most important innovation was something more subtle: the idea that supporters were competent citizens, should be respected, and should be encouraged to be inventive in their own local communities. That idea was not arrived at in a specific moment, but it came out of those months of dependency on others—others' work, others' creativity, others' intelligence. Only after we had thoroughly adopted it did we realize how controversial it would be—both inside and outside the campaign.

## Beyond the Flat Field and the Flat Website

Trippi had the mathematical obsessions of a field organizer. He wanted to know numbers of supporters, degrees of commitment, and the open-rates of e-mail sent at all times. But he also wanted to look at a mesh of social interactions and tease out the power relationships—seeing who holds power, not just who holds office, in a community. One of his core convictions was that "the Internet" was not a flat field—a collection of names and sites—but a mesh of interacting communities, a place like Iowa, where there were certain influential people to whom we should reach out. When Dave Kochbeck mentioned Larry Lessig, or Jock Gill mentioned David Weinberger, Trippi wanted to find out ways to engage them—the way a good field organizer would learn the name of the town leadership—and then to make sure to find ways to show them how their world fit with ours. Trippi asked us to help negotiate a consulting contract with Markos Zuniga and Jerome Armstrong—at a time when we believed we desperately needed a webmaster to change our website more than we needed consultants in part because he saw how Markos and Jerome, like church leaders in a South

Carolina community, were centers of gravity and power who could shape opinion and drive support as well as give advice.

Trippi asked Tamara Pogue, the field director, to build a massive database of listservs and e-mail contacts of peace groups, groups that cared about health care, groups that cared about the environment, labor groups, and gay rights groups. The project took several weeks and resulted in over 800 contact names—every time a relevant newspaper article about Dean was written, I sent a copy to all 800 names from my personal e-mail account. Every time after I hit "send" I would await the quick clatter of "out of office" replies from hundreds of peace activists' computers around the country. This was before political spam had swamped the political left, and many of these leaders were thankful and passed the messages on to their groups.

The big dream, the model, the biggest power center, was Moveon. They were organizing rallies, they were making money, and they were engaging millions of people. In mid-April, Joe Trippi invited Zack Exley and Eli Pariser—Moveon organizers—to come visit for a day. That visit, more than any other single day, transformed the way we thought about much of the Internet campaign. In that day we moved from chaotic creativity to creativity driven by the need for e-mail list growth.

Zack and Eli explained that e-mail growth—not site visits—should be the core driving most of our efforts. Websites were secondary to e-mail communications. They explained how most growth happened around specific campaigns—petitions or drives—and that we should be using our e-mail lists regularly and forcefully to share ideas and grow our list. They showed us charts of Moveon growth, and shared particular ideas about e-mail style and form. These ideas have since overtaken political communications like kudzu, but at the time they were radical, and they gave us a driving purpose. From that visit forward, we were centered around e-mail.

Zack and Eli's visit led to Zack's taking a leave of absence to help us build a simple but powerful event-planning tool for self-organizers, which we called Get Local. This was probably my favorite tool to work on, and pushing it through was one of my proudest moments on the campaign.

## Get Local

The idea for Get Local came from many sources simultaneously, but the primary inspiration came from February/March/April Meetup leaders, who wanted to have the ability to use our website to organize events outside of Meetup. Meetup coordinator Michael Silberman and I both heard from leaders that Meetup was transformative, but that they were already moving beyond it, using Yahoo! Groups' clumsy calendaring tool, simple e-mail, and even a Republican site, GOP Team Leader, to organize events. The problem with events planned independently of Meetup, they explained, was that new people wouldn't find out about them. They wanted to plan events on our site. Dave Kochbeck sketched out a model for the site, but estimated that it would cost over $100,000. We didn't have that kind of money, but put in a budget request regardless, hoping to complete it by August.

During Zack and Eli's visit from Moveon, they suggested that we think about modeling a tool on Moveon's event-planning tool. Michael and I jumped at it. They told us that we could probably hire their coder from We Also Walk Dogs, who had built their tool for them, and that the total cost—including server space—would be under $20,000. From the moment it became possible, we became convinced that the tool was necessary. It would free our people from the constraints of Meetup; events would sprout up all over the country—dozens, hundreds even. The whole Internet cave chipped in with theories and model sites as we worked with Zack to repurpose Moveon's event tool for our needs. I remember walking down the Burlington bike path one afternoon after working through the language for the tool's organizing sheets, pulling at the new vines shooting through a fence, and being completely convinced that we were changing politics forever.

We thought of this tool, which we eventually called "Get Local," as a first cut at eBay for political action. Ten years ago, someone with an old toaster would have had to accumulate a garage full of unused materials to hold a garage sale and find a buyer—someone wanting to buy that old toaster would have to wait at least until a summer Saturday to scour the garage sales for one. eBay allowed people to post a picture of the toaster within an hour of deciding to buy a new one, and a buyer could look for one on a midwinter midnight. Match.com and online dating services enabled people to find dates the moment they moved to a new town, instead of waiting for the seventh Saturday night when they finally knew enough people. For politics, however, everything still depended upon a central organizing structure, one that rarely held any kind of events in late primary states. A supporter would typically have to wait until the candidate came to town—often never—to find other supporters, or go through the local party machinery, which had developed its own arcane habits. Once found, the primary role of most supporters was fund-raising or stamp licking—roles for citizens so narrow that most simply didn't engage. It was as if, upon going to eBay, you were only allowed to trade televisions and bicycles. The opportunities didn't match the desire of citizens to contribute.

Meetup changed this, but in a very crude way: Any person could rely on a monthly meeting in a set place. We wanted to build a tool that would allow people to move beyond Meetup and create their own times, places, and types of events. The tool that we built, Get Local, allowed people to offer political events to those who wanted to attend, and turned the candidate website into a place where people could find each other—not just a place to find the candidate.

Get Local worked like a calendar that anyone could edit. Anyone who came to our website could decide to plan an event for Howard Dean, and advertise that event on the site. A featured button asked them if they wanted to host an event; if yes, they were asked to choose a category for the event, such as rally, community service, or planning meeting. They were then asked to list details and directions, and were given access to a website with suggestions for making the event a success and tools to manage attendees. Another featured button allowed people to easily search for supporter-organized events in their zip code.

As we were building, however, we did not consider the impact on other departments. In early May a senior staffer approached me and asked me to explain. When I did, she said, "We're not doing that. Forget it." She was just getting used to working with Meetup, where we were at least assured the presence of our campaign agenda, sent monthly to Meetup leaders. Though later she became one of the most creative users—and supporters—of Get Local, the idea of people organizing whatever events they wanted to didn't fit with what she'd learned about good organizing. Finance team members were similarly resistant, telling me that people would be encouraged to hold non-fund-raising events instead of fund-raising events, because it would be easier. We'd lose money because an eager volunteer would be lost on a non-fund-raising event. And there was the constant fear that it would inspire illegal political action, especially illegal political fund-raising. "Our job is to keep Howard out of jail. They'll do fund-raisers that violate the law and he'll be the one in jail." Finally, when Deputy Campaign Manager Bob Rogan reviewed the budget he'd approved for the tool, he told me that he'd changed his mind and we couldn't afford it. His resistance was more simple: "I don't see how this helps the campaign."

Nicco, Dick Rowe, Dave Kochbeck, and I finally lined up in formation in the doorway of Bob Rogan's office, and we all argued—somewhat disingenuously—that if we backed out now, Moveon would leave us for violating our contract, and we would get a bad name for future efforts to work with Moveon, and he relented. In fairness to Bob, we didn't answer his question—we didn't know how it would help the campaign. We had only a rough faith that as an insurgent our only chance lay in the people who supported us, despite mainstream media mockery. We believed we needed to serve our most active supporters, trusting that they would help figure the tool out along with us. But tactical concerns were not the only motive: We were also driven by a sense of responsibility to these people who wanted to be active citizens.

Get Local was immensely popular. Within two months, more than 2,000 events a month were held on it—in September it was closer to 3,000 events. People organized and went to basketball games for Dean, went to blues festivals for Dean, and cleaned up beaches for Dean. They held regular planning meetings outside of Meetup, always wearing T-shirts and sharing literature, and included concerts and fund-raisers on the Get Local site.[6]

## Summer

I think of summer as starting in May, when our webmaster Nicco Mele set up his desk with piles of plastic toys, pictures of flowers, and Caribbean music. Every night after most of the staff went home he would shift from his daily role of smoothing social tensions to tinkering with shapes on the homepage and testing and retesting e-mails before they were sent. Summers in Vermont last half the night with long, patient chiaroscuro sunsets well past 8:00 P.M., and he would put on Olu Dara singing "Your lips, your lips, your lips, your lips, are juicy" or blast Gil Scott Heron's "The Revolution Will Not Be Televised," and bellow along at full operatic pitch: "The revolution will not be brought to you by Xerox/In four parts without commercial interruptions." With Nicco there, we could actually act on our dreams—we could change the website, we could send out e-mails. The cold broke, as did the feeling of fishing in mud.

We moved to a horrible suburban building, but with ample room for staff. Dick Rowe arrived and became the senior staff person for the Internet team, trying to bring order and management to an entrenched chaotic culture. On June 10 Matt Gross and Marc Chadwick unveiled the new blog—with comments—and we all sat and scrolled in awe as enthusiastic humans wrote sentences on our website.[7] Trippi held a birthday party where we all threw baseballs to dunk him, to show the other campaigns how loose we were—he asked Matt to put the pictures of him soaking wet up on the new blog.

Dean hired a communications director and a political director, but Trippi continued to make decisions through the Internet team. We sat outside his door, like a scrum, and sent out finance e-mails and field e-mails, and talked constantly about giving meaning to power. In June we asked our supporters to "Double Dean" from 58,000 e-mail subscribers, and hundreds of people set up sign-up tables and forwarded requests to friends, reaching 116,000 in less than a month. The ideas hatched in the petri dish of spring were suddenly flourishing. Hundreds of groups held sympathetic announcement speech parties during Howard's June announcement speech using the Get Local tool. On June 30, we kept our supporters—and the mainstream media—in thrall with half-hour updates of how much money we were raising. Bobby's Teamraiser started raising substantial funds, creating a new model for "bundling."

Trippi took the handwritten letters ideas from Zack and Eli's visit and we sent packages with addresses of Iowa voters to each of the hundreds of Meetup groups around the country. In July, we asked Meetup groups to write to undecided New Hampshire voters. Posters for America was launched and 250,000 people created and downloaded their own personalized Dean posters. We announced an open-source policy platform, and were Slash-dotted.

## Deanlink

Zack Exley sent me a link to Friendstar in early June, a site Dave Kochbeck had talked about. For weeks I toyed with different ways of building a "Deanster," until one afternoon Volunteer Coordinator Peter Carley showed me his pile of unused offers to volunteer, a pile he did not have time to sort through. We realized, after talking, that if we could take out the middle person—somehow self-sort this pile—people could directly connect with each other and do useful work without needing Peters's intervention. The "Deanster," or "Visible Volunteer Network," would simply make the volunteer offers transparent to all.

Instead of sending in an offer to volunteer, people would publicly profile themselves, including their volunteer and policy interests. It would work like a dating site, except for people who wanted to connect with other similarly political people, instead of people who wanted romance. An environmentalist interested in doing visibility for Dean could search by zip code for the closest environmentalist with the same interest—taking the principles of selective dating and applying them to selective activism, assuming that each person would look for different things.

I had no money for a programmer to build this tool, so I put up a request for help on the blog, asking for PHP coders who could build a social networking tool for members of the campaign. The months of living without a coder had inculcated the habit of asking for help when we needed it. Thirty-five PHP coders responded within hours. One of the coders, Zack Rosen, started pinging me regularly—I finally flew down to New York to meet with him in the apartment of an irrepressible Vietnam veteran bomber pilot who supported Dean (Britt Blaser), and we stayed up all night, sketching "Deanster" designs on a large pad.

We shared the specs publicly, and a brilliant graduate student in California, Ka-Ping Yee, built a beautiful first draft version of this. We didn't end up using his version, in part because he was not American, and our lawyer became very nervous about whether this would be considered a contribution by a foreign national. I hired Clay Johnson to build the final version of what we called "Deanlink," which he did in less than a month.

Deanlink was less successful than we'd hoped—it did not grow our list by becoming a viral phenomenon—but existing organizers found it very useful. One of its most frequently used features allowed visitors to directly instant-message online Deanlink members; organizers instant-message people within close geographical range while planning an event. I also hired Zack Rosen to be the lead liaison with hack4dean and to build an open-source community-organizing website for all our local chapters to use, the tool that became Deanspace.

Our tools were working, all the campaigns were imitating our tactics—and Dean's ideas were carrying. We started to hear his ideas echoed in Kerry's words—"the wrong war at the wrong time," "this is the greatest grassroots campaign"—and, for the first time, we started to hear speculation from nonsupporters that Dean could actually win.

There was a time in that midsummer that the campaign actually set the tempo—set up movements and moments, created a cadence—that the mainstream media followed. In the spring Howard was setting his own agenda but no one was paying much attention. In the middle of summer, Howard Dean and Joe Trippi—not the *New York Times,* not CNN, not ABC's "The Note"—were telling the story of presidential politics in 2004.

In June, Joe Trippi explained the plan for the next month. It was, as was common for Trippi, in response to a mundane question that he thought was stupid—a question about why we were including a particular news article in our packets to Meetup leaders; his most riveting speeches often bloomed out of rants, like flowers from manure. The announcement speech on June 23, where Howard would lay out his vision, would be the largest in presidential campaign history. Four days later we were going to win the Moveon primary, he explained, making a huge splash and lots of money and gaining many members. At both moments, Dean would be on all national television networks—most importantly those in Iowa. Three days later, at the end of the second FEC quarter, we were going to raise more money than any other candidate, breaking records with the use of low-dollar contributions—and again be on TV. Iowans and New Hampshire residents, he said, will start paying attention. Most of them would hear about Dean for the first time during this two-week period.

The following week, 40,000 Iowans would receive a handwritten, personal letter (and a copy of the news article that inspired the question) from people all over the country asking them to consider supporting Howard Dean. The curiosity and attention raised by those three mainstream media hits would suddenly, shockingly, enter people's intimate life, like a person turning and walking off the television screen and into the living room. Those 40,000 letters were going to be handwritten by people at July 7 Meetups around the country.

We won the Moveon primary, we did have the largest announcement speech in history, we did break records for third-quarter fund-raising, and 55,000 people did meet to write handwritten letters to Iowa.

In late July, Trippi announced on our blog and e-mail list that we had a secret surprise—and asked people to fund-raise for the surprise. Trippi used a promise of a secret to get the mainstream media fascinated, obsessed even, with the secret—people were attentive—what would Joe do next? In August, tempted by the secret and the force of gravity that Dean was creating, three magazines ran cover pictures of Dean. The secret was unveiled as an ad buy in Texas—a direct challenge to Bush and a direct, irreverent inversion of the usual political process, in which all ad buys are in early primary states. As Trippi explained, we were spending several hundred thousand on the ad buy, but gaining far more in attention around Dean's political courage.

In late summer, I drove with a group of staffers to Red Rocks, cliffs that stood several meters above Lake Champlain, and we all took turns barreling into the water, afraid and happy at the same time. There are black-and-white photographs of us on the cliffs taken by someone in the water after we've jumped. In one that I find particularly arresting, we are all looking down, almost pensively, while someone's body vanishes into the water, only the arms and a splash showing.

## The Drive for Democracy

On September 17, Wesley Clark entered the race. The Draft Clark movement, built around an antiwar commitment and a decentralized model using the Internet, threatened our core support. Rumored reports from our Iowa operation were not encouraging. Half the staff was sent to Iowa. We stopped all production of new tools. The middle-aged men we called "the wise old men"—media consultants and pollsters—sat on the long couch in Trippi's office for hours, day after day. I was not privy to the conversations, although once in a while I would be called in to report on what "our people" were saying on the listservs (Gray Brooks, an Alabama student with an amazing literary flair, kept accounts on several hundred listservs) and blogs. Joe Trippi's focus would turn to Clark, to Gephardt, to the Clintons' plans, to Kucinich, explaining how each of them could beat us, talking about how we needed to go bigger to win.

Trippi called a half-day-long meeting with Matt and Nicco and me. "We're an insurgent front-runner," he repeated, as he often had that fall. "Which means we have to keep growing." The three of us sat on the floor and in chairs around a big chalkboard in a small conference room. We were the ragtag team, but his consultants weren't about "the Net," and couldn't help him grow. As it turns out, neither could we. For three hours, Nicco paced commandingly and wrote phrases on the board, and Matt argued for stronger policy stances.

At the end of October I rented a 1979 Airstream trailer that Jerome Armstrong found on eBay, took two volunteers, and went on the road to meet groups of supporters. The entire campaign energies were going to focus on Iowa and New Hampshire. I was going to focus on the rest of the country. Everywhere I went, I was going to persuade people to sign up to drive, fly, or bus to Iowa or New Hampshire in January to canvass for Dean. I set off on a trip to thirty states to visit some of the hundreds of thousands of people who were holding Meetups and the 3,000 Get Local events each month.

The full story of the two-month-long "Drive for Democracy" cannot be told here. In a cross between the Pony Express, *Fear and Loathing in Las Vegas,* a traveling ministry, and a book tour about health care, we visited twenty-four states and seventy grassroots groups. I traveled with Ryan Davis and David Welch, who took pictures, drove, and arranged call-in shows on local radio stations. At every stop we would ask people to introduce themselves; I would give a speech about the Statue of Liberty and the importance of Iowa; I would answer questions. The group would explain their tactics and difficulties and we would discuss them. That was the extent of the continuity between moments. The events ranged from a 110-person professionally organized political rally in Virginia with five speakers and a banner to meeting a lone Dean-supporter salesman in a high school classroom in Greenville, South Carolina. I cannot tell the stories of people in summary, because what was most striking about the trip was the great variety of style, of purpose, of reasons. Each group had its own culture. We slept in over forty people's homes, each with their own kitchens and families and questions.

One afternoon we sat at a southern-cooking restaurant, with cheap three-vegetable meals, for a "Seniors for Dean" event, listening to a man in his seventies with a neck like a chain of wire and a Brooklyn accent that he used like a sword to talk about health care. That night I was at a Halloween party listening to a man with a strong South American accent, dressed up as Dracula, talking about the importance of democratic speech.

Four or five times a week I would report on the blog, but the Internet connections were often too shaky to read any of the comments or responses. I'll share one blog post, however, because I think it describes the feel of the campaign, if not the Drive for Democracy:

> It started raining yesterday, a little incident we hadn't foreseen, and I tried the windshield wipers for the first time. Off they went, one after the other, completely unaligned with each-other like a flailing kid's hands, until Ryan doubled over in the passenger seat laughing. I told him if it rained again I was quitting. Just pulling over to the side and stopping, and waving our Dean signs for the next 2 months from coastal California.
>
> The driver's seat has a seatbelt, but the seat itself has a swirling tendency, so if you hit a bump you might swivel to the left—I've owned left- or right-listing cars, but typically

it's the tires, not the seat, that need alignment. There's also a fun squeegie noise that comes from no-where and rises to a nail-on-chalkboard scream if the internal wind hasn't covered your ears.

Yesterday when Ryan was driving and I was sitting in the back trying to plan, I heard a yelp from the front—the bus doors had swung open on their own (we fixed that quickly). Then every once in a while the window shutters rattle especially loudly, just for the fun of it.

The supportive honks keep coming though, from little cars that you could pile like plates inside this thing, and families and old people and young people and pickup trucks keep waving and smiling, so the terror appears to be all internal. With the CTA endorsement and labor rally and Jesse Jackson Jr. and the beginning of Iowa and New Hampshire road trip planning, the California excitement just keeps growing.

There was a strong sense of the absurd most times we encountered the media. Many seemed stuck on a vision of "grassroots" that involved waving and cheering and enthusiasm, instead of the quiet dedication of the notebooks and the precinct charts that we saw at every visit. A professional photographer brought together twenty volunteers to take a picture representing the Dean campaign—she had three assistants, and gave us all T-shirts to wear. "Get in the Airstream and wave out of the windows," she told the volunteers. "Yell, Democracy!" She lined us up in the front row in front of the volunteers and told us to jump and smile at the same time. I asked her if we were making an ad for Toy-o-ta! I swore I would never agree to a photo shoot like this again. "Jump!" she said. And we jumped again.

On December 9, Al Gore endorsed Howard Dean. We stopped the car and honked and ate mashed potatoes at the next diner to celebrate. That day I became convinced Dean would actually win the primary.

## Icarus

I returned to the office in late December, and in January, I flew to Iowa and joined the press bus. I hardly saw Trippi—one of his new deputies told me that I could not write about falling poll numbers in Iowa, or disorder or anger in the Iowa office. During the Drive for Democracy I had become a trusted voice of hope on the blog, but I'd been comfortable with it, because what I saw was hope. In Iowa, I saw a campaign full of fear and a press bus that was tired of the same speeches, but I kept writing about the hopeful moments.

In retrospect, I wish I'd pushed harder for honesty. Having used our blog to open up the office when we were moving upward, we continued to use our blog as a narrative of infinite ascension. We didn't trust people enough to engage them when things were going badly—we didn't ever write, "The TV news story about Howard dismissing Iowa caucuses in 1994 has really hurt him this week." I don't know that it would have helped, but it might have, mostly by setting lower expectations for the press—we paved the way for the Icarus-like fall by only telling stories about reaching toward the sun.

Dean came in a distant third in Iowa, far below even the worst expectations. On the day before the caucuses, Michael Silberman and I had gone door to door, finding few people home and many uninterested, but we had not expected these numbers. And then, within two weeks, the campaign was effectively over.

It is hard to understate how profoundly I misunderstood the presidential electoral process. In March, Trippi had explained that New Hampshire was critical, but at some level, I still didn't believe him—I believed that our support was so deep, so active, in so many states, that even if the general rule was that only two—or maybe three—candidates survived New Hampshire, our campaign would easily break that rule. That doesn't mean I thought it was inevitable that Dean would win, but I actually couldn't imagine happening what happened—the press stopped reporting on Dean as a serious candidate in South Carolina and beyond.

We were gone, invisible the way Kucinich was invisible, mentioned but not "a serious candidate." The campaign office became like Rome—video games and drinks at night, and the senior staff meeting that had once been held once a week was now held every day, all day, and gradually expanded so that it was held in the main conference room, with dozens of people joining in the never-ending meeting.

The night Dean dropped out was hard, but oddly relieving—the false hope disappeared from the website. We started a project that night called "Democratic Wings," challenging the grassroots to identify 100 Dean-inspired candidates who would run for local or federal office in the next week. A week later, 110 people had committed to running.

About thirteen months after the campaign ended, Nicco and Zack Rosen and I were on a fancy panel together at some retreat/conference event in the wine country outside of San Francisco. The panel didn't ask much of us—we each spoke for a few minutes—and then we took questions. As people started asking intelligent questions, I noticed that all of us were getting sort of hostile. When someone asked, academically, whether we thought "the scream" killed it, Nicco, who is usually the image of unperturbed, launched into something that was almost a rant, trying to communicate that these are not the questions—there is something much more there than the scream, than the tools, than the numbers.

Afterward, we decided that our anger came from having to speak in calm terms about a true heartbreak, in public, in front of hundreds of people. Who can do that well, and who can do that within a year of having lived it? I forget sometimes that we did, but we really believed. As mechanical and jaded as we were about some of the operations—how to get the press to write about "the Net" so that more people would join so that the press would write about the Net, and so on—there was a core passion that we all shared about actually changing the shape of political society.

There's no clear answer to me about why that happened—it wasn't the moment that Trippi started expressing an archetypal narrative that we all keened to, and it wasn't the moment that John Sykes, Adam Smith, and Steve Chaffin started the National Dean Network listserv, either, although both of those were essential. It's not so simple as the DNC speech or the NYC Meetup flipping a switch. I don't remember when I first started believing that it was possible—this restructuring of society—but I know I don't believe it the same way now, not with the same conviction that it will happen soon.

I like to think some of the tools I had a hand in were instrumental—Get Local and so on—but I can really imagine the Dean campaign without all of these things, except perhaps Meetup. What I can't imagine is the Dean campaign without that conviction and belief, the culture of passionate, pragmatic work toward something much different and bigger than a candidate—the tool that made up the molecular structure of everything we did—in a deeply contentious, anxious environment, the one tool that held us all together, if barely.

## Notes

1. A listserv is an e-mail-based mailing list. Yahoo! provided a free service (with ads) that was widely popular, within which it was easy to create groups, and which was easy to join.

2. This later became the Dean Coordinators Council.

3. A few of the people I "hired" during this period stayed on as state or county coordinators as the campaign grew—several others faded as local Meetups produced their own leadership. I now think the most important part of this practice was that it signaled that we were not going to interact with volunteers in the same way, and that we were going to expect real taking of responsibility across the board. For people who had never been involved in politics, this was a natural response on our part, and they immediately seized onto their new roles. For people who had been involved previously, they were shocked and resistant—I got many calls from friends of those I volunteered with, experienced political operatives, warning me against this method.

4. Despite fears that "the grassroots" would create embarrassing flyers and press releases, the Dean grassroots were fundamentally conservative in their communications—far more conservative than the campaign. I believe this is because they were grounded in local Meetup groups, and face-to-face communities tend to caution—and because they did not want to hurt the candidate.

5. http://wireless.deanforamerica.com (accessed December 1, 2003).

6. Despite that, we had thought we would gradually phase out Meetup, but we couldn't. Get Local never surpassed Meetup in its importance to the campaign. Meetups, with regular events in public places that new and curious people could comfortably attend, created a core community, and Get Local allowed those communities to do more imaginative and effective organizing. Get Local was used where Meetups were already active—few people used Get Local as an entry point, and few people went to a Get Local event as their first event. Get Local required a motivated, connected person to find a venue and invite people. Meetup at the time (this has changed) had identified thousands of public places willing to host events, and required no leader, just mass—fifteen people signed up, and they were all invited to a leaderless event, in a venue already discovered. And the culture that Meetup inspired was therefore unique—the people who showed up at the early Meetups all became equally responsible for their local success, simply by showing up. The first meeting was a meeting of equals.

7. http://www.blogforamerica.com/view/276.

# 6

# Swept Up in "The Perfect Storm"

## Bobby Clark

*Bobby Clark, the first web strategist for the Dean campaign, describes the chaotic, almost absurd early days of Dean's Internet campaign, including stories of borrowing icons from* The West Wing *to create a hasty mockup of a website. He explores in detail a few critical technological choices around contact management tools, and the development of online tools that enabled people to become their own fund-raisers in presidential campaigns. He describes how his background in technology start-ups influenced his approach to the nascent web campaign, and argues that the open-source ideology played an important role in the campaign's early commitment to using the Internet to connect people, instead of to broadcast. An Internet campaign, he argues, is ultimately, a reflection of the group of people who make it up.*

In the early days of the Dean campaign, Joe Trippi described what was happening as "The Perfect Storm." Having seen the movie, I wondered at the time whether that was the best choice for a metaphor. Looking back, however, that description seems as good as any.

A storm as big and powerful as the one that inspired the movie leaves everyone in its wake changed forever. The Dean campaign certainly did that for me.

In the fall of 2002, I had no plans to extend what I assumed was a temporary political career beyond that November's election. After completing my gig as a deputy director of a statewide ballot initiative to institute Election Day voter registration in Colorado, I assumed I would return to a career in the high-tech world. But my life took an unexpected turn when a friend burst into our Election Day voter registration campaign office one afternoon and invited me to a gathering with "the civil unions guy" at the Democratic Headquarters down the street. I knew little of Howard Dean other than the fact that he'd been the first governor to sign into law any measure of equality for gay couples, but that was more than enough reason to go meet him.

Following Dean's opening remarks, one of the first questions to him was whether his decision, as Vermont's governor, to sign into law the landmark legislation that created civil unions would hurt him in more socially conservative presidential primary states like Iowa and South Carolina. Governor Dean didn't hesitate. He said, "If someone questions me about the civil unions bill, I'll tell them that on September 11, when those buildings came down, they came down with every religious conviction, every ethnicity, and every sexual orientation inside—we died together as a country on that day, and we will live together."

He had me. By Monday I had researched enough about Dean to believe he could be our next president. I was certain that I had to help him in some way, so I scheduled lunch with the political consultant who had managed Dean's visit to Colorado, Rick Ridder. Later that week, I was sitting at lunch with Rick, expecting to talk about helping out the next time Dean visited Colorado. But fate intervened when Rick informed me that just that morning Dean had hired him as national campaign manager. At that point, our conversation changed completely.

They say that to a carpenter, every problem is a nail. I was a dot-commer, having spent the last four years helping start Internet companies in Colorado and California. So to my way of thinking, the only way a little-known governor from a tiny New England state could get elected was to use the Internet more effectively than any presidential campaign had before. And an opportunity to help shape the campaign's Internet strategy had just fallen into my lap. Rick agreed that the campaign would have to be Internet savvy, and he agreed that my Internet start-up experience would be valuable. So he invited me to join him in Vermont when the campaign got rolling in January, with two caveats. He couldn't promise that I'd get to do Internet work, and I would have to deal with all the more mundane technology issues because the campaign would not be able to hire IT staff for a while.

That was enough for me, and three months later, in January 2003, I put my life in Colorado on hold and boarded a plane for Vermont.

## The First Website

"Welcome to Burlington! It's not usually this cold."

My one-person welcoming committee at the small airport on the edge of town was Abbey Trebilcock, a bright-eyed and energetic recent UVM graduate. I liked Abbey immediately. In the short drive to the office, I learned that subzero weather was unusual even for early January in northern Vermont, that her best friend at UVM was gay, that she had once shouted down a religious right anti–civil unions protest at the state capitol, and that she was "employee number one"—the first hire on the Dean campaign.

I wasn't sure I believed Abbey about the cold. On the last leg of my flight—from New York to Burlington—I had stared out the window to take in the sights of my first trip to New England. All I had seen was a vast expanse of snowy white. But despite Abbey's suspicious optimism about Vermont's weather, she seemed to have the scoop on what I should expect when we reached the office. As we wound our way past the UVM campus and the students bundled from head to toe, Abbey told me that the staff consisted of about a dozen people. A few had moved over from the governor's office. The rest were professional campaigners from out of state. Abbey warned me that because the campaign had very little money lots of things had been patched together on a shoestring, including the office network. Consequently, nearly every one of those dozen staffers was experiencing a technical crisis of some kind or another. Most importantly, Abbey told me that a project to create the campaign's first real website was already under way. Governor Dean's brother had been working for several weeks with volunteers on a proposed design for the site.

In the dot-com world of Internet companies your business essentially is your website, and success rests on getting a lot of people to visit your site and stay there. So to my way of thinking the first step in building an Internet campaign, naturally, was to create a site compelling enough to draw and hold people on it. I was eager to start working on that, but I would have to bide my time before I would get that chance.

After my first few days on the campaign, I appreciated that delay. The campaign's technical challenges were worse than Abbey had described. Many of the computers had been purchased from UVM surplus. The only server was also being used as the desktop computer for the reception desk, and it was riddled with viruses. So I spent most of my time trying to play substitute for a real IT staff.

I was in between putting out technical fires one afternoon when Rick Ridder emerged from a meeting with Governor Dean and informed me that I would get a shot at designing the site. That was the good news. The bad news was that I would have very little time to propose something. In two days Governor Dean would compare whatever design I proposed with the other alternative that was already in progress and then make a decision. Two days wouldn't be enough to go through any kind of serious design process. A design process is supposed to be thoughtful and thorough and, realistically, should involve multiple iterations. But in the hyper-condensed timeline of a campaign, you rarely have the luxury of fretting about how things are supposed to work—you just have to get it done. Fortunately, I had already worked with some designer friends to create a demo Dean for America website to gain Rick's confidence and prod him into letting me work on Dean's Internet effort. With no time to do anything else, that demo site would now have to become my proposal to Governor Dean.

There was just one problem. When we created that demo, we had no images or other content to work with. There was an existing campaign website of sorts, but it had almost nothing on it—a logo, minimal copy, and only a couple of photographs that weren't particularly good. So we had created the demo site using images from various *West Wing* sites. The Bartlets had stood in as the Deans.

I spent the next day scrounging through the office looking for any other photos or other images that I could use, and I learned that most of what existed was already on the existing campaign site. In other words, there wasn't much to work with. So we did the best we could with very little content to modify the demo site and turn it into a Dean for America design, using the real Howard Dean instead of Jed Bartlet.

Governor Dean picked our "West Wing" design, and we launched the site the next day. There was no money to pay for web design at that point in the campaign. In fact, the campaign had budgeted only a few thousand dollars for work on the website for all of 2003. Thankfully, my friends had been willing to volunteer almost all of their time. But there wouldn't be an opportunity to redesign the site for another couple of months, when Nicco Mele came to the rescue to serve as our webmaster.

By late January, with the campaign staff having grown considerably, we were still desperate for IT staff. I lobbied for any amount of money I could get to hire some help. Unfortunately, any new hires would have to wait for our fund-raising operation to get going and first quarter Federal Election Commission reports to be filed. Even if you have the money to do things the campaign really needs to do, spending that money before the end of the quarter means that your cash-on-hand number won't look as good. And because the Dean campaign had started the first quarter with almost no cash, we needed to limit first-quarter expenses as much as we could. Spending any of the money we had raised on things like IT was going to have to wait until April, after the first quarter had ended.

But we had too many critical IT needs that couldn't wait until April, and I knew someone who would be perfect as our IT director. I had previously worked with Dave Kochbeck at an Internet start-up in San Francisco. Dave was extremely smart and experienced, and having worked at start-ups he knew how to start from scratch. Even better, he also was a Dean fan. Better yet, he was taking a break from the corporate world, so he wouldn't be deterred by how little the campaign would be able to pay. Dave agreed to volunteer for the month of March with no pay in exchange for Rick Ridder's agreement to at least consider hiring him in April. A couple of weeks later Abbey drove with me to Montreal to pick Dave up at the airport, and in April he officially became the campaign's first IT director.

I can't describe how relieved I was to have Dave on board. Although I had worked with start-ups and had learned a lot about IT, my experience was primarily in marketing and law. Dave was a heavy hitter, and I knew that he would get the campaign on the right track. Dave knew how to build infrastructure, and he helped lay a foundation for the campaign to grow dramatically. He led our move to a much larger office on the outskirts of Burlington, installed a more scalable phone system, and built a real server room. He also got our Iowa and New Hampshire offices up and running, and he did all of it, for the most part, with no staff.

Dave also served, essentially, as our campaign's chief technology officer (CTO), as he had for our San Francisco start-up. A CTO doesn't just manage the technology operations. A CTO also becomes a bridge between the technology and business operations for the organization, translating business needs to the IT department, and explaining the IT implications of decisions to other managers.

The Dean campaign pushed the use of technology more than any presidential campaign had done before. But even on our campaign, most of the people on staff, including the managers, had very little prior experience with IT. We desperately needed a CTO, but that proved to be a very hot seat that was never filled for long. Dave left the campaign in late summer, and at least two others would attempt to serve in a CTO-like role. But their roles and authority weren't clearly defined, and they experienced mixed results.

One of those men, Jim Moore, made an astute observation near the end of the campaign. Jim told me that our campaign reminded him of the business world in the 1980s, when the use of technology began expanding rapidly. Jim observed that in that environment the tech people have disproportionate power because the rest of the organization doesn't have sufficient understanding. Businesses faced a tremendous management challenge in that environment. Now, for future campaigns to better manage the explosion of new technologies, they will need to draw from the experience of the business world in the 1980s and learn how to deal with the same challenge faced decades ago.

## Campaign-Centric versus Network-Centric

After the site redesign was completed, I focused my efforts on improving the site infrastructure. Just about anything would have been an improvement. Our site was being hosted by a small company that was charging us $49.95 per month. Even the least technical person can probably imagine that a presidential campaign needed much more than $49.95 worth of hosting services. I'll never forget sitting with Zephyr and Dave in our tiny little web team office on the last night before the end of the first quarter, praying that the site would stay up.

Larry Biddle had crafted a fantastic end-of-quarter fund-raising e-mail, and people were responding. We had already topped $400,000 in donations with hours remaining before midnight. Then it happened—our site went down. For more than an hour. We still ended the first quarter by raising more online than any other campaign—$760,000 total—but losing an hour of donations at a critical time was a big lesson.

One might ask why we hadn't simply moved to a better hosting provider by that point. Part of the answer is that there was a freeze on any expenditures before the end of the quarter. But the more important reason was that our hosting service was only the start of our infrastructure problems. We also had no good way of e-mailing our supporters. When I first arrived at the campaign in January, the unluckiest of our staffers, Chris Canning, had the unenviable task of sending e-mails to our list in batches of a few hundred e-mails at a time—using Microsoft Outlook. Every time we wanted to send an e-mail a look of dread would cross over Chris's face. We also needed to make some changes to the way we were taking online donations to make it easier to collect the information we would need to compile our FEC reports.

All of these things needed to be addressed, and it wasn't clear to me which was more urgent. But it was clear to me that most of the campaign's resources in the first quarter were committed to the finance staff, given the fact that if we weren't able to raise money quickly the campaign wasn't going anywhere. So I decided to focus first on solving the problem that had to do with how we bring in money. I looked to the other campaigns to see how they were managing online donations. Kerry's campaign seemed to be further along at that point than anyone else with their web presence, so I was particularly interested in what they were doing.

Kerry's campaign at that time was using Convio, a service provider based out of Austin, Texas (of all places), to manage their online donations. As I investigated Convio further, I began to think that they could perhaps solve more problems for us than just our online donations. The reason for my optimism was that Convio touted themselves as an "eCRM" company for nonprofits. The "e" was just marketing-speak that meant they were web-based. "CRM" stood for "Constituent Relationship Management," the nonprofit equivalent of "Customer Relationship Management." I had been a CRM enthusiast for years while working for Internet companies. CRM is all about connecting all the applications that help companies interact with customers on top of a single, common database. Moving to a CRM platform had helped all the various company departments have a much more complete view of the company's customers when they interacted with them.

After getting a demo of Convio's tools, it was clear that they would move us forward dramatically. They would be able to host and support our website, enable us to take online donations in all the ways that we would need, easily create and publish forms on our website for things like online petitions, and easily create and send e-mails to tens of thousands of supporters in minutes. I was especially excited about a fund-raising tool that Convio offered that would enable our supporters to create their own personal fund-raising pages. Using this tool, our supporters would be able to raise money for the campaign and get credit for it publicly. And I was excited about the fact that we would be able to segment our database and send more personalized e-mails to our supporters. I imagined being able to send the same e-mail appeal to all our supporters, but with the information that appeared most relevant to them, such as the issue they seemed to be most concerned about.

I was convinced that we needed to sign a contract with Convio right away, so I began my own campaign within the campaign. As with all spending decisions in the early months of the campaign, getting the two leaders of the finance department on board was key. Stephanie Schriock was our finance director, and Larry Biddle was in charge of all our smaller-dollar direct-response fund-raising programs like direct mail. I had more than a few conversations with Larry and Stephanie about all the ways Convio's transaction processing system would help us raise money online. They were persuaded.

But Zephyr also needed to agree to the deal. And although he was still in his initial thirty-day volunteer window, Dave Kochbeck needed to agree. After lots of meetings and internal maneuvering, we did sign a contract with Convio. And Dave's opinion probably was key. He expressed legitimate (and prescient) concerns that we would outgrow Convio's services. Convio simply wasn't set up at that time to host organizations as large and active as we would later become. Dave also didn't like the fact that Convio wouldn't allow us to connect to their system any new applications that we might later develop. However, Dave did acknowledge that Convio would solve huge, immediate problems for us and move us much further ahead. With enough of us in alignment, we were able to get the top-level approval we needed to move forward.

For the most part, Convio's tools did for us what they had promised. That included processing nearly $25 million online by the time the campaign ended a year later—a presidential primary record at that point. But Dave's concern about Convio's having a closed system was justified almost immediately.

With my dot-com, it's-all-about-our-site mentality, I had been surprised a few weeks earlier when Joe Trippi had asked me to put a link on our homepage to Meetup.

com. He had learned that a growing number of Dean supporters were using that site to connect with each other at local restaurants, bars, and coffee shops. I added the link to the homepage as Trippi requested, but I thought perhaps this might hinder our ability to grow our own e-mail list and build traffic to our own site. Within a couple of weeks, of course, the *New York Times* wrote a story about Dean's visit to the New York Meetup, and Dean Meetups around the country were off and running.

When we moved our site into Convio's system, Meetups were growing at such a rate that we wanted to be certain that all of those Meetup supporters also were finding their way onto our e-mail list. So Zephyr and Dave worked out a deal with Meetup.com to create a joint registration system so that anyone who registered for a Dean Meetup also was added to our database in Convio's system, and vice versa. But because Convio's system wasn't open to outside applications, this proved to be a very challenging, and largely manual, process.

At this point in the campaign, my perspective about what it meant to be "the Internet campaign" was changing dramatically. I had been focused entirely on enabling our campaign to communicate to our supporters and enabling them to communicate back to us. What Zephyr and Dave realized before I did was that the power of the Internet, essentially, was in its capacity to foster interconnectedness.

That concept became one of the big topics of conversation among Zephyr, Dave, Nicco, and me. We had all witnessed the meteoric growth of Dean Meetups, which clearly was fueled by the way that Meetups brought people together. Yahoo! groups also were growing by leaps and bounds. This also was essentially about connection. But at that time, there was no way for any of our supporters on our website to connect with each other in any way.

We had put in place the ability to send e-mails more effectively. We had addressed our needs for taking online donations. And we could publish updates and new pages on our website quickly and easily. But there was no way for one of our supporters in Boise to connect to another one of our supporters in Boise easily.

One of the many ideas we kicked around was something akin to a Dean campaign Friendster service. Something else Dave likes to say is that if you have an idea, you can bet that others are having the same idea at roughly the same time. I always referred to that concept as a "dispensation." Dave referred to it in computer terms—you're not the only one getting the same inputs, and the same inputs will result in the same output. Input/output, dispensation—however we described it, I imagine that more than a few of Dean's tech-savvy supporters were having that same idea as Dave about connection, because over the next few months there seemed to be an explosion of software projects all geared toward enabling connection. And projects like Deanlink, Deanspace, and Get Local became part of the Dean campaign's online landscape. And like Convio's tools, none of these newly developed tools linked to each other. Ultimately we created a situation where we had multiple databases that weren't connected, and we hired a staff of four to manage all the data.

If it sounds like a mess, that's because it was.

And it wasn't our only mess involving data. Having a campaign take off the way the Dean campaign did means that you receive lots and lots of e-mail from hundreds of thousands of people. We were literally overrun with e-mail, and it took a team of dozens of retiree volunteers working night and day just to keep up. Dave saw a train wreck coming and began looking for solutions to our data challenge by midsummer. He concluded that the only way we would address our data issues and create the kind of capacity needed to win the nomination and defeat George Bush was to implement a real CRM solution.

Convio is partial CRM. Their tools only deal with web-based constituent interactions. True CRM companies have systems that also can manage many of the other types of interactions with constituents, such as inbound e-mail and phone calls.

Dave researched the best options, and then brought in a team from ePiphany to make a presentation. Companies like United Airlines and Microsoft were ePiphany customers. And using a true CRM vendor like ePiphany would solve more than just the challenge of connecting all our web applications in a common database. We would also be able to effectively turn the Burlington office, and all our state offices, into call centers. This would mean that when a staff member answered a phone call from someone in our database, there could be a screen on that staff member's computer that told him or her about that constituent's prior interactions with the organization. It would mean that we could keep better track of problems that a constituent might encounter, such as a mistake with an online donation. It would also mean that we could better manage inbound e-mail, one of the biggest challenges of any campaign.

Our campaign received thousands of e-mails every day. We had a team of volunteers in a portion of the office dedicated just to this task, to read and respond to every e-mail, hopefully within a couple of days of having received each e-mail. Imagine if every inbound e-mail automatically went into the campaign's master database, automatically becoming part of that constituent's record, and created a notification that a response was required.

All that would have been possible with a CRM solution. Unfortunately, the price tag would have exceeded $1 million. And, for a campaign that began the year with virtually no IT budget, spending that amount of money on one IT vendor was unthinkable.

Even if the price tag was too expensive, Dave's instinct was right. As businesses did before, campaigns are going to have to find a way to deal with the vast and painful challenge of managing data. Because of the scale involved, presidential campaigns are especially challenging in that regard.

And CRM will be the solution.

## Building Connections

As the primaries approached, our focus was increasingly placed on the two earliest states—Iowa and New Hampshire. Using the Internet and unconventional tactics, the Burlington office had accomplished our task of elevating Dean to contender status on the national stage. But now it was all about the decision that people in a particular state would make on one particular day. And in December 2003, I read a story in the *New York Times* about how our New Hampshire campaign also had been using technology and unconventional tactics to propel Dean to a huge lead.

For months, it seems, our New Hampshire campaign had been relying on a very unconventional field program. Our state director, Karen Hicks, wanted to try something different. Instead of relying exclusively on poorly paid kids to make calls and knock on doors, she had worked with a mentor of hers, the legendary organizer Marshall Gans, to come up with a field strategy that would utilize social networks. Their plan relied on supporters who would host small meetings in their living rooms. The host would follow a plan provided by the campaign to invite at least fifty people to their living room meeting. The reason for fifty was that was a number that would probably force the host to reach out beyond his or her most comfortable, immediate network. Another reason was that if fifty were invited, the host could probably count on having at least fifteen attend. The purpose of the meeting was solely to foster connection. Connection with Dean, certainly. But also connection with each other.

The meeting always began with a short video about Governor Dean that told his story. Then, the host would tell his or her story. And then everyone in attendance would, in sequence, tell their stories. There was no discussion of policy or politics. Just people sharing who they were, what they cared about, and why they had come to that meeting. The only "ask" at the end of the meeting was whether there were at least two people in the room who would consider hosting a house meeting such as that in the next couple of weeks.

From June 2003 until early December, more than 50,000 people attended these small house meetings in New Hampshire. The New Hampshire staff and supporters were so enthusiastic about them that I had to learn more. I began talking with other Vermont staffers about what was going on in New Hampshire, and the next weekend we organized a field trip to Manchester to attend a living room meeting. After experiencing one for ourselves, we immediately began strategizing about how we could create software that would enable such a program in other states. People were so enthusiastic about living room meetings that they called them a "spiritual experience."

In an age when we are losing our social institutions and feeling more and more disconnected from each other, people are starved for connection. The Dean campaign found many ways to offer that, and we were rewarded for it.

## Reflecting on What It Meant to Be "The Internet Campaign"

Becoming "the Internet campaign" was, in part, a deliberate strategy. It was also just a reflection of who we were as a group. I've heard it said that campaigns are a reflection of the candidate. From my experience, they're more a reflection of the entire community of people who show up and become part of their culture.

From the very beginning, there were people on the Dean campaign who lived and breathed the culture of the Internet. And that, inevitably, helped chart the direction our campaign would take. By now, everyone knows about Joe Trippi's role as an Internet evangelist on the campaign. But there were others who brought an infusion of Internet culture near the beginning of the campaign. Dave Kochbeck had been very much a part of the slash-dotted, dot-com culture in San Francisco. Matt Gross had been an early pioneer of the blogosphere when he arrived in Burlington offering to start a campaign blog. Nicco Mele also had been a blogger and a tech junkie before he came to Burlington to be our webmaster. Zephyr says that she wasn't really an Internet person at the beginning of the campaign, and she might not necessarily like being called an Internet person now, but she took to blogging and Internet organizing authentically and passionately. And, of course, there were many others who found their way to the campaign and helped it navigate uncharted territory online.

More than a passion for technology, one thing that the Internet crowd shared was a belief about power. It has been said that the Internet distributes "power to the edges." And we had all experienced that. Dave and the other programmers had experienced the power of open-source programming to take on software giants like Microsoft. We had all experienced the power of words on one web page to take on the establishment, in both politics and business.

Essentially, the Internet is about distributed power. By our placing significant focus on Internet outreach and fund-raising, the narrative of our campaign was inevitably altered. And no matter what the hook was for anyone to become involved in the Dean campaign—for me it was Dean's stance on civil unions; for others it was the Iraq War—ultimately the campaign for all of us was about redistributing power. That was the real legacy of becoming the Internet campaign.

But becoming the Internet campaign involved adopting some unconventional ways of doing things. That, inevitably, led to conflict among the staff. So one huge key to our success became the ability of everyone—the Internet people who had never worked on campaigns before and the professional campaign staff—to learn from each other and adapt. One example of an early conflict came in April. There was a growing community of Deaniacs who were using Meetup.com to connect with each other monthly in local bars, restaurants, and coffee shops. One of our largest groups was in San Francisco. April 26 was going to be our first major fund-raiser. It would be a celebration of the third anniversary of Dean's signing civil unions into law. There would be three events, in Los Angeles, San Francisco, and New York.

These were real fund-raisers, so you weren't able to attend unless you made the required donation of several hundred dollars. Somehow, our Dean Meetup group in San Francisco learned that the governor would be in town, and they naturally assumed they were invited. And when they showed up for the event expecting to see him and not expecting to pay hundreds of dollars, the finance staff was livid.

From the perspective of many campaign staffers, Meetups probably made little sense. But they were willing to suffer this sideshow because it wasn't impacting them. Now, all of a sudden, it was. The finance staff had a job to do—raise money. Having people crashing their events like this would impede their efforts. Fortunately, our finance team was blessed with great leadership. Our finance director, Stephanie Schriock, and her deputy, Linnea Dyer, were two of the best leaders on the campaign. And Larry Biddle wasn't just a direct-mail genius. He has an uncommon wisdom and provided sage advice that helped the campaign navigate more than one potential pitfall.

Stephanie's team learned from that event, and their solution was to embrace rather than resist the grassroots and the new ideas about using the Internet. Their solution was that every fund-raising event to follow would have to include a low-dollar portion so that nearly anyone could afford to join in and be part of the event.

The belief that our campaign, like the Internet, was about distributing power was never more validated than in our fund-raising. I'll never forget a comment I read on the blog on June 30, 2003—the day we shocked the political world with an $800,000-per-day close on the second quarter. It simply said, "Finally a candidate WE own."

Every political pundit, and every other campaign, was watching our website obsessively that day to see just how much money we would raise. And to try to figure out how we were doing it. We had taken a very unusual step for a presidential campaign. We were deliberately trying to create a sense of ownership among Dean's supporters, and Joe Trippi had the idea that in order to do that we needed greater transparency. And we needed to trust our supporters to get engaged and help the campaign reach our goals.

Traditionally, the way presidential campaigns approach FEC reports is that they try to downplay expectations, and then surprise the opinion makers with numbers that exceeded expectations. Trippi wanted to try something different, and one night in June 2003 he asked Stephanie Schriock and Larry Biddle what they thought about setting a fund-raising goal for the quarter that we would publish on our site and invite Dean supporters to help us meet. This was another example of how quickly Stephanie and Larry were able to adapt fund-raising strategies to incorporate new thinking. They agreed, and Larry Biddle had the brilliant idea of using a baseball bat as our fund-raising campaign thermometer.

The rest is history. "The bat" took on a life of its own, and it became the perfect metaphor for how the Dean campaign sought to empower Dean supporters and encourage them to take ownership of the campaign.

The finance team came up with two more fund-raising programs that helped our supporters engage in and take ownership of the campaign. One of those programs was our Dean Team personal fund-raising web pages. Convio's suite of tools included the ability for people to create their own personal fund-raising page on which they could tell their story and include a couple of photos. There was a link to a donation page, and every donation made through that personal page was tracked to that supporter. The supporter could set a personal fund-raising goal and then work to reach that goal.

We gave out small pens that looked like baseball bats to the first 1,000 people to set up a Dean Team personal fund-raising page. Thousands of people ultimately set up those pages, and the program brought in more than $1 million for the campaign. And we know, anecdotally, that this program brought in money that we otherwise would not have raised. One of my favorite examples of that involved one of our campaign staffers, Parag Mehta. Many Dean staffers, including Parag, set up their own Dean Team pages. At the end of every quarter, in the push to raise as much as possible for our FEC report, a friendly rivalry would inevitably arise among the staff. Although Parag was on the field staff, he was a formidable fund-raiser. In late September 2003, as we were finishing the third quarter, Parag had an impressive personal fund-raising push. Among those he persuaded to donate was a former rival who had been a member of the College Republicans at their alma mater. One of the great lessons of fund-raising is that people give to people. Parag's College Republican friend gave to the Dean campaign for one reason, and one reason only—Parag asked. By giving Dean supporters the opportunity to make a very public "ask" of their friends and family, we gave them an opportunity to take ownership of our fund-raising effort and do the work of the campaign. As always, they responded.

The other fund-raising program that afforded a similar opportunity was David Salie's house party fund-raisers. By June 2003, David already had succeeded in getting a number of supporters to host house party fund-raisers for Dean. Some of the feedback he received was that it didn't feel terribly significant to raise a few hundred, or even a few thousand, dollars for the campaign on your own. Taking that feedback, David began recruiting supporters to host house party fund-raisers in groups, following a theme. He learned that it felt more significant to raise a few hundred dollars if several other parties were also raising a few hundred dollars at the same time. As 2003 proceeded, those events grew larger and larger. David took an additional step to help those party hosts feel more connected to others by joining all the parties together on a conference call with Governor Dean. Finally, on New Year's Eve, David organized the largest house party night yet—A New Year for America. There were more than 2,000 parties that night alone. David's house party program was another important way for Dean supporters to engage, take ownership, and do the work of the campaign. That program brought in another $2 million for the campaign.

Jodi Wilgoren, a reporter for the *New York Times*, had followed all that was happening on the Dean campaign for months by the time the campaign reached the end of its run in March 2004. All the more incredible, then, that she could have gotten it so wrong when she wrote her postmortem of the campaign. Jodi wrote that other campaigns would try to re-create the Dean campaign's success in online fund-raising, but they wouldn't try to copy other ways that the Dean campaign used the Internet.

What Jodi didn't understand was that online fund-raising wasn't a thing unto itself. Making a donation was simply one way that Dean supporters engaged with, and took ownership of, the campaign. If the campaign hadn't done all the things we did to provide people an opportunity to engage with and take ownership of the campaign, we wouldn't have been as successful at raising money. Dean supporters were as passionate as anyone on staff, even the governor himself, about the campaign's promise of empowering ordinary citizens and returning power to the hands of the people.

My mother provided a great example of that on the day of the Wisconsin primary. We all knew that our only chance of continuing the campaign was to win in Wisconsin. If we lost, the campaign would end. But on that day my mother, a staunch Dean supporter, sent me an e-mail to let me know that she had just made another donation to the campaign. She asked me to go around the office and urge everyone to keep their heads up and fight on. And she concluded with these words: "We must have a government of, for, and by the people."

That, Jodi, wasn't a response to a clever fund-raising tactic. That was a bone-deep belief in the movement that the Dean campaign had become.

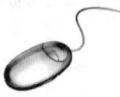

7

# A Coder Becomes a Political Activist

*Aldon Hynes*

*Aldon Hynes was a professional systems analyst who volunteered for the Dean campaign and, among other things, helped build the social software program Deanspace. He has subsequently become a political activist who played a key role in Ned Lamont's successful Democratic primary race against Joe Lieberman for the U.S. Senate, among other efforts. Hynes's story of this journey nicely illustrates how the Dean campaign did not just draw upon existing activists or groups with known and fixed opinions, but instead drew new people into the campaign and eventually into politics. His story also nicely illustrates how the Internet's evolution as an alternative news source during the 1990s created a context for both different and more interactive relations to politics to develop. Finally, Hynes's gentle, personal style of narration points to a little-understood fact about the character of the campaign: The campaign offered a kind of supportive community that was not just about youthful bonding, or some kind of heroic or radical vision of change, but that was very broadly humane and welcoming.*

## My Life before Dean, Online and Off

I grew up in a fairly conservative household in a fairly liberal town. I had little access to the news and relied mostly on what my parents said and often found myself at odds with my peers. In the school mock election in 1972, I was probably the only person who campaigned for Richard Nixon. I had heard of Kent State. It was some horrible thing that happened in a remote, faraway land called Ohio.

When my high school years came around, politics became a little more personal. I went to a superb public school that every year brought in students from disadvantaged communities around the country through a program called A Better Chance (ABC). The school had always waived tuition for these students, yet as I entered high school the school board was taken over by more conservative board members and they voted to end the waiver. The students were outraged and I joined the demonstrations in support of ABC.

I ended up going to college in Ohio, yet remained fairly apolitical in college until my senior year. That year, I helped organize groups of students to go to antinuclear demonstrations and I became involved in John Anderson's campaign for a brief while. I majored in philosophy but after four years dropped out. After college, I moved to New York City to be a poet and support myself working with computers.

In 1982, I took a computer consulting position at Bell Laboratories. I spent my working hours writing programs to help optimize the design of telephone circuits. I also spent a lot of time playing speed chess during lunch, and exploring new electronic worlds after hours. Some of the time was spent playing Rogue, an early computer game. More of the time was spent sending e-mails and writing Usenet posts.

I had an account on a computer that was connected over phone lines to a computer twenty miles away. It, in turn, was connected to another computer a little further up the line. By following the links properly, I could get to Arpanet and send e-mails to people around the world. I didn't know it at the time, but I was among the first generation of people to venture into the just-emerging online world. And it was becoming part of my offline life as well. For example, in October 1982, I sent a post to the net.singles Usenet newsgroup announcing a Halloween party I was having at my apartment in New York City. Several people I had known online but not face-to-face showed up and I experienced what you might call my first Meetup.

I continued to pursue my career in New York and ended up on Wall Street in 1987. I voted in every election, but that was about the extent of my political involvement. Instead, I focused on work, church, and family and argued that if you really wanted to change people's lives, it was perhaps best to do that through church.

In 1991 I moved to Connecticut and the following year became interested in the presidential campaign of Paul Tsongas. I put a Tsongas bumper sticker on the back of my car and wrote my first check to a political campaign. After Tsongas lost in the primary, I returned to my normal level of political indifference.

The ensuing years brought on the explosion of the Internet into popular consciousness, and the online world grew ever more populous. It was not until New Year's Eve 1998, however, that I went to what I would consider my second Meetup. Members of an online community that I participated in held a New Year's Eve party in Washington, D.C. I took a train down to Washington and spent New Year's Eve with a bunch of people I had met online, had shared interests with, but had never met face-to-face.

There is something frightening yet tantalizing about meeting people you have met online face-to-face for the first time. There is anticipation about finally getting to see someone who has become a good friend, and yet there is a fear that they may not be at all like what you imagined and that the friendships might not survive the face-to-face meeting. At the party in Washington, I found that the people I met were in fact very different than I had imagined, at least in terms of mannerisms and appearance. However, I found that the friendships were actually strengthened and not weakened by the experience.

I have always been a news junkie of sorts, and when I started working on Wall Street in the late 1980s, I had the good fortune of being able to access news wires through various trading systems. Instead of relying on an edited-down version of the news that I would find in the local papers or on the evening newscasts, I could explore the news that was interesting to me and form my own opinions. And then in the 1990s when I was able to get news via Yahoo! and then later via Google News, I found it wonderful. By early 2003, I was getting most of my news online.

## Discovering Dean: "The Real Thing"

In February 2003, I felt I should become educated about the different Democratic presidential candidates. I had heard of Joe Lieberman—he was from my home state; John Kerry was from the next state over and Richard Gephardt had been speaker of the House for many years. None of them particularly excited me, and I felt that John Kerry was probably the best of them. However, there were a bunch of others: Governor Dean from Vermont, Senator Edwards from North Carolina, Senator Graham from Florida. I didn't really know much about any of them.

I started searching online for information, and I found that I really liked the policies of Howard Dean, who was socially liberal yet fiscally conservative. In my mind he carried the mantle of Paul Tsongas quite well.

Not only was there information from various news sources about Howard Dean, but people were writing in blogs about him. In March 2002, I had started writing online journal entries on LiveJournal. I started using Blogger and Ecademy in August of that year. I enjoyed my online writing and reading what other people were writing about on many topics. It was particularly interesting for me to read what other ordinary people were saying about Governor Dean and his campaign. Politics started feeling personal again.

Through LiveJournal, I discovered a site called Meetup.com. The goal seemed to be to get a bunch of people from a shared locality with a shared interest to meet one another face-to-face, the way I had met people from the net.singles Usenet group in 1982 or from the online community in 1998. I had signed up to go to LiveJournal Meetups in the fall of 2002. Unfortunately, there weren't enough LiveJournalers in my immediate area to have a Meetup, and it didn't seem worth it to travel down to New York City for a LiveJournalers Meetup.

On February 20, there was an article in one of the weblogs stating that "Dr. Dean is scheduled to attend the March 5th Meetup in New York! The New York Meetup is the second-largest group after Washington DC, with 92 supporters, so this will be a very exciting opportunity for Dean to see for himself just how strong his netroots are." It went on to say, "Dean has 1,590 supporters signed up, whereas Kerry and Edwards have 499 and 298, respectively (as of this writing). Dean has pledged to try and attend as many Meetups as possible, so it is clear that he understands and appreciates his netroots support."

By this time, I had already made my first financial contribution to the Dean campaign and my wife and I decided to go to the Meetup. We had no idea what to expect. Unlike in my previous meetings with people from online communities, I didn't have a clear sense of the personalities involved. There wasn't anyone I knew of who was going to be at the Meetup, and other than the fact that Governor Dean would be there, I had no idea what the agenda would be like.

I think it is useful to keep in mind that most people going to their first Meetup, whether it was in March 2003 or today, have no idea what to expect. For some, Meetups were viewed as a chance to meet someone new at a bar and have an interesting discussion. For others, it was an important time to organize, much like a Democratic Party Committee meeting.

The Meetup was taking place in what sounded like an interesting restaurant, so we decided to make dinner reservations an hour ahead of the Meetup. That way we could have a place to sit and something good to eat. So we ended up with a great place to sit and a good meal. However, we didn't end up interacting very much with any of the other folks attending the Meetup. The crowd was overwhelming and they cleared most of the tables from the restaurant so they could fit more people in. Still, the room was packed and there were long lines outside.

I was struck by the twentysomethings who had gotten inside and were talking on their cell phones to their friends outside. "Yeah, I made it in. I'm standing near the back wall. Where are you?" I was also struck by the same people talking about the importance of balanced budgets. I had always thought balanced budgets appealed to an older crowd.

My wife and I had never been in a crowd being addressed by a presidential candidate. The energy was overwhelming. Was it because Governor Dean is a particularly powerful speaker, or was there that sort of energy in a crowd anytime a presidential candidate addressed a crowd? My wife and I didn't know at the time, but afterward we decided that we wanted to be more involved with the Dean campaign.

I still get asked very frequently why I got so involved. Was it because of Governor Dean's opposition to the war? Was it because of his campaign's innovative use of the Internet? I was opposed to the war, but it wasn't a crucial issue for me. Governor Dean gained a lot of respect from me for being willing to say what he thought instead of what the polls said he should say. I think the authenticity was what was so appealing to me. Likewise, his use of the Internet, while fascinating to a computer executive like me, wasn't important in and of itself. What was important was that Governor Dean was coming across as a candidate who listened to and engaged with the people.

As a result of being involved with the campaign, my wife and I started watching *The West Wing*. There is a wonderful episode where there has just been an assassination attempt and Bartlet's staff are flashing back to how they got involved with the campaign. Josh heads up to New Hampshire to hear Bartlet speak at a small gathering. On his way, he tries to convince his friend Sam to come along. Sam has sworn off politics, having given up his search for an authentic candidate. Josh goes up, hears Bartlet speak, and returns to let his friend Sam know that Bartlet is "the real thing." Sam leaves his lucrative legal career to join Bartlet's campaign.[1] I think that is what the Dean campaign was like for many of us. Dean was authentic. He was the real thing. Many of us left what we were doing to participate in something real and meaningful.

## Getting Active: Coding and Community

My wife and I read the blogs and signed up for e-mail lists. Through this, we heard of another interesting idea, house parties. Although I had given to a presidential campaign once, a decade earlier, the idea of organizing a fund-raiser for a presidential campaign never occurred to us. That is, until we read about house parties on a blog or mailing list.

We decided we would have a house party. We contacted David Salie up in Burlington and received information about how to host a house party. I talked on a mailing list with other potential house party hosts. Just as we had never hosted a presidential fund-raiser before, none of our friends had ever attended one, so we weren't sure whom to invite or how to get a good crowd.

It was around this time that I discovered the Federal Election Commission listing of donors to former presidential campaigns. I started gathering names from this list, and posted to the mailing list what I was doing and how I was doing it. Before I knew what had happened, the mailing list was shut down and David Salie was on the phone telling me that I couldn't have the house party. It turns out that it is against the law to use names from the FEC listings for fund-raising purposes. I protested that I hadn't actually used the names yet, but had just started gathering them. No good. The lawyers in Burlington wanted to play things incredibly safe. They didn't want to risk anything; better to just cancel my house party. So I sent out notes to everyone whom I had already invited, mostly on the assorted mailing lists that I was on, saying that something had come up and I had to cancel the house party.

It was a heartbreaking disappointment; our first chance to really be involved with a presidential campaign was dashed because of a technicality. Nonetheless, I let David know that we still wanted to be involved and asked him to let us know when the next set of house parties was being organized and that we would help.

Meanwhile, we helped lead Meetups. In May, Joe Trippi wrote in a blog entry saying that "in 4½ months Dean Meetups members have grown from 432 to over 24,000 and are still growing."[2] We joined various groups, such as a statewide group of Meetup hosts and a national mailing list of Meetup hosts.

Another group that I joined was called hack4dean. Hack4dean was a group of programmers, mostly young guys still in college, interested in coming up with the one great tool that would revolutionize the way campaigns work. We would develop online portals for interconnected groups tied together with RSS, bit torrent, FOAF, and every other kind of cool tool that could be imagined. It would replace the reliance on Yahoo! groups that had become so commonplace in the early days of the campaign. They decided to rename the group Deanspace and to settle on using the open-source content management system Drupal as their framework.[3]

It was a wonderful group. We interacted primarily via e-mail. There wasn't a clear membership or clear leaders. Instead, the members were anyone who subscribed to the mailing lists. The leaders were people who were getting the most done. It was very empowering and it is a great model for defining true leadership. Zack Rosen got a lot done and ended up working for the campaign in Burlington. Most of us, however, remained volunteers, doing whatever we could.

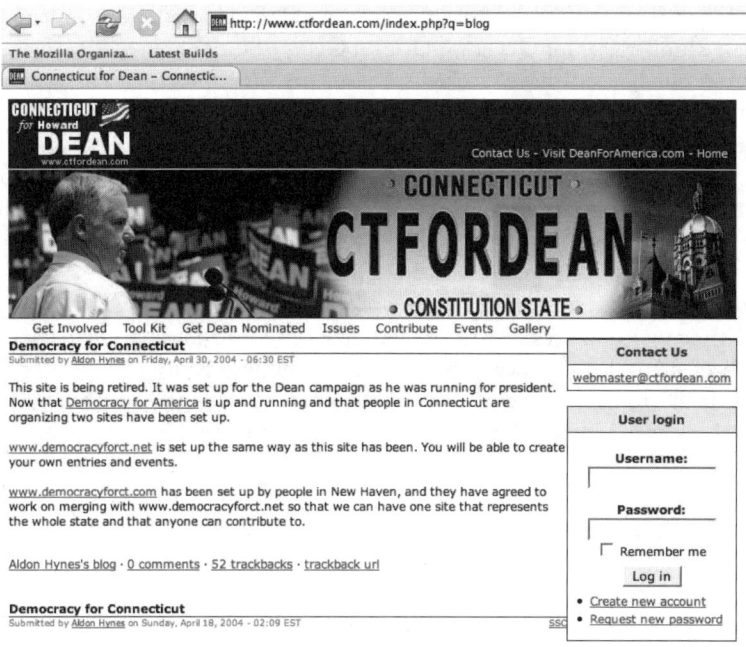

I set up some test websites using Deanspace, including the Connecticut for Dean website. Connecticut for Dean was not an official organization. A lot of things were done on an ad hoc basis. There weren't a lot of people working with Connecticut for Dean that were web savvy, so I had leeway in what went on with the website. I wrote whatever I could and used it to promote any and every event in Connecticut that I could. It turned out to be a very successful website and for a period it was getting more traffic than Joe Lieberman's national campaign website.

In June, we traveled up to Burlington to be with the crowd of 5,000 people who had traveled from many different places to celebrate Governor Dean's officially declaring his candidacy. On the drive up, we saw many cars with Dean bumper stickers. We felt like we were part of some grand convoy. Looking out over the landscape of Vermont, I thought of the famous Ronald Reagan advertisement, "Morning in America." It felt like a new morning, full of hope and joy.

It was hot at the announcement. People passed around bottles of water. One man lent a bandana to us to cover our two-year-old daughter's head. We saw a few friends from Connecticut. That afternoon, we wandered around Burlington to find the campaign headquarters. The offices were fairly empty; everyone was either home recuperating or off at one event or another. The names that we knew at that time were Zephyr Teachout and David Salie. Neither of them was around and the volunteer passed us off to Michael Silberman. Michael showed us around the office and we chatted for a little while. Then we headed off back to Connecticut.

During the summer we did everything we could to help with the campaign. There was a large fund-raiser for Governor Dean at George Soros's house. Soros lives a short drive from our house. I have worked for years on Wall Street, and it seemed like a wonderful opportunity to support Governor Dean, visit a very interesting house, and do a little networking as I tried to find my next permanent job. Kate O'Connor took a great picture of us with Governor Dean at the event, which we later got Governor Dean to sign. When Governor Dean gave his stump speech we pretty much knew all the words by heart.

As the summer rolled on, Governor Dean came to New York City for a big rally in Bryant Park. I volunteered to help register people as they showed up. I sat at the side of the event and took down people's names and contact information and entered them into a spreadsheet on my laptop. Since we were there early, my wife Kim and my older daughters ended up in the front row, and were shown in some of the broadcasts of the event. Afterward we went backstage and talked with a few different people from the campaign.

## Who Are We? Campaigning and Social Life

A personal interest of mine is the Association of Internet Researchers. It had become clear over the months that the Internet was having a large effect on the Dean campaign, and that the Dean campaign was having a large effect on the way people used and understood the Internet. I proposed to present a paper at the association's annual conference, which was scheduled for October. I set up a survey online. I sent out e-mails; posted to websites, blogs, and bulletin boards; talked in chat rooms; and encouraged people in every possible venue to fill out my survey. Some people asked on the mailing lists who I was, if I could be trusted, what I wanted this information for, and so on. Others vouched for me and talked about their interaction with me in various online venues.

Many of the results were unremarkable. The respondents were pretty closely split between male and female. A third of the respondents had attended graduate school, which seemed particularly high, but fit with the stereotype of Dean supporters' being highly educated. The income distribution tracked national averages, as did the percentage from different states, with a few exceptions. There was a disproportionately high number of respondents from Connecticut, which made sense, since I was from Connecticut and got a lot of people from Connecticut to respond. There were a lot of respondents from Vermont, where the campaign was headquartered, and states like Oregon and Washington had a high percentage of respondents, which I assumed reflected the strong online organizing activities there.

In the survey, people reported that they went online to gather information about Governor Dean. They also reported being online to organize. Meeting people socially was another important reason people were online. This appeared to be a significant part of what was going on with the campaign.

A quarter of the total group said that they had met a lot of new people or developed a lot of new friendships face-to-face as a result of being online with the Dean campaign. This certainly rang true for Kim and me. Our social life had shifted to being very focused around the Dean campaign. Our social activities were Meetups, house parties, and steering committee meetings, and that is where we spent time with our closest friends.

My survey showed that people in their thirties were particularly likely to find social connections through the Dean campaign; 40 percent of them had established new friendships as a result of their involvement. One blog specializing in political humor had an interesting parody of the campaign:

> Welcome to Howard Dean's Meetup! The first Wednesday of every month has now become the source of exciting new social opportunities that will open up your lifestyle to everything true romance has to offer!
>
> There are maybe 79,999 people out there just waiting to "meet up" with you. You're hot, you're sexy, and people find it appealing that you're involved and positive about an individual's ability to influence national elections at the grassroots level.[4]

Yet this parody was not without some basis in truth. The official blog announced, "Congratulations Are in Order ... for Laura Elaine Katzive and Daniel Lee Ackman, who were married today. According to their wedding announcement, they 'met a year ago at a talk given in New York by Howard Dean.'"[5]

How important was this social aspect, this meeting people face-to-face at Meetups, and the potential of a meaningful relationship? The most interesting statistic I observed was that the highest correlation to the amount of money donated was not income level, how committed a person was to the campaign, or how active he or she was with mailing lists or blogs. The highest correlation to the amount of money donated was the frequency that people attended Meetups. Although we cannot say for certain that going to Meetups is what caused people to donate, it is clear that there is a strong relationship between financial giving and meeting people face-to-face. I am sure that an experienced fund-raiser wouldn't be surprised by this, but it seems to be something that too often gets forgotten when people talk about the Dean campaign.

This is not to say that all was rosy with all the relationships that occurred online and face-to-face with the Dean campaign. The *New York Times Magazine* did an article on the Dean campaign that portrayed many of the volunteers in Burlington as college-aged boys who couldn't make it with the girls so they threw themselves into computers and politics.[6] Needless to say, the article was not well received by many Dean supporters.

Around September, an e-mail appeared on an international Dean supporters' mailing list. One person was threatening to sue another over who should run Meetups, who could register domain names including the Dean name, and who should speak to the press. Having spent a lot of time extinguishing flame wars online, I sent an e-mail to the mailing list suggesting that this sort of stuff didn't belong on a public mailing list. I suggested that if people needed to work this out, they could contact me and I would attempt to mediate the dispute. Contact me they did! The amount of hatred and bile was astounding. They appealed to anyone in authority they could find, and as a general rule, everyone in Burlington said that for a variety of reasons, they couldn't be involved. Slowly, they reached a point where they agreed to disagree and as much as possible stay out of each other's hair.

Other online organizing activities were much more enjoyable. One morning, reading various news and comics online, I found a *Doonesbury* cartoon where Alex was planning a flash-mob at the Space Needle. In the cartoon, she was sitting at the computer typing in the instructions. Everyone should gather at the Space Needle in Seattle at 10:25 Saturday morning and hop up and down chanting, "Howard Dean." They should then disperse. Alex's mother looked over her shoulder and commented how she just didn't understand her daughter's political activities anymore.

I sure understood it. Here was an event to raise Governor Dean's visibility, to get people together in face-to-face community, and to have fun. Using tools created by the Dean campaign, I scheduled the exact event Alex had described in the comic strip. I sent e-mails to anyone I could find in Seattle. I posted to the blog about it. Other people picked up on it. They spread the word. Some people complained that it wasn't a real flash-mob. It was too planned. Others complained that it wasn't really addressing the issues of the campaign. Some folks in Seattle questioned why some guy from Connecticut was organizing the event, and not the people in Seattle.

To that, I had a quick and easy reply. I made them co-organizers in the system, and handed the ball to them. In the end, around 150 people showed up. People brought food for a food bank and went and helped clean up a beach afterward. (During the Dean campaign, many people wanted to promote the view of Dean supporters as people who really cared about what was going on around them by contributing to food banks, donating blood, or doing other important civic actions.) The event got national news coverage and was deemed a great success.[7] One person even e-mailed me a video of the event.

## The Personal and the Political

Tuesday, November 4, 2003, was our third wedding anniversary. It was also a special day for Kim and me in many different ways. Kim's mother would have turned sixty-one on Tuesday. Kim's mother had died of cancer four years earlier on Kim's birthday. I never got a chance to meet Kim's mother, as we had only been dating a few weeks when her mother died. A year later, Kim and I got married on her mother's birthday. Eleven months later, our daughter Fiona was born and we baptized her—on her grandmother's birthday and her parents' wedding anniversary. Tuesday was also the day that I learned that my aunt had died over the weekend, the day that we received the invitation to see Governor Dean in New York, and Election Day for local municipal elections. It proved to be a very interesting week.

The next day, Kim and I stood behind Governor Dean as he delivered a speech announcing his plan to ask his supporters whether he should accept public financing or not. If he accepted public financing, he would reach an end of his fund-raising, since he had already raised about as much as he could and still accept public financing. However, if he declined public financing, that would mean something like $19 million less money he would have available. This amount would need to be made up for by additional fund-raising.

I was a strong supporter of his declining public financing, since the fund-raising was an important way in which people could feel involved. It wasn't about the donors who could give $2,000 each. It was really about the donors who could give $25 or $50, donors who had never been involved in a campaign and had certainly never given before.

After the speech in New York City, we went to the subway to head back to Grand Central Station, and from there back to Connecticut. On the subway, we ran into Governor Dean's mother, who had been at the speech and was taking the subway home. With all of the issues about Kim's mother, it was great to talk with Governor Dean's mother and for the campaign to become that much more personal to us. People too often forget that candidates for national office are regular people with families who love them.

The next day, numerous people talked to us about how they had seen Kim on television standing behind Governor Dean.

During these few days, there was a big discussion about how Governor Dean had talked about needing to reach out to people with Confederate flags on the back of their pickup trucks. Many people seemed to misinterpret his remarks and I wrote a letter to the *New York Times* about this. I was pleasantly surprised when they contacted me to tell me that they were publishing my letter.[8]

The bigger issue for Kim and me came up with what was to happen Saturday. Michael Silberman had invited us to go up to Burlington for some big event. He couldn't say what it was, but he talked about how it was related to Governor Dean's speech in New York City. He did say that it was going to be a small group of people who were specially invited from around the country.

The problem was that Saturday was going to be my aunt's funeral. We looked at schedules; we talked about what was going on. I spoke with people in my family. In the end, we decided to go to a viewing for my aunt on Friday. From there, we would drive to my mother's house and spend the night with her. In the morning we would drive up to Burlington.

Kim's car had been acting up. We had taken it to the shop and it was repaired in time for our trip north. Friday, we drove to my cousin's house in Greenfield, Massachusetts. One of the first things my cousin said when we got there was that she had seen Kim on the news. We talked about the campaign and my letter to the editor. The family viewing was small and quiet. We shared memories of my aunt and talked about how everyone else in the family was doing and about desires of getting the family together.

We then drove to my mother's house in Williamstown, Massachusetts. The Mohawk Trail is a beautiful road winding from Greenfield to Williamstown. It is especially beautiful on a clear autumn day. However, we were driving in the evening, after the sun had set. Then, it becomes a dark and twisty road that is much more of a chore to drive.

My eldest brother had come up from New York City, and we spent the evening with my mother, having dinner, looking at pictures, and talking about the family.

We got up early Saturday morning to drive from Williamstown to Burlington. The car had been acting okay, but when we stopped to get gas, it had problems getting going again. We briefly worried about whether we would make it to Burlington on time. Yet it was a short aberration, and the car was fine for the rest of the trip up.

We arrived in Burlington around ten in the morning. We looked around for Michael Silberman, who didn't seem to be around. I also tried to find Zack Rosen, whom I had met through Deanspace and who by then was working in Burlington. He wasn't there either. Finally, someone came along and herded us into a large conference room. There was getting to be quite a crowd, mostly from Vermont. This was neither a small group nor a group of people from all over the country. I wondered, were we in the right place? Had plans changed in some way? Was this a mistake, and should I have gone to my aunt's funeral?

Michael showed up and directed Kim and me to a different conference room. We had been in the room with the people from Vermont who had been doing great work and were invited to be in the audience. We went into a smaller room with the other "signers." None of us, I believe, yet knew exactly what was going to go on. There was a PC Tablet there that we could all practice electronically signing on. Each of us signed our name, and finally the whole explanation came out.

We would be signing our Declaration of Independence from the special interest groups that had been destroying U.S. politics. We got our briefings. Joe Trippi spoke about the importance of each of us speaking in our own voice about why we were involved and why we felt that it was the right thing to do to opt out of public financing.

We then all drove over to the University of Vermont in Burlington for the announcement. We went off into another room, where there were more briefings. We did get a chance to speak briefly with Governor Dean. Kim asked him if he would sign the picture that had been taken of us and him at a fund-raiser at George Soros's house. Later, Governor Dean posed holding Fiona. One of the pictures came out particularly well and we printed hundreds of copies of it on card stock, which we sent to all of our friends as a holiday card. Inside, we printed, "In this Holiday season, Let us all work together to help Hope, Joy, and Prosperity Triumph over Fear and Oppression (Fiona with Presidential Candidate Howard Dean)."

When we got home, we received a phone call from ABC Nightly News. They wanted to do a piece on people who had gotten involved with the presidential campaigns, and figured that Kim would be the perfect person to interview. They came to our house, interviewed Kim, and filmed her writing a comment on the blog, sending a letter to a voter in Iowa, and then serving dinner. It ended up being a short spot on the nightly news that captured the new ideas of Governor Dean's campaign and tied it to the life of ordinary people.

## After the Dean Campaign: Politics as a Way of Life

When the caucuses in Iowa rolled around, we couldn't work things out to go to Iowa. We were disappointed by the results, but we headed up to New Hampshire to help with the primary there. We drove around Hanover dropping off literature. We then

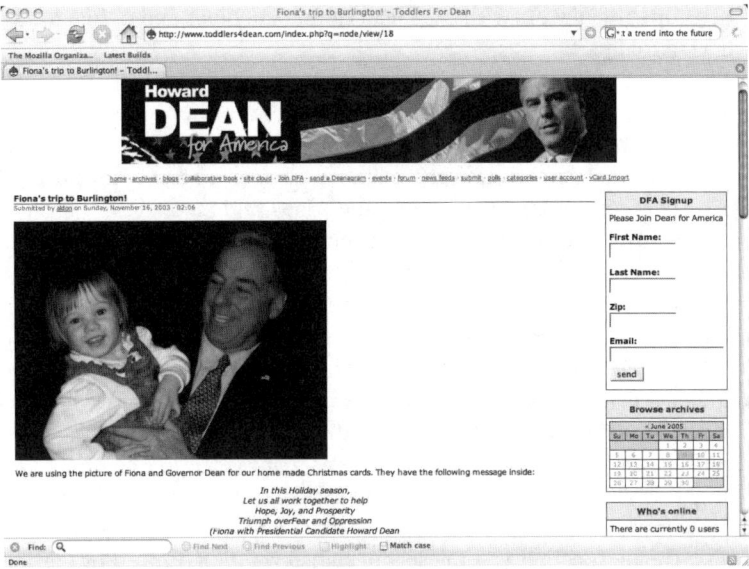

went to Manchester to do more literature drops on Election Day, coupled with vis-ibility events, standing on corners chanting slogans for Dean. In the final hours, we did phone banking and then we went to an Election Night party. The results were better than Iowa's, but still not what we were hoping for.

As the campaign wound down, Kim and I wondered what would happen for us next. Governor Dean encouraged all his supporters to stay involved and to consider running for local office. Kim decided to run for state representative. I continued to blog, and ended up receiving press credentials to cover the Democratic National Convention as a blogger. Kim didn't get elected but did better than anyone expected. More importantly, she has, like Governor Dean, inspired other people to get more involved and run for office. For me, political blogging has become a paying job, as I blogged for a gubernatorial campaign in Connecticut and then became technol-ogy coordinator for Ned Lamont's U.S. Senate run (in which he defeated pro-war Democrat Joe Lieberman in the Democratic primary; Lieberman reentered the race as an Independent and successfully used the support of moderate Republicans to win against Lamont in the final election).

As of this writing, Lamont's campaign was the closest parallel to Governor Dean's campaign that has occurred. Many of the people who worked on Ned's campaign were, like myself, former volunteers for Governor Dean. Lamont was a come-from-nowhere insurgent, going much farther than the common wisdom would have thought pos-sible at the outset of his campaign. The campaign was very much driven by citizens searching for a candidate who would express their views and fight for their beliefs, instead of the way so much politics is done these days, when candidates go out and search for a constituency. As with the Dean campaign, blogs and online fund-raising played an essential part.

After having worked in the business world for years, I still look at campaigns as a very special type of business start-up. When they start, they have an idea and little support. Everything gets built on a shoestring, with an eye toward the day when the company or campaign gets traction and makes it. The role of technology in campaigns remains a battleground among field, communications, and fund-raising. The transition from being an insurgent to being a front-runner is difficult. I'm not sure that either the Dean campaign or the Lamont campaign made that transition effectively.

Some of this may have to do with the nature of movements and communities. In the early days, there is a fierce camaraderie. It is necessary for an insurgent campaign. Yet as the campaign grows and the candidate becomes a front-runner, the movement needs to transform itself into a welcoming community that makes space for latecomers who may not be as fiercely passionate about the cause.

I've realized that even after a campaign is over, many facets of a community remain. As people gather and talk about their experiences, they may present radically different views of what happened. However, one of the most important things that happens, no matter what the perspective, is some sort of transformation. Governor Dean did not get elected president, which is what many of us had hoped for, yet he did change the country and continues to do so. Ned Lamont did not end up getting elected to the U.S. Senate, but he too helped change the country and our political discourse.

Joe Trippi talked a lot during the Dean campaign about transformational leaders as opposed to the transactional politics that seem to dominate our current politics. He is still talking about it on the blogs today.

The long months of the Dean campaign, then Kim's campaign, and finally Ned's campaign have transformed not only our country, but Kim and me individually. We have much stronger voices in the political process now. We have close friends around the country who grew out of the campaign. On our refrigerator, as on many people's, we have pictures of our extended family. For us, it includes a campaign card from Governor Dean and a Christmas card from the Lamonts. We have hope. We keep our eyes open for new candidates who will exude hope and authenticity. There will be other transformative candidates, and hopefully they can learn from the experiences of people who became caught up in the Dean experience.

## Notes

1. Aaron Sorkin, "In the Shadow of Two Gunmen, Part I," *West Wing* (first aired October 4, 2000).

2. Joe Trippi, "Taking Back Our Country: Planting the Seed of Change—Growing to Victory," Dean Call to Action Blogspot, April 13, 2003.

3. See http://www.wired.com/news/politics/0,1283,59497,00.html (accessed June 1, 2007).

4. Tom Burka, "GOP, Most Democrats Miss Bold New Internet Strategy for Grassroots

Support," Opinions You Should Have (August 6, 2003), http://tomburka.com/archives/2003_08.php#000230 (accessed June 1, 2007).

5. Mathew Gross, "Congratulations Are in Order," Blog for America (October 12, 2003), http://www.blogforamerica.com/view/1642 (accessed June 1, 2007).

6. Samantha M. Shapiro, "The Dean Connection," *New York Times Magazine* (December 7, 2003).

7. Joe Rospars, "Seattle Flash Mob Reports," Blog for America (September 13, 2003), http://www.blogforamerica.com/view/1255 (accessed June 1, 2007).

8. See *New York Times*, November 7, 2003, Section A, p. 26, column 5.

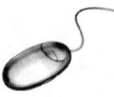

# 8

# Blogging for America

## Mathew Gross

*Mathew Gross left his home in Moab, Utah, to launch the first presidential campaign weblog for Howard Dean in March 2003. As director of Internet communications for the Dean campaign, Gross helped to develop and implement the online strategy that raised more than $25 million online and built Blog for America into one of the top weblogs in the world, attracting more than 100,000 readers per day at the height of the primary season.*

### West of Rome

The story of how I came to join the Dean campaign became both an anecdote and an archetype.

In the winter of 2002 I was an unemployed former river guide and waiter living in Moab, a small tourist town tucked into the canyon country of southeastern Utah. Winter in Moab is a normally placid time, a time when the wider world—or at least the hordes of tourists who besiege the town for nine long months of the year—recede, leaving behind the ineffable stillness and solitude of the high desert. But this particular winter was a restive one. During the days I would go up onto the mesas north of town, where thumper trucks—the physical manifestation of George Bush's energy policy—crawled over the bunchgrass and saltbrush and pounded the desert floor, listening for the telltale echo of natural gas deposits on the edges of the national parks. At night I would sit in my office in my half-gentrified duplex next to the trailer park, reading at 56k (there was no television reception in the valley, and cable was a garish luxury on my $113-per-week unemployment check) the news of Bush's imminent invasion of Iraq. That winter, the larger world—the world of politics and the East and world affairs—had refused to recede, and the silence of the desert had grown maddening.

Through those long winter nights I would surf the Net, starting first with the mainstream media sites—MSNBC.com and the AP wire and Drudge—and decamping from there into a thin wilderness of liberal websites like the Smirking Chimp and

Buzzflash, which aggregated opinion pieces and news from disparate print sources. An errant click one evening brought me to a little orange oasis called Daily Kos, and from there I made my way to a site called MyDD, which stood at the time for My Due Diligence.

I had first discovered Howard Dean online in early October, soon after Democrats in Congress had voted to authorize the president's invasion of Iraq. While his fiscal discipline and his libertarian stance on guns appealed to my western sensibilities, his nascent criticism of the president's plans for Iraq appealed to my common sense. At the time, however, his closest rival in opinion polls of likely Democratic candidates for president was the margin of error, and a Google search turned up perhaps two or three articles of any real depth or relevance. Yet following the vote for the Authorization of Use of Military Force Against Iraq—and Democrats' subsequent trouncing in the midterm elections—mentions of Howard Dean began to pick up in the press, albeit in passing. I began to collect each press mention, and each week I would send an e-mail to a few dozen friends around the country—an e-mail that, through the mirage of collation, gave the carefully crafted impression that Howard Dean was actually making headway in his quest for the nomination. (My friends, bless them, politely humored my notion that this guy from Vermont, whom nobody had ever even heard of, and whose "momentum" at the time could best be measured by an increase each week in dismissive refutations from the press, was the Democrats' best chance to win the White House.) Jerome Armstrong, the proprietor of MyDD, was also writing about Dean, and I would send him the press mentions as soon as I found them, until he eventually invited me to write directly for MyDD as his first guest poster.

And so the story that I had told a handful of friends once per week via e-mail I now told every other day on MyDD—a story of how Howard Dean could win the nomination, as well as why he should. This wasn't cheerleading but a narrative—a story of possibility and momentum that was completely different from the dismissals his candidacy was garnering in the mainstream press. It was a long story, to be sure—first he had to vault from the third tier into the second tier before he could even reach the top tier, much less have a realistic chance of capturing the nomination. But as I wrote that winter, small events kept happening that added a little bit to the story I was trying to tell about the potential for his candidacy to catch fire: Al Gore announcing formally that he wasn't going to run; a little bit of movement in the polls, from 2 percent to 4 percent; a glowing reception (from fifty people or so) in Iowa. With each passing week, more people showed up at MyDD wanting to know more about Howard Dean, and the growing interest in his candidacy was measurable in the growing lengths of the comment threads.

The Dean campaign website at the time was absolutely horrific: threadbare, rudimentarily designed, with a terrible picture of the governor in a light blue blazer that made him look like a trainee at a Century 21 sales conference. I wanted the campaign to benefit from the interest we were helping to generate at MyDD, and to do something to engage with the growing support for Howard Dean online. Yet as those weeks of quiet winter passed, and MyDD became a greater center of gravity for Howard Dean online, nothing changed on the official site.

And then came Howard Dean's speech at the DNC Winter Meeting. Even through the jumps and skips of Realplayer on dialup, one could feel the seismic shift happening in the race. No longer would I have to rely on collation and hyperbole to justify movement in Dean's bid for the nomination. The reaction online, among the still-nascent political blogs, was ecstatic: No Democrat in recent memory had delivered a clarion call like that speech. And yet on the Dean website—again, nothing. I made a few calls to campaign headquarters, and spoke to a few random staffers who nonchalantly told me that, despite the new energy from the DNC speech, they were "just moving chairs around the office, and just setting up."

The winter was coming to an end. Some obscure governor from Vermont had delivered a good speech on my computer, but his website sucked, and no one was trying to tell the story online of how and why he should be elected. But spring and the tourists would arrive soon, the callback signaling the end of my seasonal layoff from the burrito joint was imminent, and the snowpack in the mountains promised a good spring runoff and some great river running. What I wanted to know was, what to do? Blogging from Utah no longer seemed sufficient. Surely any campaign would want to find a way to speak directly to its burgeoning and eager cadre of supporters online, wouldn't it?

That I left Moab and made my way to Burlington to say "I write for MyDD!" to Joe Trippi, who had been reading my posts and who bellowed "You're hired!" in return, became arguably the most popular anecdote of the campaign season. But how I got to that point—how I found Howard Dean and the medium I used to get involved—was the archetype, and within a year it would have manifested itself in the lives of hundreds of thousands of Americans in all fifty states, each with his or her own story to tell.

## Deride and Conquer

Trippi loved baseball, and he loved a good line, and one of his favorite aphorisms for the campaign—endlessly repeated by the rest of the Net team—was imprecisely borrowed from Kevin Costner's *For Love of the Game.* "The truth is, we suck," he'd say. "But right now, we're the best damn team in baseball."

That line is like a signal post, drawing one's memory back to the summer of 2003, after the campaign had unveiled the famous bat and raised $7.6 million in the second quarter—an amount that stunned those consultants in Washington who had thought we were wasting our time on the Net.

Yet before that summer—before we became the juggernaut that everyone remembers, hitting home run after home run before collapsing in the final inning—we were barely even a team. We didn't have a communications director. We didn't have a webmaster. In early April I wrote an op-ed for Howard Dean, and we couldn't even get it placed. The other campaigns, meanwhile, were taking note of our endless sniping of their support for the war, and had begun to strike back. Trippi, dismayed by the greenness of the staff and the thin skeleton of the operation (for who with any salable experience wanted to go work for a guy who stood at 4 percent in the polls?), feared that the seasoned operatives on the other campaigns would destroy us before we even got off the ground. "I'm fighting murderers with children!" he cried late one night, as we sat in his office bemoaning the state of affairs.

Incredibly, it was during this time of threadbare deprivation that we were able to deliver a series of counterpunches that fundamentally altered the course of the race.

It was late April 2003, in the week before the first Democratic presidential debate in South Carolina—which the press had dubbed the "Collision in Columbia" because of rising tensions between the Dean and Kerry campaigns. Dean had been lambasting Senator Kerry for his waffling on issue after issue, and the Kerry campaign was growing increasingly irritated and alarmed by Dean's gathering momentum and excitement. Normally a perceived front-runner avoids engaging a lesser-known candidate directly, but it was around this time that Dean, on a visit to New Hampshire, said that the United States had to take a different approach to diplomacy because "we won't always have the strongest military."

Surprisingly, given many opportunities to take Dean on, the Kerry campaign chose this comment as its casus belli against our ragged little campaign. Chris Lehane, Kerry's communications director, issued a broadside on Monday, April 28, claiming that Dean's statement "raises serious questions about his capacity to serve as Commander-in-Chief." Our initial response—undoubtedly a historic first—was put out on the Dean Call to Action Blog. And since Lehane was widely disliked in the liberal blogosphere at the time, and viewed as emblematic of the corporate political consultant class, I naturally added the old blogger standby—the derisive ad hominem—to the response:

CHILL, CHRIS LEHANE, CHILL
by Mathew Gross
Published Monday, 04/28/03 @ 11:54 A.M.

Is Senator John Kerry getting desperate? Apparently his campaign found it necessary to put out a full-court press [in response to Dean's statement]. The hyperventilating response from Kerry Communications Director Chris Lehane, in the Kerry campaign's press release:

"Howard Dean's stated belief that the United States 'won't always have the strongest military,' raises serious questions about his capacity to serve as Commander-in-Chief. No serious candidate for the Presidency has ever before suggested that he would compromise or tolerate an erosion of America's military supremacy."

Okay, Chris. We'll make this simple for you:

(1) Governor Dean has never suggested that he would tolerate an erosion of American military supremacy. Governor Dean has repeatedly stated that he is committed to supporting the U.S. military and to protecting the national security of the United States. What Governor Dean has suggested (and stated) is that the reckless foreign policy of the Bush administration—a foreign policy that has alienated some of our nation's closest allies and exacerbated tensions between the US and the world community—fails to promote the long term national security of the United States.

(2) The long term national security of the United States cannot be built on military supremacy alone. As Governor Dean has said, the current Administration has defined the concept of national security too narrowly. For example, the Bush Administration's

failure to develop alternative sources of energy and fuel creates an over-dependence on petroleum imported from the Middle East. As well, the Bush Administration's cavalier attitude toward the United Nations during the build up of the war in Iraq undermines the effectiveness of that multilateral body. Is John Kerry suggesting that he shares the myopic view of the Bush Administration when it comes to foreign policy? Is that what his vote for the President's preemptive war in Iraq meant? If so, then that raises serious concerns about John Kerry's ability to lead this country forward into the 21st century.

(3) You see where this goes, Chris? Tit for tat? Never mind that our first instinct was to send you a few history books for your edification. The U.S. will continue to have the strongest military in the world under President Dean. The difference between President Dean or President Bush or Kerry, apparently, is how that military will be used, and in what context, and to what end. Get back to us when Senator Kerry decides where he stands on that issue.[1]

We were immensely proud of that post—in-your-face, derisive, and rapid—and it sparked a full-scale firefight, with the campaigns exchanging press releases and comments throughout the day (we accused Kerry of supporting Bush's doctrine of preemptive invasion, while Dean told a reporter that Kerry didn't "have the courage" to attack him directly, instead choosing to hide behind his political operatives; Chris Lehane hit back that Dean was skiing in Aspen while Kerry served in Vietnam; we returned the volley with a press release consisting entirely of the retort, "Who the hell is Chris Lehane?"). Despite several solid punches on our part, however, the next day the press—who had been shaking their heads over the wisdom of Dean's recent comments that it remained to be seen whether the people of Iraq were better off following the U.S. invasion—viewed the victor as the Kerry campaign. "Team Kerry has shown more tactical and strategic nimbleness than Team Dean in the battle," wrote ABC's *The Note.*

The fracas wasn't quite over, however, thanks to some serendipitous web browsing and a right-wing comment thread. Throughout the following day I posted a series of blog entries designed to amplify—again, through the mirage of collation—the disparate media commentary that argued the Kerry campaign's attack on Howard Dean's remark was specious at best ("Backfiring in Print," "Backfiring on Air"). And then, curious to learn what the right wing was making of the dispute, I made my way over to the conservative community site Free Republic. And there I found it.

Amid the comment threads, a right-winger was arguing that Dean's comments about the transitory nature of U.S. military power were par for the course for Democrats. To prove his point, the commenter pointed to a transcript of a speech that President Bill Clinton had given in Australia, in which he said, "This is a brief moment in history when the United States has pre-eminent military, economic and political power. It won't last forever.... This is just a period, a few decades this will last, and I think that all of us who are Americans should think about this and ask ourselves how do we wish this moment to be judged 50 years from now."

There it was, right there on Free Republic: the damning retort to Chris Lehane's comment that "no serious candidate has *ever* before suggested that he would compromise or tolerate an erosion of America's military supremacy." At 1:38 A.M., we put

Clinton's quote on the blog, along with a picture of the Big Dog himself, under the title "Know Your History."

Earlier that week, in anticipation of the upcoming debate in Columbia, *The Note* had invited each campaign to write a 200-word piece each day for an online segment called The Notepad. Long after midnight, after most of the campaign had left, Trippi and I would laugh ourselves silly writing pugnacious, snarky posts that stood in stark contrast to the restrained submissions of the other campaigns, delivering the political equivalent of a titty-twister to John Kerry and the mainstream press by calling Kerry "the Anointed One" and joking, "What's debate prep?" We delivered our Clinton counterattack through The Notepad, linking to the blog, and the next day I hopped on a plane to do rapid response at the debate in Columbia. It was there that we won the behind-the-scenes "paper primary" (running press releases and opposition research to the national press corps watching the debate), and for the first time the press looked at the Dean campaign not just as upstarts but as talented upstarts, capable of upsetting the race.

Two other things came out of the South Carolina debate: For the first time, Dean articulated our central message of "You have the power" in a closing statement that was written the afternoon of the debate in Columbia. And, though there were few actual sparks between Kerry and Dean in the debate itself, for the first time the press began to reject its own notion that Kerry—"the Anointed One" as we had dubbed him—was the heir apparent to the nomination. And although it would be reductionist to say that a series of snarky blog posts and press releases alone changed the course of the campaign, it is difficult to look back upon that series of events in the week leading up to the Columbia debate without recognizing how fundamentally the race was altered. Within the small realm of Washington journalists, nearly all of whom read *The Note*, two things happened. The other campaigns, in The Notepad that week, followed our "web savvy" lead and started using links, and in imitating us gave us credibility; and the media narrative of Kerry as the front-runner collapsed. By being pugnacious and irreverent while making substantive arguments, we undermined the entire narrative of John Kerry as the presumptive nominee—which created the opening for Dean to surge ahead.

All at once, in one week in April, the Dean campaign had found its medium and its message.

## A Story to Tell

Time is the one thing you can never replace. On a campaign, you can get more money and get more staff and buy more ads, but you cannot get more time; and so from the beginning everything we did was driven by a sense of desperate urgency.

As early as April we were in a sprint. Trippi sensed that the web was at a place of maturity that would allow it to be a disruptive force in the race, and so we pushed like madmen from the beginning, blogging at midnight, writing e-mails at 1:00 A.M., and working to develop and refine the message of empowerment. We knew that the other campaigns were making a massive tactical mistake by deriding our efforts—one Gephardt aide said in May that Dean Meetups "looked like the bar scene from *Star Wars*"—yet we also knew that the fruit of our labor would soon become apparent. Trippi feared that as soon as we demonstrated the success of our model, our tactical advantage would be over, and the other campaigns would adopt our techniques. Our only shot was to get bigger than everybody else before they caught on, to prevent them from catching up.

And so while they mocked, we pushed, launching a campaign in May to "Double Dean," which doubled the size of our e-mail list; building out a network of local Yahoo! and MSN e-mail groups; and launching the Dean Wireless Network. The blog, in truth, occupied perhaps only a third of my time—there were an endless number of e-mails to be written and other experiments to attempt—but from the beginning it was my intention to make the blog the focal point of the campaign's website. I wrote furiously, and often with fury, pushing to grow the audience by providing an endless stream of content that would keep people coming back.

I had remembered reading once an admiral's recollection of witnessing the formal surrender of the Japanese aboard the USS *Missouri* in Tokyo Harbor. The admiral commanded another ship anchored in the bay, and early on the morning of the ceremony he had leaned on the railing of his ship, watching the *Missouri* with envy and curiosity; he wanted to be in the midst of the action. Yet as the morning wore on, the admiral realized that he didn't really need to know what specifically was being said on the *Missouri*. All you needed to know about the proceedings, he realized, was that the conversation was taking place on *our* ship; the language and the location had already dictated the terms of the debate. My view toward the blog was analogous; I wanted it to be more than a player in the campaign, but a stage. As long as people came to talk about the election on our site, we were 80 percent of the way—actually we were 99 percent of the way—to telling them our story, which was ultimately what we wanted to do.

And so I began, from the beginning, to report not simply on what the campaign was doing, but on what was happening elsewhere in the press and the world at large. I developed a morning news roundup to get people to come to the blog first thing, to allow us to play a role in setting the agenda of the day. As soon as something good hit the wires or another blog, I linked to it, hoping to amplify the positive coverage and create a sense of media momentum, just as I had done months earlier on MyDD. And the ensemble had grown: Zephyr Teachout wrote energetic posts about the growth of Meetup and the campaign, while Kate O'Connor, who was traveling with the governor, wrote breathless reports from the road, punctuated by an endless stream of exclamation points. You could never blog too quickly or too often, in my estimation: The steady stream of fresh content would ensure that people returned frequently.

The strategy worked: With each passing day I watched the metrics of our site visitation grow, from 3,000 visitors to 5,000 visitors to 10,000 visitors. In June, after months of late-night development, we were finally able to relaunch the Dean Call to Action Blog with the ability for readers to leave comments. (It was then that we rechristened it Blog for America.) I remember visiting Daily Kos that day and reading a discussion thread about our relaunch: "A presidential campaign weblog," one commenter wrote with an unmistakable tone of disbelief. "*With comments.* We've broken through the glass ceiling, folks." A few weeks later, when we unveiled the bat and pounded our e-mail list with an endless string of solicitations at the end of the second quarter, those new comment threads rapidly filled up, and nearly every political reporter in the country (and, undoubtedly, a large number of staffers from our rival campaigns) anxiously hit Refresh to watch the numbers climb. It became, as one reporter put it, like a Jerry Lewis telethon, and everyone tuned in.

As the campaign progressed, the volume of information pumping out through the blog increased; by the end, more than 3,400 posts—an average of more than 10 per day—had been written, and the audience had grown to nearly 100,000 people, who left thousands of daily comments. Much of the time the blog was like a circus, all spectacle and entertainment and excitement; the joke on the writing team at the end was that we had exhausted our lifetime's ration of superlatives, and we could never use the word *amazing* again. There were, of course, many people—usually communications directors on rival campaigns—who thought it shouldn't be fun, that politics, and running for president, should remain an exclusively *very serious business.* Yet by being entertaining as well as informative, Blog for America was able to consistently attract the attention of voters and the press. That attention gave us the platform to play a role in shaping the stories written by the media, as when *we broke* the story of a Democratic 527 group attacking us in Iowa with a television ad that used a picture of Osama bin Laden to raise doubts about Howard Dean. Because we had built the blog's readership among both voters and the press, we were able to ensure that the outrage over the group's use of bin Laden's image was central to the story when the traditional media repeated it.

Yet the blog was more than a spin machine, or a broadcast vehicle, or entertainment: It also became, through the comments, a community and a source of endless ideas and language. Some of the most memorable phrases ("The Tea Is in the Harbor!") and events (the July fund-raiser in which we raised $500,000 online by putting Howard Dean in front of a computer with a turkey sandwich, in contrast to a $2,000-a-plate luncheon with Vice President Cheney that was taking place the same day) came from the community of supporters who interacted with the staff and each other in the burgeoning comment threads.

By the time of the Sleepless Summer Tour in August and all through the fall, the narrative of individual empowerment—first articulated in May at the Columbia debate—had grown beyond mere political rhetoric, thanks to the blog and Meetup, and become a true story. And the story was telling itself.

## Days before Iowa

It is eleven days before the first caucus. Clark is closing in on New Hampshire. The internal polls from Iowa don't look good. Every day we are under withering fire from the media and other campaigns. Inside headquarters in Burlington, it is like moving in a dream. The TVs blare frenetically even as the crawler at the bottom of the screen appears to be losing momentum and coming to a halt; eternities pass between movements of the creeping minute hand of the clock. One afternoon NBC teases, "The Dean Tapes" and the entire office raises pale beleaguered faces toward the screen. "What the hell is this?" someone calls out. At first it seems miniscule, a dramatic report of nothing of any import—Dean, four years earlier, had gone on Canadian public television and observed that many voters couldn't afford to spend a full day participating in the Iowa caucuses—and we watch it quizzically and little bemused as if it were a flare launched over a field at night, slowly drifting down. But the report, like the flare, signals something new—a sustained, coordinated attack. Almost immediately the pundits are on the air, breathlessly discussing what Dean had said years earlier, and to us it is the sound of an artillery barrage, incessant and unnerving—there's a feeling of animal helplessness before the media bombardment, and awe at the power of it.[2]

With the first promo on NBC I argue that we should put up the full transcript of Dean's interview on the blog, to tell the story first from our perspective. But the campaign has grown layered and cautious, wants to consider the message, make a few calls to reporters. Sure enough, NBC edits the interview to give the appearance that Governor Dean doesn't care what voters in Iowa think. We should have beat them to the punch, I say. This is why we built the blog, specifically for moments like this—to push back instantly on the emerging spin, to tell our side in its entirety. Yet the whole strategy is suddenly at risk because of the notion among others that what we say to the press or in a release is more important than what we say directly to the entire world.

Trippi returns from Iowa the next morning. Movement. I blog rapidly, posting every twenty minutes. The flow of the counterattack swirls around the war room—a press release on casualties in Iraq, an overheard comment from a press secretary about the mere 1,000 jobs created by the Bush economy in December—and each overheard snippet becomes a part of the blog post, of the narrative, of the story.

Trippi pulls me over.

"Matt, remember how we used to do it? The journalists read the blog."

"I know it."

"What you should do is the *Des Moines Register* story. The twelve Iowa guardsmen injured in Iraq. That's the news—"

"That's what I'm doing."

"—and the bastards are talking about what the governor said four years ago? About whether he likes the Iowa caucuses?"

"That's exactly it."

"This is what the media has come to?"

"That's right."

"Write it," he says. "Something with heart. Like we used to do."

And so I do, a beautiful post taking all these snippets that goes out instantly into the world and into the chaos of the politics of the moment. Just as I hit publish, MSNBC reports that Harkin is endorsing Dean. An oppressive weight is lifted. The office erupts into cheers.

"Jesus Christ," our spokesman says behind me, hanging up the phone. "I swear that guy has a lucky rabbit's foot up his ass that he pulls out whenever he's about to go down."

Later that night, Trippi goes on with Paula Zahn on CNN. She asks him about the NBC report. "Just read the transcript," he says repeatedly. Zahn looks sideways at the producer off camera, is handed a piece of paper. "Read the transcript," he insists. She refuses to read the full quote, a visceral demonstration of the gotcha game of the media. "Read the transcript," he repeats. A chastened Paula Zahn abruptly ends the interview. For the second time in a day Burlington erupts with shouts of joy and laughter. Score one for the American people, someone says. The media, at least for the moment, at least in the form of Paula Zahn, at least this once, loses.

## Notes

1. http://www.blogforamerica.com/view/83 (accessed June 1, 2007).
2. For an example of the minor news frenzy about the tapes from Canada, see transcripts of CNN's "Judy Woodruff's Inside Politics: The Howard Dean Tapes: Dissing Iowa?" Aired January 9, 2004, 15:30 ET, available at http://transcripts.cnn.com/TRANSCRIPTS/0401/09/ip.00.html (accessed June 1, 2007).

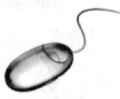

# 9

# The Meetup Story

## Michael Silberman

*Michael Silberman, Dean's National Meetup Director, was more intimately involved in the Dean Meetup phenomenon than any other staffer, landing as a recent college graduate in the middle of the most explosive part of Dean's campaign. In close detail not described before, Silberman explains the evolution of the intensely demanding processes set up to manage 1,000 different local chapters of active Dean supporters. More like a help desk than a director's chair, the Dean Meetup structure he describes is fundamentally about supporting local, on-the-ground activity, and includes creating software to track packages, regular conference calls, and systematic reports. He shares critical lessons learned through trial and error, and discusses the core question at the heart of Meetup: "How do we keep these leaders engaged with campaign goals while continuing to organize them to take further action? And how do we balance our national campaign needs and priorities with their local autonomy?"*

When I first joined the Dean campaign in mid-February 2003, Meetup did not exist as far as the campaign was concerned.

The Burlington, Vermont, headquarters was an exciting, tiring, and terrifying place to be in those early days. Each of the approximately two dozen staffers there, including me, was busy filling holes as best we could. We seemed to have enough people to run a skeleton operation—one or two people for every campaign "department"—but not nearly enough people to do everything that we should or could be doing to keep pace with the momentum our candidate was generating as he traveled the country asking questions that no one else seemed to be asking.

Resources were tight and meager. What we did have went into fund-raising. Furniture was recycled or donated, and we had one 13-inch TV/VCR combo that was usually balanced on a couch in the finance office. During Dean's February speech to the California Democratic Convention, we stood together in silence, shock, and admiration as our candidate began asking the questions that put him on the map and gave him a standing ovation at the DNC Winter Meeting a few weeks earlier: "What I want to know is what in the world so many Democrats are doing supporting the president's unilateral intervention in Iraq."

I quickly began to understand the meaning of an insurgency campaign. We had started with almost nothing and Rick Ridder, our campaign manager at the time, was fond of describing our situation to us this way: "The plane is taking off, but we haven't finished adding the doors, seats, or steering wheel, so we're doing it as we go." We knew that this wasn't going to be a typical political campaign.

But it also wasn't yet the type of place where the Internet was anything more than a conduit through which supporters would send us some several thousand e-mails per day. Yet on March 5, 2003, over 550 people came together at New York City's Essex Lounge to meet Dean at an event organized through a website called Meetup.com. The following Thursday, the *New York Times* ran a story in its Circuits section about the Dean campaign's Internet-driven event. Then it became clear that these self-organized Meetup events were something that the campaign was going to have to deal with one way or another. Which meant that someone was about to take on some more work. I had been hanging around the field team long enough in my first three weeks (and apparently demonstrated enough basic competence) that I was assigned to look after this strange new aspect of the campaign.

I promptly moved my desk from the front room into the "field office" (a small room housing three political/field desks and the entire two-person scheduling department), where I became initiated as the "virtual field desk." The three other field desks each covered a third of the country's states and regions, and I was to cover the national online population—a position that *Maclean's* magazine described as "ambassador to the wired legions."

No one was really sure what that meant since there was no precedent for such a position. I was instantly in the very awkward but exciting position of filling a role for which there was no previous model. In short, there was no precedent for success or failure—but plenty of room to do both!

## Beginnings of an Online Network

As Meetup.com founder Scott Heiferman will tell you (with a wry smile), he started Meetup.com after seeing *Lord of the Rings* and realizing that there was no good way for fans to find each other and get together locally. During the winter days at the end of 2002, William Finkel, an enterprising staff member and political junkie, had the creative idea to expand the company's topic offerings into politics, so he created Meetup groups for each of the presidential primary candidates at the time.

At the beginning of the month, on January 1, 2003, one person had signed up to Meetup for Dean. Will was already following blogs like DailyKos.com and Jerome Armstrong's MyDD.com. And Jerome was already blogging about Howard Dean. William posted a comment on the site in mid-January 2003 and ultimately got in touch with Jerome to let him know about the site, suggesting that he encourage readers to visit Meetup.com and sign up to Meetup for their favorite candidates. Jerome concurred and sent his readers over to http://dean2004.Meetup.com, asking them to sign up. These courageous souls were our early adopters.

At the time, Meetup.com had a database of venues that were willing to host group meetings. They assigned, randomly, a monthly time at which any given group would meet—for Dean, it was the first Wednesday of every month at 7:00 P.M. Anyone who signed up for a local Meetup group was notified to attend their monthly Meetup meeting if at least five other people in the same geographic region signed up and RSVP'd for the same group. My job was to increase the number of places in which there was a Meetup group, and the number of places where we had a trusted contact.

In March, we pursued a fairly typical campaign approach to the events: Find some trusted person in each of the cities in which these Meetups were supposedly happening, get in touch with them, and ask them to be there to either run the event or answer questions on behalf of the campaign. In short, we tried to get some sort of official campaign coverage at each location. We developed a spreadsheet of all the Meetup locations that were active for the Dean topic on Meetup.com, and we sporadically listed whatever contact information we could find for the people that we tried to "send" to the Meetups. Unfortunately, these volunteers were usually busy with other campaign work, like hosting fund-raisers or doing political work, so we quickly discovered that their appetite for any grassroots work was fairly limited. We were sending people who were generally less interested in being there than those who had signed up to organize the events themselves.

So we quickly realized that a far more effective approach would be to try to establish communication with self-identified volunteers who had indicated some interest in attending or organizing a local Dean Meetup. These people were far more likely to put in the time and energy necessary for building a great event.

My primary objective for the remaining weeks in March leading up to the April 2 Meetup date was to continue filling in this spotty (and growing) spreadsheet of cities and coordinators and to start *talking* to these folks so that they knew we were paying attention and there to help. The Meetup message boards were both the most obvious and the most complicated solution. Like many third-party tools and online systems, the campaign had no way to communicate directly with the people signed up for our "topic" on the Meetup.com system. The boards were a clunky thing, and they definitely weren't designed to be used the way we tried to. But they were all we had—especially in the absence of a campaign blog, which Matt Gross was just getting off the ground.[1]

Although I don't think we realized it at the time, being forced to go out to where the people already were was a good lesson in switching from broadcast politics to the old-fashioned, person-to-person, word-of-mouth politics that we were getting ready to revive via this new online medium. The Meetup message boards for each city within the Dean 2004 topic were like the coffeehouses that used to be essential to politics. Unlike what would have been possible with television, we had no way to broadcast a message into each of those regional coffeehouses or Meetup groups; rather, we had to get in the weeds and show up on each message board (many of which were inactive) and participate to try to identify a local leader.

We ultimately inked a deal with Meetup.com to provide us access to the e-mail addresses of website users who had signed up for our topic and opted in to receive updates from the campaign. In the interim, this was the best way to get the pulse of the community and to communicate with the grassroots leaders who were making Meetup happen.

## Our Strategy: Effective Community Organizing Online

Several reporters covering the campaign picked up on a common campaign phrase (and ultimately joke): that you either "got it" or you didn't get it in campaign manager Joe Trippi's worldview and, therefore, in the campaign. Fortunately, it wasn't hard to figure out where you stood on the spectrum.

Despite what I thought I was doing in tracking down Meetup hosts and sending e-mails to the group, I definitely didn't fully "get it" during my first few weeks, and Trippi made that perfectly clear to me in early April 2003. He had called me into our windowless kitchen-cum-conference room, along with the two people I had been working with to develop this new program: Tamara Pogue, our national field director, and Zephyr Teachout, our new head of Internet outreach.

With his head half-cocked, Trippi started drawing circles on the meager whiteboard. He had spent weeks just trying to get someone to put the Meetup button on the homepage of our website, so he sure as hell wasn't going to let us screw up one of the potentially most important tools to this insurgent campaign. And I was about to receive the single most important piece of education that I would receive throughout the entire campaign.

"Okaaaay. This is what traditional campaigns look like. And the military. And broadcast television." On the whiteboard, Trippi drew the outline of a hierarchical organizational chart—sharp horizontal and vertical lines at ninety degrees that expanded downward like a family tree. "You have the campaign manager, state field directors, county organizers, precinct captains, etc.—all taking orders from above. Nothing happens until someone above them says to jump. Okaaay?"

After a typically uncomfortable pause, he pointed to the bull's-eye pattern that he had drawn earlier on the board, while staring at us. "This is what our campaign looks like … concentric circles. If I drop a pebble into the center of the pond, the waves ripple out, self-propelled. That's how we did it with Gary Hart—but we didn't have the advantage of the Internet then. We don't have the money or name that John Kerry has. We're never going to have a huge field staff, and we're not going to pump millions of dollars into TV and mail, so we have to rely on our supporters to carry the message, to create their own ripples. When I send out an e-mail to 25,000 people, we need everyone to drop pebbles in their own ponds, forwarding it on to their listservs so that really we're reaching 100,000 people. That's how we're building this thing. Get it?"

This was probably one of the first of many talks Trippi gave on what would ultimately be defined internally as "concentric circle organizing." Trippi used less than half the number of words and twice as many nods as he could have to explain what we were doing, but it was clear to us. Our job was to use every tool available to us to empower the grassroots to run the campaign, and Meetup was going to be one of the primary vehicles for making that happen.

Our campaign was going to be different because it was going to mirror the web, taking advantage of the fact that our country was networked, along with our social and interpersonal relationships.

He also made the decision to clear up some of the organizational challenges we were wrestling with regarding the appropriate place for Meetup (i.e., me): Is it part of the Internet team? Field team? He didn't give a damn what team I belonged to or where I sat, but I was to report directly to Trippi when it came to Meetup.

In May, we prepared and sent our first national Meetup Agenda, which was broken into "before," "during," and "after." The idea was to create a cheat sheet that organizers—with busy lives outside of Dean—could use to prepare for and run their Meetups. The key part was to leave enough wiggle room in the agenda for local creativity, additions, and revisions. As soon as the agendas became too detailed or specific, local leaders would ignore them.

Beyond the general organizing tips ("introduce yourself," "mail us your sign-in sheets") and campaign updates in the agenda, we included one element that would become a mainstay in every future agenda: the national action item. Rather than just giving people things to do to keep busy, we wanted to help foster the long-term growth of these local community groups. Following what had worked in a few of the more established Meetup groups in Atlanta and in the Bay Area to develop local committees, we asked Meetups to break into four groups—flyering, constituency outreach, media, and "double your numbers."

Here's what we wrote in the agenda:

> BREAK OUT AND GET LOCAL …
> During the month of May, Howard Dean needs your help to reach out to all the potential Dean supporters in your community who are not yet connected to the campaign. Divide your Meetup into several Local Action Groups for several minutes of brainstorming and goal-setting. Meetup members should choose the group with which they are most comfortable and meet for 10–15 minutes in various corners or parts of the room. (If you are hosting a small Meetup, each Action Group might contain one or two people.)
> [Description of each break-out group]
> Swap contact information so that members of each Action Group can stay in touch with one another about their project throughout the month of May.
> After the break-out session, ask one individual from each group to present a summary report (1 minute) to the collective Meetup group.

At the end of the agenda, we did something unique. Zephyr had been talking all month about the Meetup Challenge, where grassroots supporters challenged others to donate $10, which had evolved from the New York Meetup. She suggested that we help keep it alive by including something in the agenda. So, in a large box at the end of the May agenda, we explained how the Meetup Challenge had evolved from the New York Meetup and highlighted it as an example of grassroots ingenuity.

Rather than simply smile and ignore the effort, this was one of the first examples of the Dean campaign's listening to supporters and working to support creative efforts. It's also an excellent example of how the campaign—at least the Meetup team—strived to create positive feedback loops that demonstrated the real-world impact of individuals' actions and initiative.

Several months later, we tried to make up for being physically absent from each community by expanding my virtual field desk into a full-time staff of three or four people who responded personally to e-mails and calls from Meetup leaders, as well as followed up with leaders when necessary. We divided the country up into regions, so that we could become more familiar with the volunteers we were working to assist. More than half of our grassroots leaders were new to politics or local organizing and were eager for tips and organizing assistance.

The major difference between our operation and typical field desks was that ours ran a bit more like a computer help desk. We were working with many more people than a typical field desk might oversee, and none of our field contacts were trained staff. Of course, this inexperience came hand in hand with unbridled enthusiasm and willingness to do whatever was necessary or most helpful to the campaign. But it put us in the position of providing a great deal of support, which could have consumed all of our time as well as that of a dozen additional employees had we not made a concerted effort to balance our team's help desk time with our other priorities.

## Social Networks

As we continued building the Dean Meetup program, we benefited heavily from the hundreds and thousands of people who were looking for ways to get involved in the campaign every day. Every campaign website, e-mail reply, and phone response funneled supporters to their local Meetup group. Not only was it the most scalable solution to the ever-increasing (and unmanageable) number of inquiries, but it was also among the most effective ways of engaging volunteers and supporters in meaningful activity.

If a Dean Meetup didn't exist in or near a supporter's community, our program and associated web tools encouraged people to start their own. Volunteer Meetup leaders continued to emerge in places where none had previously existed. These local grassroots leaders almost instinctively tapped their own local networks to grow their events and local Dean presences. They reached out to other people they knew, forwarded the campaign's e-mails to them, and ultimately invited them to join their local Dean Meetup groups.

Local Meetup groups flourished and grew as a result of our volunteers' built-in social networks. Almost every e-mail message encouraged supporters to pass the message along to five friends, and every Meetup agenda encouraged leaders to remind attendees to bring one or two new friends with them to the next Meetup. Increasing media attention and press stories only facilitated this process by providing third-party validation for their friends' personal requests.

Our ability to funnel supporters into this self-generating and self-organized Meetup program allowed us to rapidly circumvent more traditional campaign practices of going out into the field to recruit volunteer organizers by hand. The Internet also enabled us to provide a direct link and connection to the official campaign, which provided a good balance to the more local, decentralized engagement that they had via the Meetups.

We were also wary of the Internet's shortcomings in replacing these high-quality face-to-face interactions, so we made a concerted effort to maintain constant dialogue with our grassroots leaders using every available technology (i.e., phone, conference call, mail, instant-message, and digital video).

As the campaign took off and our Meetup program really started growing, we started seeing gaps in some geographical areas. We saw, for example, that the state of Florida lacked substantial coverage. The campaign needed to grow, so we asked ourselves what we knew about traditional organizing and traditional social networks that we could apply to the online world.

As field organizers, we could ask a supporter, "Who do you know in your circle of friends that might be willing to join us?" As a national online campaign, we could ask a similar question, "Who in our supporter database might be likely to organize a Meetup in their area, given their previous engagement with the campaign?" We called and e-mailed those very specific subsets of people, and many agreed to help (and were happy to have been asked!).

We knew that we needed to find the online equivalent to Rotary Club membership. These are the types of group members who know everybody and everything in town and are respected for that. We targeted people who did more than just sign up on an e-mail list. These were supporters who took an action online, donated money, or showed an indication that they were more than just e-mail activists. Once we found them, we called or sent them an e-mail about Meetups and invited them to build a Dean community in their towns and counties.

We also asked Meetup leaders to ask their groups for a show of hands for everyone who traveled more than twenty, thirty, or forty-five minutes to get to the Meetup. If there were at least a few people in common from the same distant area, they were encouraged to *not* come back next month and to start their own local Meetup group in their area. We made this ask an explicit addition to the suggested national agenda and reinforced it on conference calls and in our organizing guide.

Our strategy worked: Dean had more Meetup groups across the country than almost all of the other Democratic presidential candidates combined. Many of them still meet today as chapters of Dean's new organization, Democracy for America.

## Behind the Screen

As the Meetup leaders network grew and strengthened, the Dean Meetup team in Burlington necessarily became an increasingly more important anchor. The Meetup operation doubled and tripled in size during the early summer months of 2003, when David Temple, Alex Mackay, and a rotating group of interns joined our team full-time.

On the wall of our four-person Meetup cube in the office, we pinned up a copy of an old *New Yorker* cartoon showing a dog seated in front of a computer, looking over at another dog: "On the Internet, nobody knows you're a dog." We all thought the cartoon pretty much summed up our team and much of the entire campaign operation. Given my young age at the time—and the fact that the rest of my team was still in college—I don't think there's any way that we could have been nearly as effective without the veil of technology and the Internet to put us on equal footing with our network of volunteers.

It wasn't until the final months of the campaign, beginning in late 2003 and early 2004, that I began to meet large numbers of our volunteer leaders either in the field in Iowa and New Hampshire or at the dozen Grassroots Summits we organized around the country in November 2003. After months of interacting with these folks via every digital medium from phone to e-mail, instant-message, blog, discussion list, or confer-ence call, it was always great to meet one of these heroes in person.

The encounter was always amusing. I was usually surprised to discover what someone *actually* looked like (versus what I had imagined). But the other person was generally shocked—something for which I quickly learned to prepare myself. Without fail, the first words out of my new acquaintance's mouth would be "Oh, I can't believe how *young* you are!"

We didn't really have time to apologize for our ages, but we did invest a great deal of time acknowledging the years of organizing experience that many of our leaders had. The humility we were forced to embrace as a result of our age had the effect of making us more effective organizers, as far as I can tell. Fortunately, the technology-based methods we were merging with those old-school community organizing skills were new and different, which helped to validate our young Meetup team.

Being young also ensured that our threshold for burnout was pretty high. Like the rest of the campaign, we were a pretty high-octane team, operating almost twenty-four hours a day and seven days a week. But I found our work to be considerably more rewarding since we usually saw a near-immediate return on our investments of time and energy. We were in direct, regular contact with a network of energetic folks across the country eager to help us improve. Every chance that we had to be more effective in supporting their efforts would translate into more effective local Meetups and, therefore, stronger or better support for our candidate.

The positive force of the Meetup leaders network was contagious both within our team and throughout the entire office. In conjunction with the Internet team, we provided a live link to the most hard-core supporters at the center of our campaign and, therefore, to the pulse of the entire effort. We were often among the first to hear or deliver the most inspiring supporter stories, such as new volunteer efforts like "Doctors for Dean," and among the first to receive the most useful and immediate feedback, such as total number of voters contacted by phone or mail.

## Wrangling Decentralized Energy: A Volunteer Program Run Like a Field Program

A key part of our strategy was identifying real things that Meetup groups could do to legitimately help the campaign. Not telling them what to do, but giving them ideas—our most enthusiastic leaders knew that they were in charge of their Meetups, but they also wanted to be as useful as possible.

I quickly learned that the best Meetups—the ones that people returned to month after month—were ones that did more than give people an opportunity to hang out and drink beer. When people left their Meetup feeling like they had made some contribution to the course of the campaign, they were more likely to return and bring others and, therefore, help to keep their Meetup strong and active.

Early on we brainstormed a handful of activities that we could suggest for Meetups and put together a menu of options called "Taking Meetup beyond Meetup: 12 Things You and Your Meetup Can Do to Elect Howard Dean in 2004." We turned it into a PDF, put it on the website, and asked all Meetup leaders and participants to download it.

It was our way of communicating with Meetups and acknowledging their importance and potential. We didn't ask for anything specific during those first few months of Meetup, and we didn't ask for any data back, so we didn't really know what was happening on the ground—yet.

Once we assembled this core group of grassroots leaders, which ultimately included over 2,000 people volunteering to build and host Meetup events every single month, we had to figure out how to organize and support them. How do we keep these leaders engaged with campaign goals while continuing to organize them to take further action? And how do we balance our national campaign needs and priorities with their local autonomy?

## Taking the Network Offline

The first big test of our online grassroots network occurred on July 2, 2003, when we launched a major letter-writing campaign to voters in Iowa. We asked our grassroots volunteers to organize letter-writing parties at Meetups. (We later expanded the program to include voters in New Hampshire and other states, as well as encouraged letter-writing parties between Meetups.)

We knew that the burnout rate could be high, so we tried to make it easy for the leaders to organize their events. After all, these people weren't full-time organizers; they were volunteers. We sent each group every item they would possibly need—sample letters, stamps, envelopes, paper, pens, and even information about the county in Iowa to which they were writing and a DVD message from Howard Dean about the program.

Then we stayed in close contact with Meetup leaders before, during, and after the events. We did the usual preparation calls and e-mails, but at the last minute, we did something different. We sent an e-mail to all the Meetup leaders asking them to call us with some results as soon as they could. We had no idea how the night was going to play out, and we wanted to do more than just cross our fingers.

On Meetup night, the entire headquarters staff was out celebrating the previous quarter's historic fund-raising success from June 30. You could usually find someone working the phones until at least 10:00 P.M., and someone from at least every department was required to staff his or her department until midnight.

But on this night the office was barren, save for David Temple, me, and the six-pack we had purchased to complement the celebration happening on Lake Champlain. We took over the phones in the main reception area and started reading the early blog comments on the open thread to find accounts from people who had already returned from their Meetups.

Then the switchboard started to light up, and we started receiving ecstatic reports from our grassroots leaders on the ground—some of whom were calling us directly from their events. I don't know what was better: hearing the real voices behind the e-mail addresses and names we had been looking at for months or vicariously experiencing the rush of energy that these leaders were conveying about what they had just achieved.

The impact of this reverse phone bank was far greater than we initially intended. We set it up to get an early survey of the data, for ourselves and for the rest of the campaign staff, who would be asking for it the next morning. We also realized how powerful that connection to headquarters was for these leaders. It showed that they weren't alone on this campaign. When you can pick up the phone and hear a familiar name or voice on the other end of the line, interested in your last three stressful volunteer hours, that means a lot.

## Meetup Central

Everyone in Burlington knew when Meetup time was coming because boxes upon boxes of shipping supplies, flyers, stickers, and other materials for that month's national action would show up in our offices weeks before Meetup day. We lined the hallways with our boxes because there was never nearly enough room in our area. The other clue that Meetup was coming was an unlucky printer assigned to several daylong print jobs. Depending on the national action for the month, our team could be found reloading reams upon reams of color-coded paper into the printer to produce mail-merged printouts of letter-writing kits containing names and addresses of voters in key states.

The process of collating Meetup kits for each local leader with organizing guides, sample agendas, DVDs, and the supporting materials for that month's action item was a mind-blowing multiday effort, even with the assistance of a dozen dedicated volunteers who knew the process better than we did by the end of the year. Meetup groups in different states might be matched with different counties or precincts in Iowa, New Hampshire, or New Mexico. And the right number of letter-writing kits, pens, stamps, and voter addresses had to be matched with the appropriate Meetup group. New coordinators received the twelve-page organizing guide but veteran organizers did not. We developed an assembly-line system of constantly changing volunteers that generally relied upon a quality control person double-checking packages before they were sealed to be sure that the right mixture of everything was on its way to the right people.

In order to ensure that all leaders received their package in time for their Meetup, we prioritized shipments based on UPS ground shipping zones and how long it would take to get from Burlington, Vermont, to that part of the country. I can still tell you what "zone" each state (or part of a state) is—a skill none of us expected to have picked up on the campaign. The UPS driver even agreed to do our pickup last in order to give us that extra bit of packing time, and then we'd still have to race a carload of packages out to the sorting facility and onto the conveyor belts in south Burlington before the 7:00 P.M. cutoff.

At the end of a weeklong sprint and overwhelming logistical challenges, we'd ship between 800 and 1,200 packages each month for at least six months, and the ingredients for each month's mailing were always slightly different. All of it had to take place at the last possible moment so that we could prepare a meaningful national action, record and burn to DVD a timely message from the governor, and get materials to organizers a few days in advance of their Meetup.

We joked that the Meetup team often served more like a customer service help desk than a campaign team. Our phones would ring off the hook with questions from coordinators about when their kits would arrive, or why they only received thirty writing kits if they expected fifty people to attend. Our e-mail inbox was no different.

During the early summer months, our "help desk" operation started to face some serious issues, in the form of a bursting Excel spreadsheet. David, Alex, and I had used just about every color, row, column, and tab that we could to keep track of the constantly changing contact information, names, event locations, and data associated with the Meetups. And our bloodshot eyes and tired fingers were creating serious errors with data we had. The system was so unstable that our inability to keep up with the growing amount of information generated by this leader network was actually becoming a critically serious limit to growth.

Fortunately, a talented, snarky web developer named Justin Pinder joined the campaign and engineered a web application that saved us from our bloated spreadsheet and played a critical role in the ultimate success and scalability of our program. The new Meetup Central website and database consisted of a fairly simple set of web pages that enabled coordinators to "claim" responsibility for organizing their Meetup location each month and update their information—something that was impossible via the Meetup.com site at the time and that we could no longer manage by hand.

Ultimately, toward the end of the campaign, Pinder surprised us with a beautiful feature that imported the tracking numbers from the UPS shipping software into the Meetup Central database, enabling coordinators to look up the tracking numbers and track their Meetup package directly via the website. It was all about using technology to continually enable the program to scale.

We did our best to stay upbeat and make up for any errors that would undoubtedly occur in this massive shipping process, but at the end of the day it was fascinating to observe the contrast between coordinators who held us to the lofty standards of their airline's customer service departments and those coordinators who were more familiar with political campaigns and, therefore, were overjoyed to be in contact with someone at the campaign, let alone receive a bundle of materials each month.

## Three-Dimensional Communication

There were lots of ways for us to communicate with our grassroots leaders in the typical broadcast or hub-to-spoke model. Moving into a two-way conversation model was a no-brainer because we needed to know how Meetups were doing across the country so that we could provide good support, but we also quickly learned that spoke-to-spoke communication was just as critical to the viability of our network.

One of the first and most successful things we did to facilitate this communication between and among leaders was to create a Yahoo! Group discussion list for Meetup hosts, where leaders asked questions of one other, swapped success (and horror) stories, and shared resources or best practices.

I had also digested Trippi's "concentric circles" lesson well enough to realize that Meetup organizers needed to start talking to one another, connecting, and helping each other out. As Meetup continued to grow in the early days, there was no way that I was going to be able to continue having personal relationships with each leader and also prepare the strategy and logistics behind the next month's Meetup. My peppy one-way e-mails from Burlington to coordinators were not going to be enough to sustain this, and they weren't going to help us grow.

In late April, a Meetup organizer in California by the name of Dan Robinson agreed to start and moderate a group called DeanMeetupHosts. The discussion list is still alive and active today, under the name DFAMeetupHosts. The group's ongoing existence is a testament not only to the leaders currently involved with the new DFA effort but also to Dan's relentless commitment to moderating the group discussion and ensuring that the discussion stay on topic.

We also had dreams of more advanced networking opportunities, some of which were realized in the Deanlink social networking tool developed for the entire Dean network. Deanlink proved to be useful in a variety of ways, but it wasn't an effective way to provide other Meetup leaders with a way to see who was doing great work in a certain area or part of the country and directly connect with them. Much of the mentoring that happened within the network took place either via regional meetings or discussion lists or via the national DeanMeetupHosts list.

In the absence of the regular face-to-face meeting that a typical organizer might hold in a community, we held a series of monthly conference calls just for our grass-roots leaders to help everyone prepare for the upcoming month's Meetup. The purpose was threefold: provide an insider's campaign update, discuss the suggested national action and agenda, and share best practices across the network or receive feedback in an open forum.

We hosted the maximum 100–125 people per call that our conference numbers would allow, usually at four different times each month to accommodate varying work schedules and time zones.

I'll never forget the intensity of the first few minutes of every call, hearing the computerized chirps of dozens of people joining the call at once, followed by an explosion of exuberant voices announcing themselves:

"This is John in Fairbanks, Alaska!"

"Mary in Pheonix"

"Viki in Fresno—hi, Mary!"

"Oh, hi Viki!"   ·

These intros would continue without pause for several minutes as local leaders dialed in to the conference.

We would recognize almost every name, but hearing that person say his/her *own* name was an important reminder for us that there were *very real* people at the core of this effort. The downside of online organizing was that we spent so much time looking at names on a computer screen or on shipping labels that the names quickly morphed into identifiers for Meetup groups and locations rather than people. (We often had fun quizzing each other randomly on the city that matched a Meetup leader's name, or vice versa.)

The chaotic sound of everyone talking at the beginning and end of each conference call when the lines were unmuted in many ways mirrored our entire program—much like the beginning of a road race where all are doing their own thing and with their own color but moving in one single direction.

The energy of these calls was like a drug for me. No matter how tired or irritable I was before the calls, which usually took place at night after a long day, the calls always left me with more energy than I had before.

After the first few calls we began taking rapid attendance by running through each state and asking who was on. This was just one more metric that we thought we could use down the road. For example, do attendees rate more highly the Meetups whose leaders participate in the conference calls?

Most importantly, these calls built accountability and trust. The ability for us all to hear each other's voices made the program so much more real for everyone involved, and it deepened the relationships we had established via e-mail.

Phone calls and personal e-mail gave our grassroots leaders access that other people didn't have. We sent them immediate updates, even in hard times. For example, when Joe Trippi left the campaign, we delivered the news immediately, so that they could be prepared to discuss it with their local networks after it broke on the evening news. We treated them like high-dollar donors. As far as we were concerned, they were the most important people in the campaign because they were doing all of the heavy lifting—without getting paid.

Our incredibly close contact with leaders gave us real-time feedback on what was working and what was not so that we could make large-scale adjustments to the way we were doing things or pursue technological fixes with the folks at Meetup.com. We were also able to distill common concerns into solutions and ideas that we could recommunicate back out to the leaders network.

## Feeding the Network

Back in May, Meetup energy was just beginning to snowball, and I was determined to match the energy of the grassroots organizers and Meetupers (we never really did figure out what to call Meetup attendees). I was also set on getting some materials out to the people who, it seemed, were doing as much heavy lifting as many of the campaign staff in Burlington. We weren't getting paid much at headquarters, but they weren't getting paid at all.

We had ordered a box of "Meetup for Dean" stickers. We barely had a campaign logo at this point, so whoever ordered the stickers didn't hesitate to use the juvenile "Comic Sans" as one of the fonts. There was something beautifully authentic about these stickers, whose simple—and borderline audacious—design helped to teach me the importance of getting it done, and not letting the perfect be the enemy of the good.

I was determined to get these stickers out to every Meetup group before the next Meetup. The package of materials was an important way for us to show Meetup leaders how important their efforts were to the campaign. Many leaders had already spent hundreds of dollars on Dean stickers and banners, which they used at their events, so we were already somewhat indebted to them for their personal expenses.

At the end of 2003, we wanted a simple way to thank and acknowledge our leaders for all the hard work they had done that year, so we mailed physical thank-you letters from Governor Dean, all of which were accompanied by limited edition "Grassroots Leader" lapel buttons printed in the campaign style. The cost to the campaign was minimal, but the impact was far greater than I ever could have predicted. Once a few showed up in the mail, some leaders on the discussion list grew frantic that theirs hadn't arrived yet. And when volunteers from around the country arrived in Iowa to help with "The Perfect Storm" volunteer canvassing effort during the final days, the button showed up on many people's chests as a much-discussed badge of honor. (The buttons also had the unintended effect of helping my team and me find and personally meet leaders from around the country.)

## Numbers, Numbers, Numbers

We were all obsessed with numbers. We had to be, or else there was no way to know how we were doing or what was happening short of nice anecdotal stories about good times had at the local Meetup. The membership numbers listed at http://dean2004. Meetup.com quickly become one of the easiest ways to monitor and measure the support we were receiving—hence Trippi's and Kate O'Connor's almost comical obsession with refreshing the Meetup website every hour.

Most people, when describing Trippi as an Internet genius, fail to understand that he was first and foremost a field organizer—someone who values the importance of knowing, at any given moment, how many supporters you can count on in your precinct or county or state. Instead of residents in Jones County, Iowa, my universe was all Americans, everywhere—everyone with access to the Internet across the country and around the world, all of whom were managed in neat little Excel boxes and later in a database.

Not surprisingly, one critical element of my job was to obsess over this number day in and day out for the campaign. It was one of several metrics that were needed to run an effective program. Organizing online didn't mean that we were going to abandon traditional organizing standards. Effective political organizers live, breathe, and sleep by the numbers—precinct captains, committed voters, possible voters, unlikely voters, and so forth.

When you didn't see someone on the field, finance, Internet, or even communications teams grumbling about numbers—crowd numbers, e-mail addresses captured, dollars raised, blog comments posted, Meetup leaders reporting back, letters sent, etc., etc.—you'd realize that the person was new or just didn't, well, "get it."

We tracked all of the Meetup groups on a giant map on a wall behind my desk at the back of our cube. Since we didn't know the faces or voices of most of our leaders, the map was one of the only ways that we could anchor ourselves to the real people across the country. The Meetup Map also became somewhat legendary and one of the top things that reporters and camera crews seemed to gravitate toward when they toured the headquarters.

The map was nothing more than a large poster of the United States upon which we added tiny translucent dots. Red dots represented active Meetups with confirmed leaders. Yellow dots were locations of Dean groups listed on Meetup.com that didn't contain enough group members to be considered "active." And green dots represented possible future locations for Dean Meetup groups because they were "locales" on Meetup.com or areas that we thought should have Meetup groups.[2]

As beautiful as the map was, we soon learned that its analog form prevented us from running any queries or doing any sophisticated GIS analysis on our network. What's more, all of the dots were the same size, unlike our Meetup groups! So whenever we had spare hands or skilled volunteers, we asked for help digitizing the map from our database so that we could compare and visualize average Meetup attendance numbers by state, Meetup sizes by location and state, and per capita Meetup memberships across states.

One of the lasting imprints that Trippi made on me was an early interaction where I entered his office to get approval for something or another, or to let him know what the Kerry campaign had done at some of his New Hampshire Meetups. Then he asked me a basic question about the state of our Meetups—how many did we have contacts for?

"Close to XX," I replied. "I can go back to my computer and tell you in, uh, a few minutes. It's all there on this Excel—"

Cardinal mistake. The glazed look that Trippi shot back at me (he looked up from his laptop, which meant that this was important) suggested that I may have just as well said, "Sorry, Joe, but I'm a complete idiot and have no idea what my name is or what I'm doing here."

"Don't ever, *ever* walk in here again without knowing *exactly* how many f—n people there are on f—n Meetup, okaayyyy?"

The next day, I prepared and circulated our first weekly Meetup status report, which I would proceed to prepare every Friday night for the next ten months. These reports became one of the most useful and rewarding tasks I performed on the campaign, because it gave us a sense of how we were doing compared to our goals as well as enabled my team to provide some public accountability for what could otherwise have been seen as an obscure and unquantifiable use of campaign resources.

I began implementing a series of feedback loops into our program that would generate the data points necessary for monitoring the pulse of the network. We bolstered our anecdotal feedback system and the user-generated event and venue rankings for each event that Meetup.com provided with a twelve-question web survey that we sent to all coordinators immediately following each month's Meetup.

We asked about everything from the total number of people attending to yes or no questions about whether or not they played the DVD message from Howard Dean or attended one of the planning conference calls. Then we asked for anecdotal feedback about what they'd do differently next time or advise new Meetup leaders to do in planning their Meetups. We included many of these results in the weekly Meetup status reports. After summarizing the quantitative results, we'd page through all of the qualitative data and post as much as possible back to the group or share it with new leaders in hopes of distributing the wealth of knowledge across the network.

## Bottom versus Top

As the campaign grew heavy with additional field staff in the final months, one of the biggest challenges our program faced was managing the clash of cultures between newly hired field staff and grassroots Meetup organizers who had emerged locally.

Throughout the campaign I had unwittingly served as one of the Dean grassroots' key ambassadors and representatives within campaign headquarters. Between our Meetup team, the house party crew, and the campaign bloggers, we had a pretty good pulse on what our key supporters were saying. The other campaign departments were generally content with this arrangement because they didn't need to have direct contact with the grassroots in order to do their scheduling or communications work, for example.

That changed, however, as our campaign operation expanded into early primary states and grew heavy with field organizers. As we neared these primaries, my cell phone would ring with increasingly frustrated grassroots leaders who couldn't understand why, after pouring their heart and soul into the campaign for so many months, the newly placed campaign staffers in their states weren't taking their suggestions seriously or bringing them on board to help more officially.

Washington state was a particularly bad case. We started receiving reports from our longtime Meetup leaders about tense interactions with the new campaign staff, or about field organizers showing up at local Meetups with the intention of running the events. In short, our veteran grassroots leaders and new field staff came from different worlds of organizing and weren't sure what to make of one another.

At one of our lowest points, I worked with our national field director to draft a one-pager for field staff entitled "How to Communicate with Dean Supporters and Grassroots Organizers." I imagine it's not much different from the type of guide that soldiers in Iraq receive before going into towns and villages—one of those essential things that we all wish shouldn't have to exist.

Here's an excerpt of what we advised new field staff, which also nicely summarizes our broader campaign approach:

> The *tone* and *language* you use with supporters and volunteers defines their role in our campaign, affects their willingness to engage, and informs their communications with others. The DFA-grassroots relationship is based upon mutual trust and respect. Supporters will trust your ability to set strategic goals provided that you respect their ability to meet them.
>
> This is a different kind of campaign—unlike any you may have worked on before. Our supporters built this campaign from the ground up and remain responsible for every success. This is their campaign, and it's our job to support their efforts by providing them with as much guidance, resources, and direction as possible.
>
> *Our goal is to empower supporters to take ownership for the work that needs to be done* in order to win this campaign. We need to support active, energized volunteers who will turn out new voters and continue to virally grow our support base.
>
> In practice, we're using a combination of traditional and nontraditional field strategies (i.e., both phone canvassing and house-meetings) to achieve specific, concrete vote goals. Regardless of the technique, our supporters will be responsible for each plan's success. In short, we're *supporting leaders* rather than ordering troops.

As future campaigns and organizations begin to embrace and support the energy of their volunteer and supporter networks, we are likely to see some repeat culture clashes. The lesson for me in observing traditional campaigners approach our grassroots model was this: When a campaign open-sources its operation and invites its network to grab on and run with that power, there's no way to easily take that power back.

## The Day That Meetup Died ... and Then Played On

I was probably among the last few people on the campaign staff to accept or realize fully that our ship was sinking. I spent the majority of my waking (and nonwaking) hours working with the most enthusiastic grassroots organizers and volunteers I'm likely ever to meet. A literally tireless and unstoppable bunch.

Losing Iowa and New Hampshire during that short, eight-day stretch in late January 2004 was a tremendous blow to the entire campaign staff. The official word was that we were marching on—fighting the good fight in Michigan, Washington, South Carolina, Wisconsin, and, well, we all remember that speech.

But most everyone inside the campaign saw the writing on the wall after we lost seven states on February 3. Those of us in the field were like zombies at that point, just going through the motions in whatever battleground we found ourselves losing in, and the remaining skeletal crew in Burlington started taking long lunches and hitting the bars before sundown. Not a good sign when the most dedicated, hardest-working people on the planet start knocking off early. There was nothing more that they could do from there, they would explain, but someone had to keep the main office open.

But our grassroots leaders fought on, which meant so would we, at least on the Meetup team. The Meetup mailings and conference calls for our February and March Meetups continued as planned, even as we conducted them from our dying cell phones, racing between Lavonia and Ann Arbor, Michigan, in a rental car on empty. The disconnect between our intrepid grassroots leaders and our emerging fate was more difficult for me to stomach than the prospect of losing. These were our campaign heroes: They deserved better from us, I reasoned. Then I'd find myself occasionally wanting to tell our folks to just save their energy for the eventual nominee—that we had passed the point of no return.

But then I'd see our Meetup numbers go up, or read some incredible story about something one of our Meetup groups did to build their local group or organize in their town, and I'd want to redouble our efforts. The Meetup operation would fight on, damnit, until the bitter end—until our candidate said that we were done. You just don't quit playing before the final whistle.

By February 10, we had lost in another ten states. The "game over" whistles were blowing, my colleagues were telling me. Everything was crumbling all around us; the mood of the entire campaign was grim as losing state operations shut down offices and fired field staff one after another. I recall a long conversation with some leaders in California who called me after one of our Meetup conference calls to complain about the lack of official campaign resources in their large and, therefore, well-deserving state. They just didn't get the fact that the campaign was likely to be over long before the California primary on March 2 (Super Tuesday). After an hour of bickering, I finally lost it: "Don't you realize that none of this matters if we never make it to California?"

Then, a few days before the Wisconsin primary, the unthinkable happened: Our total Meetup members started going down. Oh, our growth had slowed before between Meetups, but it had certainly never flatlined or, worse, gone down. I stared at my computer in disbelief, hit Refresh several times, and then finally ran outside to get some air.

It was really happening. I felt like I had lost my patient on the operating room table. The others had been telling me for weeks that this slow death was happening, but I had refused to believe it—I had to in order to do my job. I listened to Dean's concession speech on the radio in a Wendy's parking lot the day after we lost Wisconsin. We were somewhere in the middle of the country, unable to get back to Burlington in time for the speech, which was somehow just fine with me at the time. I imagined that my experience was similar to how my real colleagues, the volunteer leaders around the country, would be hearing the news.

I stayed on for a few more weeks to help Democracy for America get off the ground by organizing the March Meetup, which was surprisingly well attended for a campaign that no longer existed. I tried to pretend that I wasn't organizing a funeral, but the good turnout reinforced the fact that what we had built was about much more than a candidate. The concession speech was a blow, but not a death knell.

I didn't stay in Burlington long enough to get the results of the March Meetup, but I did enjoy staying in touch with Chris Warshaw, my replacement, over the following year. Warshaw did a remarkable job of keeping the Meetup network alive as it transitioned more formally into the backbone of Democracy for America and all of its local chapters, which are still active today.

## Looking Back, Looking Forward

At the end of the day, Dean Meetups were a bunch of people getting together locally—often over drinks—with others who shared this common interest for progressive politics, Howard Dean, or getting rid of Bush. The Meetup program simply provided a somewhat organized means and vehicle for these natural connections to take place.

Our network, not to mention the entire 600,000-person supporter base, was the driving force behind a massive volunteer operation that fueled the campaign in countless record-breaking ways—from sending more than 280,000 handwritten letters to voters, to traveling from all points on the globe to knock on doors in Iowa, to raising almost $30 million online in small-dollar contributions.

It's easy to point to the technology and the Internet as the source of all this success. But almost anyone on the campaign will tell you that technology was nothing more than an enabler. That's especially true in the case of Dean Meetups. After all, our most successful tactics were tried-and-true community organizing or field tactics that we simply translated for the digital age.

Technology's greatest role in Meetup was providing people with that feeling of belonging to something larger than themselves, both online and off. Technology enabled local Meetup group members to stay connected to one another (and active) between events, and it enabled local leaders and volunteers to stay closer to the national campaign than they ever could before. Most importantly, it allowed this program to grow like wildfire by reducing to seconds the time it would take for new Dean supporters to find out what was going on in their area or to start their own local effort.

One important note for campaigners: Although our Meetup program was dedicated to supporting our most critical field and fund-raising efforts (and to fueling the growth of the entire Dean movement), it was structurally independent from the true field or vote-getting operations in key states. Despite a last-ditch experiment to integrate our Meetup model into Iowa's ninety-nine counties, the Dean Meetup program was really a massive national volunteer operation that supported the campaign's field efforts—but we weren't a field operation.

Through the letter-writing campaigns and other activities, we were able to focus the limitless energy of our national volunteer network on those key early states. And the grassroots leaders' organizing efforts in thousands of communities across the country enabled Dean to build a national presence almost overnight. But the challenge for campaigns or organizations that are successful in cultivating grassroots leadership and inspiring similar levels of self-organized local activity will be to find a way to integrate those programs with true voter identification and recruitment efforts.

Well, that's my slice of the Dean Meetup story. The full story sounds more like an elaborate chorus of 189,000 different stories, each representing the motivations, hopes, and dreams of an everyday citizen who gave up countless hours every month to fuel an incredible movement.

The media spent plenty of time in Burlington interviewing staff and trying to summarize what they saw happening. But to really find out what was going on, they should have been out talking to thousands upon thousands of grassroots leaders in communities around the country. Many of us would try to explain this to the journalists, but most assumed that we were simply staying "on message" by referring to the campaign's grassroots supporters and to one of Dean's favorite lines, "You have the power!" Perhaps the only real way to appreciate the difference between talking about "people power" and believing in it is to experience it oneself, person by person, supporter by supporter, citizen by citizen.

## Notes

1. In order to post a message to a Meetup group's message board, you had to find the city's Meetup, then you had to join the group, then you could type a short message into the box. A few groups used their message boards all the time as an organizing tool, but most others quickly abandoned them to create their own Yahoo! Group listservs, which had the benefit of pushing new messages straight to the user instead of relying on users to check the website—something that your casual supporter was not apt to do. Newer versions of the Meetup site released after the campaign resolved this issue by facilitating unlimited e-mail communication between group organizers and members.

2. The original Meetup.com system was organized around a series of geographic "locales" that Meetup.com cofounder Matt Meeker had painstakingly created from an atlas of commercial development and population. Matt and his team manually matched every zip code in the United States to one of these locales so that site visitors could easily enter their zip code and be matched with a Meetup group in a neighboring zip code. Needless to say, these locales did not map effectively to the political geography and caused a handful of complications for us, including locales that were either way too large or too small for the number of separate Dean Meetup groups being organized in a region. The locale names also caused great confusion when individuals at the border of one state would find themselves placed in a locale named after the nearest large city in a neighboring state. The locale system also divided a state like Iowa into less than a dozen locales when we were trying, at one point, to organize Meetups in all ninety-nine counties. Our program, given its large size, quickly unearthed a handful of issues like these in the locale system, which Meetup.com worked with us to address to the best of their abilities. Ultimately, the "locale" system was eliminated in more recent updates to Meetup.com.

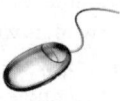

# 10

# Experiences of a Grassroots Activist

## Pam Paul

*Pam Paul, a midsummer Oklahoma volunteer for the Dean campaign, tells her extraordinary story of transformation from a disengaged voter to a committed grassroots activist, organizing over sixty events and keeping in direct contact with thousands of Dean supporters, and Dean himself. Her story is the technology from the other side—what the tools did for her, in context, to bring her into the campaign and then make her work possible. In her straightforward way, her story cannot help but inspire—she eventually set up her own website, helped organize the Oklahoma Rapid Response Network, and was involved in creating independent ads for her candidate. But she does not bring a Pollyannaish approach—instead she tells a story of action and the development of political autonomy.*

It is hard to believe that over three years have passed since I first joined as a volunteer for the Dean campaign.

My story is like that of thousands of activists I met during the Dean campaign. I am forty-two, a transplant from Massachusetts to Oklahoma City, with a background in business management. Before August 2003, I considered myself a Democrat, but I had never been active in politics or even cared about it. Even voting was a struggle. I used my computer only for online shopping and the occasional Google search; I had never participated in a blog.

In early 2003, news of the Iraq War filled the airwaves and I was quickly growing tired of it all. I felt helpless, frustrated, and overwhelmed. News of the upcoming 2004 elections, and potential candidates, was also making the headlines and—honestly—I had zero interest. But one day I heard part of an interview with Howard Dean and his message against the war. I needed to know more. The message I received that day was to stop complaining and get involved. For the first time in a long time, I felt a sense of excitement about our current state of being. I searched the Internet for every bit of information I could find about Governor Dean. Dozens of online articles later, I concluded that he was the man I wanted to become president of the United States, and I wanted to be a part of his campaign.

I had no idea how a campaign worked, how I could be of service, or if I'd even like it, but during my quest for more information, I visited DeanForAmerica.com. It was unlike any other website I had visited, with an inviting and fun energy. The blog turned out to be the heart of it all. I did not post a comment for quite some time; in fact, I watched for a couple of days. When I finally did comment, I nervously waited to see what kind of response I would receive. But my fears disappeared quickly because I received a warm welcome from those participating on that thread, and I soon found myself entrenched. I became one of hundreds participating in the various threads each day.[1] My user name was "deanforokc" and my opening and/or closing remark was always "Spread the love!"

I did all my online work from home and because I was an in-home care person, I had free time off and on during different times of the day. Through the blog, I met thousands of folks who ultimately shared my concerns, my passion, and my desire to become a part of something larger than a campaign.

This wasn't all just socializing. It is here that I learned most of what I needed to become part of an activist community. The blog let us keep up with the activities of the campaign, respond to Rapid Response alerts, and share invaluable resources. The blog was the venue I used for sharing opinions, learning about history and politics, and sharing campaign ideas. It is here that I learned that I became part of a progressive movement that would set out to change the course of the Democratic Party and of the United States.

## Becoming a Volunteer Activist

Shortly after I became virtually involved in the Dean campaign, I discovered there was an upcoming Oklahoma City Dean for America (DFA) monthly Meetup taking place at the Oklahoma Democratic Headquarters, the sixth to be held there. At that meeting I found dozens of folks, just like me, who were excited and waiting anxiously to help. Although this meeting had a lead organizer, and traditionally followed an agenda that the campaign provided, it was always a grassroots affair. Everyone was encouraged to participate. It was not long before I became part of the organizing team, connecting me to hundreds across the state, and not long after that I became the Oklahoma City Meetup organizer, a position I held for the next year. Unlike the organizer before me, Keith Smith, I had no political experience. Keith (who has since passed away) may be the person most responsible for keeping me, and hundreds of others, continuously involved at the local level. It was his persistence and his attitude toward the fight for civil rights, in every aspect, that truly paved the way for many of our accomplishments in Oklahoma City. His enthusiasm for the campaign made all my local work worthwhile.

During my time as the Meetup organizer, I followed the guidelines that DFA sent to us, but it was not always possible for us to work on national-led tasks so we tailored events, or agenda items, to our own needs. This was always a grassroots-driven meeting, so I traditionally let participants introduce themselves, share why they wanted to help the campaign, and then provide us with their ideas or experiences for possible use in future activities. We then set monthly goals and events and continued work thereafter either via the Internet or via individual meetings. There was a lot of flexibility with Meetup and this is one reason the meetings were so successful. I was always amazed that the folks who attended the meetings were so willing to listen, did whatever they could to help, and rarely caused conflict or disruption.

There were times when we had fifty or more in attendance and we began to have a very large presence in Oklahoma. The Dean staff did not usually attend our Oklahoma City Meetups, so it always continued as a grassroots effort. We also attracted local progressive candidates running for office who were seeking our support, like Bert Smith, who ran for Oklahoma's Fifth Congressional District in both 2004 and 2006. I think there were about six different Meetups across the state of Oklahoma, and three of those continue today. It is through Meetup that I met the most motivating and inspirational group of people, and made many great friends with whom I continue to work on certain issues and events.

## Dean Meetups and the Dean Committee: Dynamics

At about the same time I joined the campaign, there was also a very active Dean Committee in Oklahoma City, made up of folks who had been involved in politics already, had several campaigns under their belt, had their own way of doing things, and had political aspirations before and beyond this election. They had met several times via the previous Oklahoma City Meetups, had a large list of volunteers, and had held a couple of very successful events long before the local volunteer wave hit. Unfortunately, when the wave did hit, there could not have been a more combustible reaction had we tried to create one. I think they were totally blindsided when the onslaught of activists started pouring out from the woodwork.

As the Dean campaign in Oklahoma spread like wildfire, mostly through Meetup, volunteers were appearing everywhere, most without experience, and just raring to go. This rush of volunteers, their energy, and the new campaign technology may have disrupted the work in progress of the folks on the committee. They had been doing such a great job and now they had to deal with all the new faces and ideas. I also think they assumed we would all disappear as quickly as we had arrived, as had happened in the past. To be fair, it would have been impossible for any staff to keep up with everything because the campaign was gaining traction in such an unprecedented manner. We realized early on that it was up to us to become conduits for the campaign if we expected to have a strong Dean connection throughout the entire state. It was about this time that Burlington sent a campaign manager to Oklahoma, which may have added some confusion. I tried to work with the new campaign staff as well as the former committee people but there were times that it seemed more productive to gravitate toward the grassroots aspect, so I continued my work at that level.

Eventually the former committee dissolved. Some members still attended Oklahoma City meetings but once the Dean campaign hit its peak, many became paid staffers while others worked in their own areas. This is when it became apparent to me that we needed to find balance between the "old" and the "new" in order to gain maximum exposure, in the least amount of time with the least amount of personal disruption. The one regret I have is that we were not able to mesh everyone together in a more healthy and productive manner. It grew large and somewhat unmanageable for the local paid staffers.

## Campaigning through Volunteer Social Activism

Because of this newfound independence, and perhaps our naïveté about the political system, we were able to develop untarnished ties with our local Latino, Asian, African American, and Native American communities. I learned quickly that due to certain legalities, most groups or agencies cannot promote or endorse a candidate or party, but they can always use volunteers for their own needs. Therefore, I decided that, if done properly, we could spread the word of the campaign through volunteerism. I was able to connect with different groups by looking through the phone book, calling different agencies around the city, introducing myself, and asking if they needed any help with activities. I would also look at event calendars that I found online or in the newspaper to see if we could help. I would commit volunteers, and then create Democracy for Oklahoma City events, through Get Local, and we soon became a part of their upcoming activities. I would also post our events in the online newspapers and event calendars so we would attract folks, throughout the city, who were not already involved with the campaign. Leaders of local agencies seemed to enjoy speaking with activist volunteers. I lost count of how many times people told us that we were like a breath of fresh air.

Our particular group of local volunteers (including Amy, Curt, DeAnn, Stephen, Preston, Angela, Pat, and Sheri, just to name a few) contributed locally by volunteering for events such as the AIDS Walk and cleaning parks via the Oklahoma City Parks and Recreation Department. During these events we wore our Dean T-shirts and became physical billboards for the campaign. We supported the Oklahoma Youth Agency's talent show by raising money for a donation that secured a table at the event as well as a one-page ad in their program. We participated in the Martin Luther King Parade by purchasing float space and volunteers handed out campaign flyers while walking during the parade. We also painted "Faces for Peace" during the local Peace Festival, filled stockings for children for the Oklahoma City Salvation Army, and sent holiday gift boxes to soldiers in Iraq. All donations were on behalf of Democracy for Oklahoma City and the Dean campaign.

Maybe the most memorable of these events, for me anyway, were the Oklahoma Youth Talent Show and the Martin Luther King Parade. The Democratic Party in Oklahoma City had declined the invitation sent by the Oklahoma Health Care Project event organizer, even though Republican candidates would be contributing. The organizers seemed relieved that we wanted to help. It all worked out perfectly and we were able to raise our own money for the table we needed and get a one-page Dean campaign ad (that I created) in the program, and we had over a half-dozen Dean supporters at the event.

*Youth Talent Show: DeAnn, Preston, Amy,
Stephen, Pat, Angela, Sheri, and Pam*

(We also participated the following year and we have an ongoing relationship with the folks who work with the Health Care Project and the talent show event.)

The Oklahoma City Martin Luther King Parade event was memorable because of all the support and the work of the volunteers. I booked the spot for us in the parade, set up the event on Get Local, and arranged for us to have what we needed. One volunteer, Anthony, offered his convertible, some volunteers printed flyers, and I got decorations and candy, prepared a CD with Martin Luther King speeches and music, gathered aprons to hold our wares, and had our "Flat Howard," a life-sized cardboard cutout of Howard Dean, ready to go. Everything was in order but unfortunately my grandmother was in the hospital at the time. I called Amy, our most faithful volunteer, and asked that she meet me at my house while DeAnn, my partner, stayed at the hospital. My grandmother died while I was on my way to the house. Amy consoled me and then she collected all the gear and took over the formalities of the parade. Dozens of volunteers showed up, young and old, including many folks who were not usually at the grassroots events, and they passed out hundreds of flyers. I received many e-mails and calls of sympathy and support. Because of all I had going on personally, from that point on, the volunteers began doing more organizing, which helped lighten my load. I am forever grateful to them for helping the campaign, and me, on that day.

*Oklahoma City Martin Luther King Parade*

## Digital Tools

Most of my event organizing was possible through Get Local, my favorite tool of all. It allowed me to organize events with a simple click of the mouse. After I created an event, an e-mail went out to all those within the desired location range—hundreds signed on from Oklahoma City—and folks showed up to help each time. Within the first four months, I had organized about sixty local events, including visibility activities, voter registration, and house parties. It still blows my mind to think of all the grassroots ideas ultimately put into action that directly contributed to Dean's surge during the campaign season.

For local communicating and gathering volunteer lists, most states, including Oklahoma, also used the Yahoo! Groups tool. Yahoo offered the web space to store data, files, pictures, and e-mail lists of volunteers. It was possible for there to be dozens of such groups in one state. Other groups that proved to be extremely beneficial included the Dean Leaders, the Meetup Hosts, and the State Leaders lists/groups. Members of these lists were usually those working more specifically as lead organizers in their local areas, and they shared a plethora of information and resources. At one point, I belonged to almost fifty Yahoo! lists, in addition to other lists, and I could communicate with thousands of folks at any given moment. It could be very overwhelming but I felt that it was vital that I, and others, stay connected and that we share as much information as possible.

I used my lists to send out weekly updates to hundreds of those working on the Dean campaign and in some cases included many who were not. I kept my e-mails cordial and informative. Ultimately, I was able to get my name, and Governor Dean, recognized around the entire state. During a Democratic dinner, former Oklahoma governor Walters, who was the Dean campaign representative, was speaking about the campaign and asked the audience if there was anyone in the room who had not received an e-mail from Pam Paul. I was shocked to hear him mention me, but maybe more shocked that everyone in the room knew exactly what he was talking about.

Although the campaign offered such tools as Deanspace, Get Local, and Deanlink, and we had the Meetup tool, we still needed a local website that the grassroots could easily manage and that catered to local volunteers, so I started the Okies for Dean website. I had never created a website before but, as this was a "do-it-yourself" campaign, I decided to do it myself. I searched the web for the best tools that I could find that would allow me to produce a site without having to use html, or web script, writing, while still offering me the flexibility to add the content that I felt was relevant to our needs. I also did some checking with local activists to be sure the name chosen for the group was one that people would appreciate. After spending some time looking at all my options, I was able to find what I needed and within a few days I created the site by using shared graphics and resources, bought the domain name okiesfordean.com, and we were up and running. I then learned the copyright rules for published materials so I could reproduce materials without worry of causing any legal problems.

On the Okies for Dean site, people could find information related to the Dean campaign in Oklahoma and, in some instances, nationally. I made it as user-friendly as possible. I included information and resources on volunteering, registering to vote, and voting locations; provided links to other useful groups; and directed them to local Dean Yahoo! Groups and Meetups. I also spent time daily updating the site and provided real-time information so that people felt a direct connection to the campaign. This site was an open-source website designed to aid folks in becoming part of the political process and included resources for positive purposes only. I posted no negative articles or information about other candidates running during the primary. This became a premier Dean site for Oklahoma, linked directly on the Dean for America site, and we had several thousand visits within the few months it was online.

## Events

Volunteers attended political events, held bake sales, adopted parks, worked in soup kitchens, and traveled across the state spreading the message of Howard Dean. In Oklahoma City, we worked most closely with the volunteers of the Cleveland County[2] Dean group (Marta, Carter, Adam, Bette, Mary Beth, Margaret, and many more) and we tried to attend as many events in their area as we could. They did the same in return. Later, after Dean dropped out of the presidential race, we were able to help them by volunteering for Gail Poole, a Dean supporter who was running for mayor and who became our first post-Dean candidate. We were glad to be able to help a fellow progressive run for office.

During the campaign, I personally organized or attended as many events as I could. We always had table space at Democratic events, and I also worked diligently to place information about Dean in as many public venues as I could. I even investigated possibly getting airtime on the radio and print space in newspapers, and managed, with the help of Latinos for America, to place a quarter-page ad in *El Nacional,* the leading Latino newspaper in Oklahoma City. (To my knowledge, this type of grassroots-initiated marketing was taking place in every state in the nation.)

I also promoted the idea of having grassroots campaign offices located around the state. I asked supporters to volunteer if they could house supplies for distribution, then I posted their e-mail and physical addresses on the website so if people needed supplies they could just stop and pick them up. Our household became one of the Dean headquarters for our area. We filled our garage with Dean paraphernalia, or Dean Gear, we covered our computer table with every issue paper written, and we had "Dean for America" signs all over our yard. People would stop by at any given time of day and collect whatever they needed to aid Governor Dean. My car had "Ask me about Howard Dean" written on the back window with shoe polish. When people asked I would tell them all about him. People would even ask me questions while I was driving, or stopped at red lights. We practically lived in our Dean for America Gear. My partner and all our friends worked together regularly to spread the word. Even my grandmother supported Howard Dean.

Registering new voters was a priority and was an ongoing process for us during the Dean campaign. We registered voters every chance we could. We set up tables to register voters in front of supermarkets, near bars or clubs, during musical events, at arts and crafts fairs, and on street corners. During the Gay Pride Parade, there were so many people and it was so chaotic we felt we could not just walk around handing out registration cards, so we drove our jeep to the end of the parade float line and, with permission from the Oklahoma City Police Department, we slipped into the parade. We were passing out voter registration cards from the windows and people were running up to us and grabbing the cards as if we were giving out money, often passing them to other folks in the crowd who needed them. Soon we had nothing left to pass out. We had given out hundreds of voter cards, bumper stickers, and flyers.

These types of activities were happening everywhere across the country. I watched as, nationally, people adopted highways, cleaned rivers, brought food and clothing to shelters, shrink-wrapped their cars with Howard Dean ads, and sent phone cards to soldiers. Most of these activities fell under the Dean Corps umbrella. Dean Corps was the Dean campaign's equivalent to the Peace Corps. The South West Voter Express, a caravan concept created by the grassroots, brought supporter help to the southwest part of the country. People Power Graphics was an online site that provided slogans, graphics, and issue papers that were readily available for folks to use if needed. People started T-shirt/merchandise shops via Café Press with tailored graphics for local groups. There were grassroots-written, -created, and -produced television, radio, and billboard announcements. A group called Switch2Dean created television ads that featured folks who switched from another candidate or party to Dean. Dean Port became a grassroots center for information and technical resources, and Dean Photos was a photo album website that contained thousands of event and group photos taken from across the country. At one point, Democracy for Oklahoma City had more pictures of events in the photo album than any other group. There was even a group called Blankets for America that sent handmade blankets to hospitals for babies born prematurely. Hundreds of blankets were distributed and this was a great opportunity for folks who did knitting or sewing to get involved with the campaign.

We also tried to support any national events we could. We attended at least a dozen house parties organized in our local area, many of which we organized and held at our own home. If the media said something negative about Dean, it was a lot of fun to donate to, or hit, the bat. The amount of time, energy, and finances that we saved, and gained, by using these homegrown resources was priceless and is a reflection of a true grassroots movement and all it has to offer. There is no telling what the total income for the campaign would be if one combined the actual campaign finances with the volunteer hours and personal money spent on our own resources.

## Getting the Message Out

A group of supporters also formed the Dean campaign's rapid response (RR) team. A rapid response team is responsible for tracking the national and local media coverage of a candidate and his or her campaign, and then responds as needed with letters to the editor or directly to political campaigns. Folks would receive daily carefully designed alerts. With help from RR, we learned how to get our message across in an effective and efficient manner. We had a wonderful team in Oklahoma, whose members helped each other, and subsequently we had several Dean-related op-eds and letters to the editor published in our conservative-leaning state newspaper. This was no easy task considering how difficult it is to get any liberal or progressive news printed in the *Daily Oklahoman*. RR worked flawlessly and gained recognition from the national media as one of the fastest campaign response teams they had ever witnessed. My guess is that they thought the team comprised a paid media team rather than grassroots volunteers.

In addition to raising money and reshaping the message of the media, we needed to shape the minds of the voters. Therefore, a big part of our ability to connect with voters depended on our knowledge of Governor Dean and his position on the issues, and our ability to transfer it. We spent hours upon hours watching him during every interview, rally, and debate. If, at any time, I could not find what I needed, either I or someone would create it. With help from different groups, information translated into Spanish, Arabic, Vietnamese, and other languages was distributed to the relevant communities.

Whether we agreed with Dean on everything or not, we were able to convey his passion, common sense, and practical approach to politics. In one instance, I became a speaker at an Oklahoma City GLBT "State of the State" event because the original surrogate for Dean had a scheduling conflict. I had never spoken in public like this before, especially for a candidate, so I was extremely nervous and felt totally out of my element. There were other people, most already involved in politics for years, speaking on behalf of candidates, and I remember thinking that I was in way over my head. I brought no notes so I spoke from the heart about Governor Dean and I told about all he would offer Oklahoma, and the gay community, if he became our president. At the beginning my voice was shoddy and my palms were sweating but within minutes I felt more comfortable and at ease. It was my knowledge of, and my passion for, Governor Dean that allowed me to transfer his message of hope and practical governance. Folks came up to me after I finished, thanking me for participating, and spoke to me in great depth about Dean. As a result, I became a regular representative for Governor Dean.

## The Peak of the Campaign

Soon Dean was getting front-page news at every turn. Buses filled with thousands of supporters, arranged by the local campaign staff or the grassroots, would travel around the country to see Governor Dean. Hundreds of folks from Oklahoma participated in one or more of these journeys, including to the Jefferson Jackson Dinner in Iowa. One of my favorite pictures is of Dean standing in front of a line of about twenty buses that brought supporters to join him at the dinner in Iowa. It was mesmerizing and, as I understand it, they needed a permit because there were so many buses that it became a parade.

Of all the hundreds of varied Dean groups that flourished during this time, I belonged to Out for Dean, Latinos for Dean, Women for Dean, and Mainstreet Moms. The Dean community, as a whole, had such diversity, breadth, and depth of character that it seemed, to me anyway, a picture-perfect reflection of the United States. The hope-filled spirit of the community was intoxicating, as if it were a fix we had all been craving. Random acts of selflessness, local and afar, were never ending and ultimately we became one big progressive family. It did not matter who was straight, gay, black, white, tall, small, old, young, male, female, rich, poor, a Green, a Republican, a doctor, or an Indian chief. That, to me, was the wonder of it all. We were all connected by the Internet but somehow touching one another directly as if we were in the same room. We were one, regardless of life history, and a common thread of ideals is what held us together. Status, condition, and ego never seemed to enter the bigger picture. Words cannot accurately describe the bond, or chemistry, among all of us, and there is no one experience that stands out to me, but all of them together created a sense of hope and belonging.

No matter what group one belonged to, all supporters for Dean did their part for one another and the campaign. Folks would offer housing or help with transportation, without question, when groups of people would travel for voter canvassing events, and our home was always open if needed by someone visiting Oklahoma. Volunteers regularly sent supplies, or physically volunteered to help, whenever and wherever needed. Technical aid with website design was just a click away and all those who were asked gave information freely. If a group needed money for a project, people would contribute without hesitation. People put their lives on hold and moved cross-country to help if needed. Folks even helped others more personally. If someone needed a lift in his or her life, there was always a hand available. These acts of kindness were less noticeable than the more public efforts but they were just as important, as they were the true essence of the campaign. The slogan was "Dean for America," not "Dean for President." Getting Dean elected would have been the by-product of all we hoped to accomplish. Our commitment was to the betterment of each of us, every single person within or beyond the campaign, regardless of who they were or where they came from.

The media sold the Dean campaign as being white, rich, and in its thirties. This may be the biggest disservice ever done to any group of individuals who gave their hearts and souls for a single purpose. In my experience, the Dean campaign was the epitome of acceptance and teamwork, and included all types of folks. Maybe most inspiring were those I met along the way who are in their sixties, seventies, and beyond, living on Social Security and Medicare, and who were, in most cases, fighting harder for my rights than I: Joe and Polly Forgy and Elda and Jim Davis, for example. The truth is that it is those individuals who kept me involved the entire time. How could I complain or whine about a single thing when people the age of my grandparents were working as hard as, if not harder than, I was, and had less than I to work with? Folks directly around me were the inspiration that kept our movement alive, and I am still in awe of the intensity that our local seniors had during, and after, the campaign.

Another amazing aspect of the campaign was the direct connection I, and others, had to Burlington and to Governor Dean. Because the volunteers who staffed Burlington HQ were traditionally young and mostly new to politics, and the Internet was our primary gateway to the campaign, I was able to connect often and easily with HQ. Our primary mode of communicating was through the blog but if I needed more contact, I could just e-mail or call HQ. If I needed supplies and DFA could provide them, they would. DFA held conference calls for widespread communication and feedback and for face-to-face interaction; they started the Drive for Democracy. During this drive, folks from Burlington would travel the country and report on the activities of the grassroots and the local state campaign workers. Some states had paid staff folks and some did not, but every state they visited had the opportunity to "meet and greet" about the campaign. We, in Oklahoma, were fortunate to have been one of the visits during the "drive." I remember their visit vividly. They drove up to the Java Dave's coffee shop in a car with a plastic Dean magnetic sign on the roof. They looked like they were delivering pizza but instead they sparked the lives of hundreds of Oklahomans during their stay.

Supporters also had Governor Dean's e-mail address. Folks could e-mail him and he would answer them directly. I had several e-mail exchanges, relating to Oklahoma politics, with Governor Dean. Once, when he gave his e-mail address during a national conference call, I remember thinking that there could not have been another politician running for president who would speak to folks so personally. Governor Dean also called folks to check on candidates whom the campaign was choosing for the Dean Dozen endorsements. If selected, Dean Dozen candidates would receive money and support from the campaign. The application and selection process occurred via the Internet. One day Governor Dean telephoned me at home, unexpectedly, to ask about an Oklahoma candidate, Kalyn Free, and her possible endorsement. He wanted to know my opinion about the endorsement, he wanted to see how things were going for us locally, and he wanted to thank me for my work. It was an experience I will remember always.

Who could have imagined that I, as well as others, would become spokespersons for a presidential candidate simply by stepping up to the plate? It seemed to me that Howard Dean loved that people were just taking matters into their own hands and working so relentlessly for his campaign, or maybe more importantly for America. In fact, he always challenged us to do more. He would tell us, "You get a D for voting but you get an A for running for office." This type of unbridled activity may have somehow contributed to the downfall of the campaign itself, but it is really the only way for citizens to gain control of government and, in my opinion, should be happening more often. Maybe one day we can achieve true equality between the political and citizen tiers. To this day, I am not exactly sure whether Governor Dean realizes all that happened and continues to happen because of his campaign.

To me, this was the biggest difference between Governor Dean and the rest of the people running for office. I realize other candidates resonated very deeply with their supporters, but it also seemed to me that some micromanaged, screened everyone and everything around them, and had a total disconnect with the group of folks who were supporting them. Howard Dean treated his supporters, including me, all the same—with courtesy and respect. He worked harder than we did and he became an excellent role model for all of us. He enjoyed meeting with us during his visits and he seemed to remember every name and face. He insisted that despite our differences we all had at least one common link that bound us together. He told us that we had the power, he believed that we could create change, and he challenged us to do so. We, in turn, believed in him and responded to his challenge.

I am also still in awe at the number and diversity of people whom Governor Dean attracted. Actually, I think what happened during the campaign was somehow spiritual. I know people joked that we had been drinking the "Dean Kool Aid" but I do not feel that that description was accurate. The majority of Dean's supporters reacted to him and his campaign as if they/we were answering a calling for a greater purpose and, in turn, we rose to a higher level of awareness and participation. I know I did. I am not old enough to remember the emotional connection that John F. Kennedy, Martin Luther King, Bobby Kennedy, and even Malcolm X had with the country but I cannot stop thinking, and feeling, that this was somehow similar.

Who knew things would come to such a screeching halt because of one exaggerated and overplayed moment in time? The scream heard 'round the world was one of the most heartbreaking experiences one could imagine. I was supposed to attend the event but could not, so I watched from home and I could not believe what was unfolding. Everyone left the caucuses, emotionally, in shock and awe. People with whom we spoke who attended the event had no clue what was happening and did not know of the damage until the next day or even later. The media managed to take a celebration of thousands of elated volunteers and turn it into a story of the lunatic fringe. Heartfelt cheers for a third-place victory fell silent on the ears of America, and the dramatized replays of "the scream" became center stage. Personally I do not think "the scream" is all that bad, amplified or not, but the whole incident literally brought tears to my eyes and it was at that time that I fully understood how powerless average citizens are against the media and the political propaganda machines.

It seemed to me that America needed a positive story of an upbeat reaction during a first-place loss and instead they got negativity and manipulated sound bites. "The scream" lent support to all those who were just waiting for the demise of the Dean campaign, Democrats and Republicans alike. Grassroots activists were finally able to connect with ABC and ultimately provide the actual event audio/video footage shown during the Diane Sawyer interview with Governor Dean and his wife Judy, but it was too late. They were showing "the scream" every chance they could and there was no way to recover. To this day, I think that most people have no clue what was taking place in that room despite efforts to educate them.

## Keeping the Grassroots Alive

Volunteers across the country, myself included, continued working after "the scream," even as news of Dean's possible dropping from the race was trickling in. He said he wanted to go all the way but we could tell this might not be the case. I had never worked on a campaign before but I saw no reason to stop all the activity. We understood that the fate of the campaign could rest in our hands, so after the New Hampshire primary, supporters across the country decided that we would focus on specific states in an attempt to concentrate our energy. Groups nationally started to send huge amounts of resources and volunteers to different states. After our primary in Oklahoma, we chose to send supplies to Massachusetts, Florida, and California. By using my e-mail lists and state group lists, I connected with leaders in those states, I started to recycle our campaign gear, and I shipped our yard signs, bumper stickers, buttons, and T-shirts directly to them. Burn for Dean, another sprout group, created a Dean video and delivered copies personally to the doors of over a thousand voters in Wisconsin. TruthandHope.org created radio ads for different states around the country, and folks across the country could use the website to choose which state radio effort to donate to. At one point, there were at least eight radio ads going.[3] I worked with both of these groups directly in my attempt to keep the campaign going. I think this may have been the most inspirational time of all because although the campaign itself seemed in limbo, its supporters were going strong without any guidance from HQ or, in some cases, from the local campaign offices.

I was very disappointed when Dean finally decided to discontinue the campaign. I believed Dean could still win, or, at the very least, I felt we should participate directly in the election process in all fifty states. People gave everything for the Dean campaign and it seemed so unfair that things came to a sudden stop. Even though this was my first campaign, I always fully understood that we might not win. I was not disillusioned about the possibilities. I believed Howard Dean was the best choice to lead our nation out of the crisis we were in. But I also knew that we needed the majority of the voting population to also believe it for that to occur. I was obviously distraught about not continuing work for the Dean campaign, but I was most concerned that we might lose the progressive, or crossover, group of voters, and the community, we had garnered during the campaign. I realize now that maybe I was also concerned that not having Governor Dean to support would cause me to want to drop out altogether also.

The Dean campaign attracted such a wide variety of voters, and I felt that the lack of interest in the upcoming Democratic nominee would seriously interrupt our grassroots momentum both locally and nationally. It was at that time that I created the Oklahoma Grassroots Campaign website. This was similar to Okies for Dean except the focus was now on all things progressive rather than on a particular candidate. Through this website, I was able to continue my involvement while helping local volunteers find activities that kept them, and me, involved without compromising our ideals. I helped them find national election connections, join issue groups in our area, help to register voters, and find local progressive candidates to support. I continued to work alongside the Democratic Party of Oklahoma and in March 2005, during the Oklahoma County Convention, I received the Lecia Swain-Ross award for "outstanding, spirited service to the aims and ideals of the Oklahoma County Democratic Party." Not only was this award a total surprise to me, but it was testimony to our county party and its appreciation of the grassroots community. In March 2007 I became the precinct chair for my house district, and it is at this capacity that I will continue my work at the local level.

Nationally, I became a board member for Grassroots for America (GFA), a group formed to help bring grassroots ideas to fruition. GFA implemented the *Taking Root* online newsletter and the Grassroots Theatre Network, which brought progressive movie showings across the country. With the support of GFA and Latinos for America, I started Root Camp, which is an open-source website that offers no-cost training materials and resources to folks running for office or interested in becoming engaged in politics. I became the Oklahoma contact for America Coming Together (ACT), a group that registers voters across the country. I became a founding board member for the Progressive Democrats of America (PDA), a group started by former Kucinich supporters that works more directly with Congress. In this role, I spent a lot of time and energy trying to blend the work of activists of PDA and Democracy for America, the Dean campaign transition group. To me it was vital that the activists from these two opposite campaigns begin working together as one. I was able to help facilitate Governor Dean's appearance at PDA's first convention in Boston, Massachusetts—I consider that one of my biggest accomplishments. I also became a part of the group (first known as My Vote Is My Voice, and now DemocracyFest INC) that produces DemocracyFest, an ongoing yearly weekend gathering of progressive activists who meet for training, speaker panels, and entertainment.

The most common words I hear to describe the campaign are "inspirational" and "rewarding." This inspiration and its rewards currently carry on through the continued work of thousands of folks across the country. I think the 2004 primary, and the work leading up to it, reshaped many past decades of misguided politics. The spirit of the Dean campaign is still vibrant. Countless folks I met are carrying the torch and leading the way through the political process. Progressive Democrats, from all campaigns, have infiltrated every area of our government's leadership, from the precinct level on up, and are working endlessly to give us a chance for a new beginning.

We still have hurdles in connecting progressive or liberal Democrats with those who have already been in power. Many Oklahoma Democrats, like many other red-state Dems, believe they need to lean to the conservative side in order to win elections, so we progressives still find occasional resistance to our methods and our message. The DFA groups in Oklahoma became the vehicle by which we could play a more important role, or have a voice, in local politics. It is through dialogue and careful reasoning that we have been able to work more effectively together and subsequently elect more progressives. We have made great gains in forging a more accepting and understanding leadership, but we need to continue to work both within the party and from the outside in order to create a more socially progressive Democratic Party both in Oklahoma and in other states across the nation.

## Community Spirit

Sometimes it feels like everything happened yesterday and other times it feels like decades ago. What is inevitably missing from the headlines is any mention of the depth and breadth of the community, the scope of our contribution to the campaign and the country as a whole, the undeniable spirit that became the foundation of the campaign, and the fact that this community and its spirit still live on today.

I became involved in politics because of Howard Dean. All that happened during that primary election has changed my life dramatically. I am not a big fan of party politics because it traditionally centers on money and status, but I understand that participating in the system is the only way to change it. So when Dean dropped out of the primary race and asked us not to dwell on the past but to work toward the future, I followed his call. It is our duty as citizens to speak out loudly and often when we see or experience injustice, to vote during every election, to give of ourselves when we can, and to run for office if life permits. I will continue to work, both offline and online, in a manner that I believe is productive while allowing me to follow my principles of politics. I know I, along with thousands of others, wait for another candidate, or Howard Dean, to re-create that spark of hope, compassion, and participation that catapulted us to a level of humanism that we so desperately yearn for. I am forever grateful for having already experienced it, at least once, in my lifetime. I worked tirelessly, alongside hundreds of thousands of people, for Governor Dean, and I would do so again if I had the chance.

My gratitude goes to Howard Dean for running for president, to all the volunteers who gave of themselves during the campaign, and to my partner, DeAnn, for working alongside me every step of the way. My experiences are a direct result of, and only possible because of, the connection the Internet provided me to fellow supporters,

*Howard and Pam*

the campaign, and Governor Dean. The DFA community, its "spirit," and the impact it has had on me, the country, and hundreds of thousands of citizens are not measurable with a single sound bite, book, or movie. I hope I have expressed, through my experiences, some of the magnitude of the passion, independence, and community that were cultivated during this online/offline presidential campaign.

## Notes

1. There is a site dedicated to some of the folks who participated on the blog: http://dean2004.bmgbiz.net/blogfamily.html.

2. Cleveland County lies directly south of Oklahoma City proper, and is considered part of the metropolitan area.

3. See http://web.archive.org/web/20040401132137/www.aspenwilde.com/dfa.htm (accessed June 1, 2007).

*DeAnn and Pam at the Oklahoma County Democratic Convention*

# 11

# The Lessons of Generation Dean

## Amanda Michel

*Amanda Michel had recently graduated from college when she joined the Dean campaign. She turned out to play a central role in the development of Generation Dean, the official youth outreach arm of the Dean campaign and the most successful campaign effort to organize young people since the McGovern campaign more than thirty years previous to it. Although the story of Generation Dean has not received much broad public attention, it has affected subsequent efforts, helping to transform the tactics and tone of college Democrats and shaping the sensibilities of a generation of future political activists. The story of Generation Dean is a quintessential example of the tactics and techniques that made up the grassroots character of the campaign, welcoming outside efforts and self-presentation on the web as distinct individuals, not as a nameless organization. Another key move Amanda and her coworkers made was to redefine the effort as youth outreach instead of student outreach, thereby greatly expanding the possible audience beyond the traditional groups of students at elite colleges and universities.*

*Michel, who is now the director of Off the Bus, a new media collaboration between the Huffington Post and NewAssignment.Net, emphasizes how the complex if often creative tension between the inside and the outside efforts and events—especially chaotic growth—presented novel organizational challenges of which those planning future campaigns should take heed. Finally, she tells how her experiences on the ground in Iowa gave her a sense of how important non-Internet-based activities remain in political campaigning.*

### In Line

The lunch crowd at New World Tortilla had begun to dissipate. It was mid-December and people lingered in the Burlington eatery's warmth before venturing back out to work. Since graduating from college the previous spring, I had worked there while trying to decide between applying for a Peace Corps position in the Balkans and to the Foreign Service.

A few newcomers stood waiting at the counter. One of them cautiously stepped forward. I recognized her as Sarah Buxton, a high school acquaintance of mine, and quickly walked over to say hi. The last time I'd seen her was more than a year before, when she was collecting signatures for Governor Dean downtown. Since then, she told me, she'd continued working for him and had recently joined his campaign staff.

That night I mentioned the encounter to one of my closest friends. He quickly became insistent that I volunteer for the campaign. "When does a presidential campaign come to your town?! You always talk about how awkward you feel walking in the antiwar marches. Do something useful with your frustration. And time." I had met Governor Dean twice at summer camp and supported his run for the presidency, although I strained to see such a familiar face as my president. Even so, I agreed to visit the campaign once it transferred to Burlington from our state capital, Montpelier.

One month later, in the first week of January 2003, I waited to speak with a staffer after filling out volunteer forms at the campaign office. Zephyr Teachout bounded into the room, eyes bright and face completely engaged in a conversation she had already started in her head. After Zephyr found out I didn't have a personal computer I could use for volunteer work, she motioned to Nico,[1] another early-bird campaign volunteer, and asked him to delegate one of his responsibilities to me—reviewing the recommendations sent in to the campaign. They were strewn in a box in the corner. I pulled what was on top off the pile and stuffed it into my bag before heading out to my favorite coffee shop.

Unknowingly I had volunteered myself to read *Click on Democracy: The Internet's Power to Change Political Apathy into Civic Action.*[2] According to the authors, successful campaign strategy revolved around the concept of "interactivity." Minnesota governor Jesse Ventura had been the most innovative, asking supporters to post photos of themselves on his website during his state tour. Supporters would direct friends to the site and some friends-of-friends would attend his rallies, thereby creating what is now referred to as online buzz.

The book was immediately interesting to me even though I'd never used the Internet for anything more than e-mail or reading the news. A medium that I'd never thought of as anything more than transactional suddenly revealed itself as a whole lot more than that. I drafted notes on the book and passed them on to Nico in our next meeting. If *this* was campaign volunteer work, I'd definitely stay on through the campaign. Perhaps my college major, philosophy, would come of use, I mused. Later I'd look back on this first volunteer opportunity as an auspicious sign of what was to come.

Unbeknownst to me, Nico passed my notes to Zephyr, who passed them on to other campaign staffers. A week later, Zephyr reappeared and asked me to work with her on some Internet projects. Several weeks later Zephyr announced that I would organize students for the campaign, an offer I didn't recognize as official until she suggested we celebrate by going out for falafel.

The next month flew by. All e-mails sent to the campaign by students were forwarded to a DeanStudents@hotmail account I created. The volunteer coordinator also delegated the task of answering the campaign's main line to me. Sitting on top of a plastic tub, I worked from a donated computer so slow it frequently crashed when sending my e-mails. Occasionally the screen would go dark and I'd frantically pound the top, thinking it had crashed again mid-e-mail before realizing someone had tripped over its power cord. Hundreds of people called daily, asking me about everything from Dean's stance on health care to the national security risks of Jell-O. In the evenings, I continued working at New World Tortilla.

In March the campaign field staff asked me to organize students in California for the California Democratic Convention, where Dean emboldened the crowd and took the national press stage with his "We need to take our country back!" The student leaders I'd come to know over e-mail swarmed the scene. The fervor Dean generated brought hundreds of e-mails from students to the campaign daily, many of which began to stack up inside my inbox. I couldn't wait to move on from phone duty and looked forward to the day I'd be given a real desk and chair. As with the Internet, I'd assumed I'd have a transactional relationship with the campaign and, instead, I was connecting to it. If I continued to learn enough so that I could participate, I thought, being on the Dean campaign would be an exceptionally meaningful experience.

## Throwing Myself into the Fire

Like most army brats I know, I learned to adapt and adapted to learn. On the campaign I developed and honed my strategies as carefully as I assimilated new material. Intensely curious about this new world, I enjoyed discovering and understanding the campaign's methods. While stuffing envelopes for the finance team during an especially hectic fund-raising cycle, I peppered Larry Biddle with questions about finance's direct-mail operation and learned from him that we had to ask people often for money. After I read several historical accounts of student organizing efforts and assembled a list of new organizing ideas I wanted to try out, I went to Field Director Tamara Pogue. She dealt with my enthusiasm well, wisely cautioning me to "not put the cart before the horse. Before you can organize a large rally," she said, "you need many supporters, and not the other way around."

By March 2003 the word was out—the campaign would begin communicating and organizing via the Internet. I learned of this from Zephyr, who announced to me one morning that, as of today, she had a new position on the upstart Internet team. Since I worked for her, I, too, would need to begin experimenting with the Internet. Like Zephyr's announcement to me that she changed positions, the campaign's way of signaling our new approach revealed itself in miscellaneous decisions. There was no edict except that everyone was to support the Internet team's efforts. There was no central force dictating an overarching strategy. It was something to discover, to realize, and to learn from. Motivated in part by my desire to gain a paid position on the campaign, I knew I had to keep up with the innovation occurring at its edges.

A strategy at my disposal was Google. In March 2003 the campaign buzzed over the hire of Matt Gross. "Who is he? What is he going to do?" I asked a coworker. He told me Matt Gross was going to start our campaign blog. "A b-l-o-g?" I asked again, not even sure I'd heard the word correctly. Why someone would move from Utah to Burlington to blog about a campaign was incomprehensible to me. What was it? To get my answer, I put "blog" in Google and hit Enter.

Sometimes I learned by force that I needed to operate outside of my natural comfort zone. Early one morning Zephyr bounced over to me, inquiring why I hadn't yet set up a web page for my group. Until recently e-mail had seemed ideal; I researched student organizations on the Internet and then introduced myself over e-mail to student leaders. I answered everyone's questions one on one and enjoyed the involved conversations. Fearing that I'd lose contact with my leaders, I pushed back against Zephyr's request. "Isn't this the work of a professional?" I asked. She insisted I do it anyway, reminding me that it would cut down on my e-mail correspondence and that I could continue to improve upon the page after we put it up. Several days after I'd submitted a draft of my website to Zephyr, I came across it online—someone had put it up even though it wasn't finished! I confronted Zephyr and she confirmed she'd done the deed, telling me, "The good thing about the Internet is that you can keep improving it. You gotta sack your perfectionism." A few weeks later, I realized I'd begun to distance myself from my tendency to procrastinate, an evil habit I'd picked up to shelter me from my perfectionism, and began reveling in drafting.

Yet another strategy was to seek guidance from those with more experience. In May, Moveon's director of online organizing, Zack Exley, came into the office for a few weeks to consult us. Just two weeks prior the campaign had relocated from its crowded head-quarters to a business complex out in south Burlington and by chance, Zack decided to sit in the cubicle I shared with Michael Silberman of Meetup. I promptly took the opportunity to ask for a lesson in writing "real e-mails." Zack seemed sympathetic to my cause, but told me he didn't have time outside of answering Trippi's and Zephyr's requests. By then I already knew I had to be creatively self-reliant in this campaign to survive, so I returned to my desk and searched through my files for my worst attempts to write "professional mass e-mails." I printed them out and held them in front of Zack. "Could you just help me improve these? Please?" Zack grabbed the papers and rifled through them. "Amanda, you need a stronger lead. You need to have an explicit ask. You need to restructure these." From Zack I learned that e-mail was the most important tool we had at our disposal. Moveon, he explained, didn't even have a website at first. If I had just one hour to organize people, I should send an e-mail out to supporters rather than put up new website content. A good e-mail is difficult to write, but I could improve my e-mails if I constructed them around a single "ask" or request.

My first few months on the campaign showed me how my approach to work needed to change. Campaigns aren't easy places for people unused to blunt blows of criticism or waking up to decisions made overnight that easily erase a month's work. I was doing my best to shift my sense of gravity so that I could easily stay upright as people piled random bits of work on my back.

## Bringing the Outsiders in, and the Insiders Out

Zephyr stopped by my desk. "Let's talk about bringing Students for Dean in. Should we go out to the picnic table?" Unlike the campaign office, where people sat three to a table and private conversations were impossible, the picnic table in the office building's backyard guaranteed privacy.

Two months prior we'd discovered Students for Dean, a flourishing online effort begun by Michael Whitney, a freshman at American University, and Yoni Cohen, a senior at Washington University in St. Louis. At StudentsforDean.org the two organized several thousand students, an impressively high number for the time. The Students for Dean website organized its members via the Internet and operated a much wider range of tools than the official campaign did. Students belonging to the same school belonged to online chapters and the system offered e-mail and calendar tools. Recently they'd been joined by Ryan Beam, a programming student at Ohio University.

Inside the campaign, groups like Students for Dean were labeled "the grassroots." According to Trippi, the grassroots were absolutely indispensable because Dean was an insurgent candidate and did not have the support of the Democratic insiders, especially after he criticized them for their handling of the Iraq War. On a practical level, supporting the grassroots meant we had to do our best to service their work by, for example, fostering good relationships with their leaders.

Until then, Zephyr and I had casually entertained the idea of inviting StudentsforDean.org on board. Now that summer was approaching and Michael had accepted a student internship, we needed to decide. The thinking behind a merger between Dean's official student effort and Students for Dean was simple—combining our resources and membership would vastly improve our size and strength. Recently we'd discovered that our memberships didn't overlap and that together we reached 4,000 young supporters; Students for Dean attracted activists while DeanStudents appealed to College Dems and Young Dems members. The two organizations complemented one another; Students for Dean represented the grassroots and DeanStudents represented a more traditional student base. Although I'd gotten support to send e-mail and put up a web page, there were few resources—like the time of developers—to be devoted to student outreach; by merging with Michael, Yoni, and Ryan, we'd gain a new website and web tools. Students for Dean wanted more direction, and having direct access to campaign information was extremely appealing to them. Not only that, but we enjoyed working together.

A difficulty lay in reorganizing two separate organizations into one without sacrificing the goals and identities of either. Yoni, Michael, and Ryan were accustomed to making their own decisions and refused to merge if it meant relinquishing their autonomy. They were also intensely proud of their website and work. If merging meant becoming anonymous and losing relationships with students they'd worked so hard to create, they'd prefer to remain outside of the campaign.

At the picnic table, Zephyr and I came to the conclusion that preserving their independence would have to mean creating more autonomy for DeanStudents. We would gain valuable resources, such as Ryan's programming skills. If we were autonomous, we could send out e-mails and put up website content without running it through the campaign's normal vetting process. If we were successful, we believed the campaign would want to support our efforts. In the end, independence meant a great deal of convenience and control without any significant loss of benefits. Only later would we come to realize that the stigma of organizing students would place us at the kids' table and that independence without money or income leads to dependency.

By June, Michael and Ryan were in Burlington.[3] Ginny Hunt, Middlebury's student government president, also joined the team and shared management responsibilities with me. Her involvement in student government, College Dems, and various campaigns brought a great deal of insight into the more formal world of organizing and activism. Jeff Horowitz, a recent graduate of Pomona College, drove to Vermont from California to help out. Jan Insel, a student at UVM, devoted countless hours to student outreach, from answering e-mails to doing research. We also had student interns, like Tim Singer, who assisted in general outreach and strategy.

We now attempted the marriage of the grassroots with the official campaign. We faced the uniquely challenging task of melding a centralized campaign operation with a decentralized and ever-changing grassroots. Balancing the differences between the two meant preserving the integrity of our team. Tying these two together—ideologically and organizationally—was our ongoing focus and challenge until the end of the campaign.

When I was appointed director of student outreach in February, I learned that student outreach usually amounted to the recruitment of students from elite liberal arts colleges. Elite schools generously support student activities, which means that campaigns spend less money and time organizing students there. When I realized this, I felt immediately uncomfortable. I had attended my state university, the University of Vermont, on a four-year scholarship. I also knew many people who had never attended college, either because they planned to farm or because they were disillusioned by their high school experience. Research on youth demographics offered a solution. I learned that "youth" were untapped—many more people attended smaller public schools and colleges than elite institutions; people from the ages of twenty-two to twenty-five and young people also had a lot of time to give. Besides that, speaking to the concerns of young people—instead of "students"—seemed far more appropriate and appealing. I quickly pulled together a memo and sent it to several senior staffers, suggesting that we broaden our outreach efforts to small public colleges and to young people generally. They acknowledged that student outreach in the past had been too narrow, but noted that campaign resources were slim at the time. I could begin branching out, but needed to make sure the effort was affordable.

When I began working closely with Students for Dean in May, I shared with Michael parts of the memo I'd written in February. We both felt strongly about the impacts of Bush's policies on all young people, and began discussing ways to broaden our outreach efforts. Alex and Robert, two extremely committed students in South Carolina, had created a vibrant group called Generation Dean. We asked their permission to use their name for our umbrella effort, and they agreed. I think of the morning we became Generation Dean as the day when the youth organizing phenomenon popularized by the media officially began.

In early fall we planned a four-day, six-state national Generation Dean tour for Governor Dean, which we called Raise the 'Roots. Michael called me from the road during the tour, telling me, "You wouldn't believe it! There are thousands, I mean, THOUSANDS of young people rallying around Dean here in Wisconsin! It's madness. All the reporters want to know about Generation Dean. Even Trippi looks amazed." By the time he'd hit Wisconsin, Dean had visited Washington, D.C., South Carolina, Oklahoma, and Iowa. According to later newspaper reports, nearly 5,000 people crowded the space outside the University of Wisconsin–Madison's Kohl Center. Nearly every major daily paper, and the *Daily Show,* covered the tour. Even Rush Limbaugh gave ten minutes of his show to an excoriation of "Generation Clueless." (The next week Rush entered rehab.)

It was hard to believe just how far we'd come. Just months ago we ran Students for Dean and now we'd just introduced a new way of organizing young people through a national tour, which was—as far as we were concerned—the kind of thing only rock stars did. We'd also learned the preliminary lessons of online organizing as we designed our new website and developed a strong set of chapters. What we didn't foresee were the future challenges of balancing the grassroots and the official campaign, as well as the tremendous costs of supporting an independent brand.

When companies spin off departments, they spin them off for good, sending them off to become their own businesses with their own leadership and income. In politics, such a clean break is almost unimaginable because constituents of the new organization still share ideas and values with the former. In our case, spinning off Generation Dean meant we decided what our website looked like and how we fund-raised, but we still reported to the same bosses and got paid by DFA. Looking back, we misunderstood what would truly make us autonomous and underestimated what support we would need. If we'd only seen how we could build off their resources instead of forging a new community, we may have met with greater success.

We'd gotten our first glimpse at the problem early in the summer when the campaign's revolutionary online fund-raising efforts took off. Immediately thereafter we were asked to test our own fund-raising savvy. Knowing that many students are financially dependent and cash-strapped, we created a fund-raising appeal in sync with a student's budget:

> What better way for students to spend their first summer paycheck than to give it all to the campaign that's going to take back America?
>
> Can't find a job in the Bush recession? Use that money from end-of-the-semester book buyback instead!
>
> Either way, there should be no excuse to not participate in Going for Broke, Students for Dean's financial contribution program. The end of the second fundraising quarter is approaching quickly, and Howard Dean needs to make a strong showing. In order to track student donations, add $.18—18 is to signify the voting age—at the end of your contribution.

Here are some suggestions for how much to contribute:

$25.18 Starving Student
$35.18 Mom Slipped Me $50 for Food
$50.18 Thank Goodness for Financial Aid
$79.18 Average Student Contribution
$100.18 Sold My Bike for Democracy
$150.18 Trust Funds Rock

Join hundreds of students across the country on Wednesday, June 18, to donate to Dean for America. The average student contribution is already an incredible $79, and with your help, we can push this higher. We've already established the largest student network supporting a presidential candidate this election cycle. This is our chance to show the media, the Democratic Party, and the nation that Howard Dean is our generation's candidate.

Make your contribution by visiting www.deanforamerica.com/students4dean.

The fund-raising initiative was a surprising success. One female student from Students for Dean at Penn State University reported that she literally "sold her bike for democracy" and contributed $100. Going forward, though, it was never as simple or as effective. Since all of our students were also on the DFA e-mail list, we had to convince them to give through us instead of DFA. Oftentimes we had no idea that the Internet team would be sending out a fund-raising appeal and would scramble to send out a tailored version to our e-mail list hours later.

In late summer Michael, Ryan, and I began merging our student memberships and redesigning our website. The finished site was attractive and practical—it allowed users to create their chapters automatically; group leaders maintained membership lists and e-mail administration, and were given a new calendar feature to manage events; and the website differed enough from DFA's website to validate our semiautonomous relationship. What we didn't realize at the time was that maintaining our own website forced us to be competitive with DeanForAmerica.com. If young supporters registered as supporters at DFA, they wouldn't join our list and we would lose credibility with the campaign. DFA's frequent publishing and high-speed development set expectations for our online operations. We were expected to have every tool in DFA's repertoire and yet we were also expected to be different. Our supporters clamored for the new tools available through Dean for America. Occasionally we outperformed DFA, which we always celebrated as an enormous success. In early fall, we launched our e-postcard tool, which made it possible for supporters to send photos with customized messages to friends. In less than a week GenDean members had sent more than 10,000 postcards. DFA created an identical tool a few weeks later. Like a grassroots group, we saw the co-opting of our tool by DFA as a sign we'd arrived.

At the end of summer, the team split up as our student interns returned to high school and others, like Ryan, returned to school to finish their studies. Also determined to finish his schooling, Michael returned to D.C., where he worked for the campaign part-time from his American University dorm room. When Michael brought Students for Dean on board in June, the media paid little attention. Just three months later, hundreds of stories had been written about Dean's focus on youth and Michael had become our team's celebrity. CBS Evening News even requested an interview with Michael in his dorm room. Sitting atop his bunk bed in front of a wall of posters, Michael explained why he joined the Dean campaign and why Dean should be the candidate of choice among young people.

## The Fork in the Road

Generation Dean existed as a general organizing and media platform. People signed up because they wanted to generally get involved. On our website they could connect with other supporters by starting or joining their local chapter. They could donate money. They could share ideas and feedback. They could sign petitions, forward e-mails, send out e-postcards, and more. Our chapters were organized mostly by schools, and all were hyperlocal. Our day-to-day work involved talking to local chapter leaders.

Immediately after the Raise the 'Roots tour we were instructed to appoint Gen-Dean state coordinators and begin designing and implementing state-specific get-out-the-vote plans. This radical shift from a flat, media-Internet organization to a hierarchical and centralized organization stressed our capacity, not to mention our knowledge and skills.

Official state campaign operations organized supporters to ID voters by ranking them on a scale of one to five. Campaign staff and volunteers huddled over call sheets in their local offices, calling whole neighborhoods to inquire about their political opinions and favored candidates. Every day the state director reviewed the campaign's progress, noting where in the state its supporters were and in what numbers. At the crux of this operation are data—the ability to store and parse data, the ability to share data for ID calls and get-out-the-vote operations, and the ability to overlay such data with commercial/campaign information. Accustomed to broadly serving our membership, we were unprepared to design and drive specific state plans. We were not set up technically or organizationally to coordinate the minutiae of voter IDs, canvasses, and vote goals. But we tried.

By mid-October we had a network of two dozen state coordinators, mostly from early primary states. Nearly everything we organized offline and online started to be done with, and through, the state coordinators (with the exception of Iowa and New Hampshire). Our state coordinators started being the people talking to local chapter leaders.

At the same time as our workload increased, our staff decreased. Trippi turned his attention to Iowa in early fall and wanted to commit as many resources as possible. As part of the first shipment of campaign staff there, Ginny left to coordinate the Hawkeye State's student efforts. Like Lex, New Hampshire's state GenDean coordinator, Ginny took marching orders from the state staff and no one else, and quickly grew distant from Generation Dean. Our volunteer capacity shrank, too. An increasing number of GenDean state coordinators were hired by the state operations. Because GenDean's field plans and the state's field plans developed independent of each other, there was little room for negotiation and collaboration so late in the game.

Our state coordinators took this in stride, but many remained personally conflicted about abandoning Generation Dean. In many other cases, young voters recruited by our state coordinators were quickly assimilated into state operations and had little sense of being a member of Generation Dean.

From then on we would never be the same. Resource-strapped, we struggled to make do between two distinctly different operations and to meet all of our bosses' needs and demands. State coordination meant staffing rallies, shipping out signs, and working with the advance team to prep for events.[4] Sometimes these could take one person an entire week to do, especially when the event was as far away as Colorado. We were no longer focused on building connections with local volunteer chapters.

## Staying Connected

Back in late August Joe Trippi had sat down with Michael, Ryan, and me to review the website we had slaved over throughout the full summer. The months leading up to this moment were filled with great anticipation, but now we fretted over his reaction. Would it be good enough? Trippi was silent as we showed him the new features and tools. Just when we thought we were done, he pointedly asked us, "Who wrote the mission statement?" Confused, Michael and I both said incredulously, "We did. We all did." "Then sign your names. We're not one of those campaigns that send out generic crap because no one would dare to sign it. If you write something that's worthy of others' reading it, you sign it. That's all. Good job." Trippi got up and left.

We took Trippi's advice to heart, closely reviewing our mission statement a second time and then adding our names one by one. Michael became more liberal about injecting his personality into e-mail text. We listed our e-mails on our bio pages. In early September we created campaign alias instant-messenger screen names for ourselves. I was GenDeanAmanda. Every day countless young supporters would instant-message me, asking quick questions and telling me stories. When it became impossible for me to keep up with my work, I initiated instant-message office hours. We started a Generation Dean blog so that we could have conversations more broadly with our membership and recruited our members, including Ian Hines, an engaged and politically deliberate high school student, to write for it.

Originally we heeded Trippi's advice because we wanted to follow DFA's lead and because we believed in its authenticity. Some wrote to make sure I really existed. "You're Amanda, right? You are a real person?" Soon we came to realize that open communication also opens up conversations about bad leadership. Just days after we profiled our instant-messenger screen names, people began messaging me about their problems. Until then I had heard primarily from group leaders, who oftentimes wrote to tell me about their successes and to share tips with other leaders. One girl told me that her group leader left after a power struggle and refused to turn over the group tools to the new group's leader. Another person messaged me that we wrongly profiled only the largest of Generation Dean groups, like Tony Cani's Arizona group of more than 400. She lived in North Dakota and, regardless of how much time and effort she invested on behalf of the campaign, her group would never swell past 20.

The picture our full membership painted was of an organization that had quickly outgrown itself and never properly scaled its operations to size. When I first started organizing students, I communicated with all of them—members and leaders alike—by e-mail. After we merged with Students for Dean, we merged databases and began defaulting to mass communications. After that our membership swelled to more than 20,000 students and our shrinking staff size made it difficult to keep up. All along we'd assumed things were going well because we didn't know any better; now that members could bypass their leaders and share problems directly with us, we began to realize the quality of leadership varied dramatically across the board and that some of the tools we'd so carefully designed weren't up to par. Although direct communications with our members successfully revealed the problem, there wasn't an easy solution. With little time to remedy the problem before the election, we relayed the problem directly to our membership and began seeking out a middleman solution.

In late October a D.C. supporter named Sean Gunn approached me, telling me, "It could be as simple as educating members about good leadership." I knew he was right and enlisted him to work with me on what I called the Generation Dean Help Desk. Staffed by group leaders, group members, and staffers, the help desk welcomed all new GenDean members and provided them with guides on managing groups and getting press, and information about GenDean. By educating everyone we believed that group members would have more realistic expectations for group leaders and bad group leaders would be forced to improve. In essence, the help desk inverted the power relationship between leaders and members. I was proud of the fact that we'd come up with such a creative yet simple solution but worried over our ability to implement it. Ginny had left for Iowa almost a month ago, and I believed I'd be next.

## Internal Conflict

Situations involving group conflict or confusion occurred frequently, especially in an organization like ours that promoted people's niche affiliations. We were a home for Punx for Dean, an organization started by Kimmy Cash. In just a short time, Cash had proven herself to be an organizing wonder and touted the fact that she managed more than 13,000 volunteers. We were also home to the Young Professionals for Dean, a subbranch that sprouted up almost overnight in multiple U.S. cities. Unlike the Punx, who dropped leaflets all over town and ambushed potential supporters at concerts, the Young Professionals liked to talk politics over happy hour. We were also a home to Chicks for Dean and Snowboarders for Dean, as well as Disney Employees for Dean and American University for Dean.

The truth was, some Punx didn't like the Young Professionals. Some Young Professionals didn't like the Punx. The Young Professionals wanted to fund-raise. The other groups did not. The high school groups felt overlooked. The Law School Students wanted to help the campaign with legal matters, despite the fact that none had taken the bar or completed law school. The College Dems wanted to do things the College Dems way. Big groups wanted big attention. Little groups wanted to be seen as what they were: big fish in little towns. Grassroots groups wanted independence from state-coordinated campaigns. And sometimes, groups wanted to take over the national Generation Dean.

I found out about one coup attempt by e-mail. Unknowingly, someone included on the e-mail chain had copied me in on a related conversation without realizing that I'd scroll down to read about the planned coup. It was planned for March and people had already chosen and agreed upon their titles. It would be just in time for the presidential cycle and would save them effort in case Dean didn't make it that far. I sighed. Some of the people on the list were quite dedicated. I reread the e-mails, looking for criticism of what we'd done. There wasn't anything of the sort, just a very aggressive and positive assertion of power. Some of them were longtime organizers and, from what I understood, this was an issue of entitlement.

Admittedly I was never entirely comfortable with having found myself at the top of an organization by a great deal of luck. Although I couldn't and wouldn't ever claim I'd have been the most likely candidate from the outset, I believed I'd contributed to our effort in significant ways and met the challenge.

I quickly wrote the participants involved, asking them to report to me on their most recent efforts. One by one, I then called them. I brought up the e-mail and asked them what they'd like to see improved. Some had genuine frustrations, which I promptly wrote down and later addressed. Others didn't and I called their bluff. To each, I let them know that they were free to do as they pleased on their own time, but that staying in good standing with the campaign required getting their work done. As we approached Iowa, we'd need them more than ever. As far as I know, they dropped their coup plan, embarrassed by the fact that I'd found them out and, even worse, discovered it had more to do with them than with us.

Group conflicts weren't always so easily resolved. Unknowingly we had designed a website and an organizing platform that lent themselves to special interests' games. With the help of the Internet, group leaders were more apt to share their frustrations and conflicts with me. Some of our members planned on careers in politics and competed ruthlessly for opportunities. Fortunately for us, we could divert our members' attention to Iowa; having a singular, looming goal reunited our membership when we needed it most.

## Website Redesign

"Hi Amanda, this is Sean Gallavan. I'm a member of the D.C. Pride Group and I'm coming to Burlington to help you with the website redesign. Would you call me back?" I listened to the message again, thinking that I missed hearing when Sean would arrive, given the noise in the campaign office. Nope. I picked up the phone and dialed. Sean answered and he sounded really groggy, as if he'd been sleeping. In fact, it sounded like he was standing in the middle of a busy road; his voice was barely audible over the noise.

"Sean, this is Amanda, Generation Dean. I got your message that you're coming up to Vermont. When?" I propped the phone against my shoulder and returned my focus to my computer screen. "Hey, sorry; I'm sleeping at a rest stop in Jersey. I'll be there in about four hours. Will you be there? Did you get my other messages? I left you two other voice mails saying I was coming up." It took me a second to process all this information. I received so many calls that my voice mail frequently built up. I returned as many calls as I could in the evenings, but the truth is that I often fell behind. "Oh! Do you have a place to stay? Wow.... We need help with our website. Guess you could tell, too!" I laughed. Sean answered, "Yeah, I need a place to stay. Will you be there when I get in?" I couldn't believe our luck. We'd been fretting over our website dysfunction for months now and DFA had recently stolen the programmer I'd selected to work with us. My strategy of teaching myself all the basic web skills, like html, helped us keep pace and me to keep face, but didn't suffice for a website redesign. We were bitter over the fact that we couldn't compete with DFA's pay and offer to provide webbies a full team with which to work. Since DFA's priorities always trumped Generation Dean's, I consistently found myself at the end of the campaign's development queue. "I'll stay around until you get in. I'll find you a place to stay in the meantime. I can't wait for you to get here!"

Less than a week after Sean's arrival, a whole posse of DFA programmers and volunteers committed themselves to working on our new website. By then Generation Dean had achieved real credibility inside the campaign and some younger staffers working in other departments felt a real personal allegiance to our mission. Fascinated by the synergies between architecture and behavior, I looked forward to this task more than anything else. With the help of Zack Rosen, the founder of Deanspace and the youngest of Dean's web staff; Justin Pinder, the programmer we had recently lost to DFA; and Hunter Weeks and Josh Caldwell, two Arizona GenDean members whom I had met later in the summer, we quickly set to work. Knowing that our needs had now become a priority for so many was tremendously redeeming.

Within two weeks' time our team finalized plans for our new website. We wanted our new website to represent a form of e-democracy—with architecture like a system of checks and balances on power, including our own authority. The stories told by some of our members about their power-hungry or lazy leaders convinced us that systems permitting lateral and horizontal synergy, collaboration, and exit were the only solution. In many respects, we saw our website as a corrective to the natural imbalances between local organizers and the hungry beast of a national campaign. Fired by adrenaline and relief, we worked around the clock to realize our goal. Everything was on track until I was asked to go to Iowa for the caucus.

## Iowa

The subject line said it all. "Depart for Iowa." I saw it as I scrolled through the e-mails in my inbox from the previous night. My heart dropped and soared. All of the experienced campaign hands told newbies like me that we wouldn't understand campaigns until we'd experienced them from the ground up. "Iowa is where it's at," they'd say. "We'll win or lose this in Iowa, not Burlington." I also felt real allegiance to the members of Generation Dean. I'd worked so hard with my teammates to correct for our failures and ride our successes, and hated to just duck out.

My destination in Iowa was Dubuque, a postindustrial town in the northeast corner of the state. Hit hard by industrial downsizing, downtown Dubuque is a motley collection of well-kept office buildings and boarded-up storefronts. To calm my nerves, I reassured myself that I'd done everything possible to prepare myself for this moment. I'd been in contact with the Dubuque office several times and already acquired a log-in for the state's voter file. I'd also started reading the local newspaper.

The mood in the Dubuque campaign office was impossible to miss. People were tired. People were frustrated. The Kerry campaign, they said, had been in full swing and had recruited nearly all the Catholics and teachers right out from underneath them. Edwards was everyone's second favorite. No matter what was done, people couldn't be convinced of Dean. "Would Dean visit soon?" they all asked me. "I don't know," I replied. "Aren't you from the national HQ? Shouldn't you know?" was the most frequent retort. What was the value of being sent a national staffer, they thought, if the national staffer couldn't divulge the information they really needed? At one point, my friend Joe called from Burlington. "You arrived yet?" he asked. "Yup, I'm here." "What about getting us a blog post? People want to see what's going on. Could you do that?" I turned my head away from the phone and repeated the request to the people in front of me. It was met with blank stares. "I've got to ID voters." "I've got to help the in-house volunteers." "What about? We haven't done anything special today." That's when I knew that I'd spend the next few weeks unlearning and learning everything I thought I knew about campaigns.

The first lesson started with a simple phone bank. All I had to do was call people and inquire about their political position. If they were open to Dean, I needed to try to convince them. "Why should I vote for Dean? Tell me exactly why I should vote for Dean." the man at the other end of the line demanded of me the first night. I was the third person calling him and he wanted answers. "Because he opposed the war in Iraq from the get-go." My mind began to waver. For months I'd drafted content for our organizers explaining why Dean was THE candidate. The truth was, however, that I'd only had experience with supporters because it's supporters who visit your website. What we—online organizers—didn't experience was the tremendous courage and power it took for all of our supporters to stand out in public and bare their political souls to passersby. I wished I'd gone out in the field earlier in the year.

Several days later, I panicked. I didn't see any possible way of winning Dubuque for Dean. I'd scoured the voter file sheets instead of running up and down the town's hill to campus to organize students like I was supposed to. There weren't enough 3s to convert to 4s, not enough 4s to be counted on, and not enough 5s to help find 4s and 3s. Everyone else seemed to know it, too. They viewed any word of upcoming Dean visits as a chance to give hardworking volunteers the thank-you and goodbye they deserved. In a moment of real angst, I called the state HQ several times in a row, adamantly requesting that senior help be sent to the area or that I be sent somewhere else in the state. Several days later I received a call telling me that two volunteers who happened to be senior political operatives would arrive shortly in Dubuque. What a relief.

Carl Wagner and Tick Segerblom came the next day. Within hours, everything began to change. What I didn't know at the time is that I'd been blessed with an opportunity to work with two extremely accomplished organizers. Over the next few weeks I would learn as much from Carl about organizing as I'd learned during the entire Dean campaign.

Carl, ever curious about the Dean campaign's Internet operation, frequently demanded of me, "Can you use the Internet to get people to vote?" Almost as if I'd been slapped while sleeping, I stood still and quiet the first time he asked me and set my mind to work. The people on our website were identified Dean supporters, the types of people motivated to organize. We shared with them information about registering to vote, including their state's rules and links to important information. I hadn't had consistent access to the Internet since getting to Iowa, but I remembered that DFA had requested that our Iowa supporters confirm they would vote by e-mail. Still, I knew this wasn't an adequate answer to Carl's question. Were these people voting because of the Internet? What about the people who weren't members of Dean's online operation? Could the Internet be used to get them to the polls? We were sharing information with people about voting locations, hoping that they'd distribute the information in their areas. In this case, the Internet was one step removed; we were using it to organize people who would organize others to vote. I was stumped. The crazy thing, I realized, is that while we successfully raised a ton of money, generated tons of attention in the form of free press, and connected supporters nationwide, the Internet campaign didn't have a functioning solution to what seemed like the simplest and most obvious of questions. Over the course of those next few weeks, I kept thinking about Carl's question. No answer I gave myself or Carl was ever satisfactory enough. Just when I was about to give up, Carl asked me, "Where are the online Iowa supporters?" Yet another question that I didn't have an answer to.

When he first got to work, Carl met with all the office's organizers, asking pointed questions about the area's grassroots efforts and supporters. Over lunch his first day I described to Carl what I'd felt from the town, pointing out the numbers and the ways volunteers and staffers carried themselves. Carl nodded his head and shared with me the information he'd been given from state HQ. It was true: Dubuque was in bad shape. They'd counted on winning this part of the state, but now it looked like an impossibility.

By the next day, Carl and Tick had a plan. We needed to air out the town's organizing operation and give it new life and vitality. At times like these, Carl said, we shouldn't disperse. We needed to bring people together, identify shared solutions, and then get to work. It was going to take, he said, an aptitude for motivation and celebration. Transforming our operation required a new office space where people could congregate in larger groups. It was my responsibility to find it. "Huh," I remember thinking. This task wasn't exactly what I'd expected.

Five minutes later I'd found one. The campaign had rented an office down the road for our out-of-state volunteers and it wasn't being used. The space was a former sporting goods store that had gone out of business. The most charming feature was the stuffed animals in the window, some of which we ended up decorating with Dean paraphernalia.

Every night Carl invited people from town, like teachers and other educators, to sit down and talk. He would ask them how they thought their peers would vote and then construct a simple plan for identifying others who supported Dean. To someone who had primarily organized online, Carl's work was new to me. I watched countless people—many of whom came in looking like they just wanted to do a good deed to assuage their conscience before heading home for dinner with the kids—sit up in their chairs, reinvigorated with ideas and energy. With each group, it was important to plan, to follow up, to revise the plan if necessary, and to track progress. It was a work in progress, a continual feedback loop that perpetuated itself. I enjoyed its dynamic simplicity and reveled in my newfound human connections. I'd gotten used to thinking about things in terms of open rates, click-through rates, and sign-ups.

By the end of the week, we'd met enough people to have a party. I went out with volunteers and got decorations for the space, and spent the latter part of the afternoon blowing up balloons, recruiting people to make signs, and hanging streamers. That night, people milled around, excitedly talking to each other about their experiences on the Dean campaign and revving up for the election. They were all nervous like me, I could tell, but there was no other place people wanted to be that night. This, I remember thinking, is chemistry. The party couldn't have been better timed or planned. It made me realize that in order for people to successfully bring others into the campaign, they need to have a good experience inside the campaign first.

Generation Dean had shared successes with people through the Internet. Sometimes, it had been a quick blog post from Trippi. Other times, we had sent out e-mails, written blog posts, and featured the best work of supporters, but no time I could remember had ever felt like this. In fact, I wasn't sure how we could have achieved such a gathering. Would it have to take place in something like a virtual world? Where people could synchronously stand next to each other, stare each other in the face, and grin ear to ear? Would we toast each other with virtual wine glasses? Would that be enough? No, but we could use the Internet to organize get-togethers in our local communities and that is of tremendous value. Suddenly I understood the real magic of Meetups, these synchronous get-togethers among strangers at their local bars and coffee shops. "Chemistry," I kept repeating to myself before going to sleep. "This is all about chemistry."

Despite our best efforts, we lost Iowa. Dubuque, reported to be the worst county in Iowa for Dean, moved up to above average on Election Day. Devastated by our loss but motivated by the immense outpouring of passion and discipline and astounded by the success of our local operation, I was comforted by having done my best. I said goodbye to everyone I had met and began the long drive back to Vermont.

When I finally pulled into the parking lot at DFA, I expected the building to be falling down, imagining that DFA was a bit like the *Titanic*. Lights glared from the windows and I could see people trekking back and forth in the hallways. I wouldn't know for sure until I got back inside, so I parked and walked in.

## Aftermath

When I walked into the office, I noticed that almost everyone had their eyes glued to our few televisions. I had never seen this before. Usually people were staring down their computer screens, charging between rooms on an errand, meeting in our empty hallway spaces, or peering over everyone's head in search of an important someone. I heard a strange sound and looked up. The television showed Dean gesticulating and then, after taking in a deep breath, letting out a "yawlll." The commentator pointed this out to viewers as "the Dean scream." I looked around the room. No one looked surprised. They looked disgusted. "When did this happen?" I asked the person next to me. "Election night in Iowa." I looked back to the TV. The program replayed it again. Not thinking that much of it, though, I moved on.

The office looked grayer than I remembered and oddly small; I'd gotten used to ducking streamers and stepping on balloons while winding through crowds of volunteers. There were lots of wires and cables everywhere. I hadn't used a computer consistently since I left. And it looked drab and corporate.

When people asked me about my time in Iowa, I told them about chemistry, about witnessing people coming together and celebrating their shared visions. Once, someone interrupted me, telling me, "The election was all rigged. This is about the media attacking an insurgent. We were misrepresented." Immediately, I came to life. "No, the operation in Iowa wasn't strong. We got beat at our own game."

At the same time, I sympathized with everyone who stayed in our Vermont HQ. I was lucky to have seen things as they were so that I didn't have to overcome my own disbelief. Winning the hearts and minds of people is hard work, I'd realized. It wasn't nearly as straightforward as I'd believed it to be while working in HQ. During my long cross-country trek I'd made peace with our loss. What I couldn't come to terms with, though, was my uneasiness with how the campaign had depicted a sure win in Iowa. What is more, I couldn't make sense of the undue reverence for the media, for money, and for glamour when, in the end, none of that seemed to pull through.

I went out to New Hampshire and worked with our state coordinator, Lex. On Election Day I ran around a school, directing people to vans waiting to take them to their voting locations.

When I returned to Burlington I found the moment I'd waited for—Sean had finally finished our new website. I ran to my computer, hitting Refresh, Refresh, Refresh, until the site appeared. I scrolled down through the pages, admiring the smoothness of the functionality and the elegant text.

The site permitted users and groups to sync up so that they could collaborate and share tools and resources. Grassroots groups that joined the campaign would receive campaign communications directly, like a blog post from the state coordinator. The state coordinators could e-mail groups, and their personal calendars depicted all events

created by individuals and groups who had opted into the campaign. We would offer group leaders the tools they'd requested—a blog, a calendar, additional resources,
guides, e-mail, and different user permissions. We also designed what we termed our
"killer app"—a website-accessible voter file. All individuals and groups could load
contacts into the system and tag them with important information, such as whether
or not they were Dean supporters, their addresses, and their affiliations. Only the
contact, the group leader, and our national team had access to these data directly. The
Generation Dean homepage would also feature a calendar, a blog, tools like e-cards,
and a resource center. All of these features would be populated by content produced
by groups and individuals synced up with the national campaign.

But the admiration was bittersweet—the election was basically over. And we'd become
erratic online organizers. We had stopped using e-mail to communicate to our list and had
overrelied on our blog while Michael and I had been in Iowa. Instead of spending time
devising creative content, we had talked with state coordinators about their plans.

Did we fail because we overreached ourselves? Or did we fail because we couldn't
plan for what we didn't know was ahead? The lessons learned with our website were
hard for me to swallow. I realized that regular communication with your membership
is absolutely essential, no matter what the cost. Assuming that information will trickle
down through multiple layers of leadership is dangerous. I also realized the hard way
that we hadn't entirely fulfilled our roles and responsibilities.

As I mulled over our next steps, the campaign's vibe changed once again. By then,
we'd all become astute at sensing internal changes. Dean announced a meeting at
which Trippi declared his departure. After Trippi left, the campaign's administrators
also announced a series of staff cuts. A few days later, I learned I was on the cut list.

I packed up my things, said my goodbyes, and called Mike, the same friend who
had told me to join the campaign. "Can I stay with you in D.C.? I want to help out
the Democratic nominee, no matter who it is." Monday I was in Washington, D.C.,
with $250 to my name and a credit card. Six weeks later, I took my place on John
Kerry's Internet team, along with Zack Exley, the Moveon consultant to the Dean
campaign, and other survivors of the primary season.

It only took me a short while to realize just how special the Dean campaign had
been. As one of the first Dean staffers hired on to the Kerry campaign, I was called
on to answer any and every question about the Dean campaign. To people's curious
questions about how the Dean campaign would approach a problem, I disappointed
them by saying there wasn't any one answer. I'd spent the whole time trying to adapt
to the Dean campaign, which, in retrospect, had been adapting to the new terrain of
technology and tools it had been afforded almost by chance. The questions presented
to us by the technology, the grassroots, and our accessibility to innovation and change
taught us very valuable lessons, many of which we'd come to realize over time and
through conflict or chance. With the help of the Internet, small-dollar donations can
be contributed and processed at little cost and consequently regular people can be
stakeholders. The Internet makes innovation accessible, even when it occurs at the
edges. Campaigns can talent-scout discoveries, tools, and people online, making it
easier to influence the party. For the first time, the campaign and party could hold an

ongoing conversation with its base using communications tools like blogs, e-mail, and web TV. Campaign communications are no longer available to only select listeners. The Dean campaign didn't necessarily invent these developments, but it demonstrated their potential to the public at large.

As for me, I'd survived a hell of a ride with a man I'd always known as my governor, and I'd come into my own. Politics was no longer abstract. I'd pushed myself far beyond my comfort zone and my home, sometimes putting up with the greatest resistance from my Burlington friends and neighbors who didn't know what to make of Dean's personal changes or mine. Better yet, I realized that I, too, could make a difference.

## Notes

1. Not to be confused with Nicco Mele, who arrived in May.

2. Steve Davis, Larry Elin, and Grant Reeher, *Click on Democracy: The Internet's Power to Change Political Apathy into Civic Action* (Boulder, CO: Westview Press, 2002).

3. Yoni opted not to come and instead accepted a job on the New Hampshire field staff.

4. In political operations, the "advance" team plans and advertises public speaking engagements for a candidate.

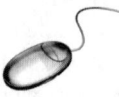

# 12

# Fund-Raising

## *Hitting Home Runs on and off the Internet*

### *Larry Biddle*

*Larry Biddle, deputy finance director for the Dean campaign, came from a nonprofit general fundraising background and provides a look at the campaign from the point of view of an experienced and relatively traditional campaigner. He tells his story of entering the wild new world of Joe Trippi and e-mail fund-raising. He also tells the history of his most famous creation—the Dean fund-raising bat—and the lessons he learned and applied in later campaigns. Wired magazine once referred to him as "the arbiter of the new hotness," about which Biddle comments, "Not bad for a guy in his sixties." He is principal of PlanningWorks, helping citizen-sector organizations develop interactive technology strategies.*

For me, it all started with a postcard.

It was March 2003 in Burlington. Even though it was spring, the air was still wintry cold. And I hated the cold.

Inside the already small office space, the Dean for America Internet operation was housed literally in a closet—the genesis of a campaign staff determined to make the best of everything. Bobby Clark was the all-around Internet guy and I was the Internet fund-raising guy.

We were at the end of our first Federal Election Commission reporting quarter, and I knew our FEC report would be regarded as a critical barometer of the Dean campaign's financial health. Howard Dean was an unknown governor from Vermont with little chance of making it through to the end: That was the conventional wisdom inside the Washington, D.C., beltway. So far we'd raised most of our funds through close friends of Dean's, loyal Vermonters, and a few thousand online donors (mostly antiwar advocates). I wanted to boost their donations for our first quarter with a different kind of e-mail solicitation, but I wasn't sure what—and I hadn't had much experience with Internet fund-raising.

I decided to make it personal—an e-mail message designed to look like a postcard, sent to everyone on our list from their new friend, Governor Howard Dean. You know, the kind of postcard people send while on vacation with a picture showing the wonders of where they were and a "wishing you were here" sentiment. We were wishing we could get Howard Dean *there*—to the White House, where we could pick out our West Wing offices. (We watched a lot of *West Wing* in those days.)

The postcard had to contain a refreshing message that would motivate people to give money. I don't remember the exact words, but I do remember the highlight: I said we needed to raise $48,326 to make our goal. Everyone wanted to know how I came up with that number. Well, I sort of made it up—it was close to, but not quite, our total goal. Most fund-raisers would have used the number $48,000—they tend to dumb down goals to round, easy numbers. For me, that line of attack wasn't going to be as believable as an odd amount.

I hadn't seen anything like the postcard used before in political e-mail, and I worried that our online constituents would view it as a gimmick, not as a fund-raising "opportunity." So we included the standard fund-raising progress thermometer, with the familiar red filler indicating how much had been raised along the way. It was the only traditional item on the postcard, but I thought users needed something that would be quickly understood. Then I decided—unaware at the time that this was a best practice—to send the e-mail to the same list three times, each time adjusting the thermometer as the e-mails yielded more money for the Dean campaign.

And it worked. That postcard raised a *lot* more than $48,326.

I was delighted it was so successful. It definitely raised my stock among the small Internet staff; up until that point, they hadn't been quite sure I knew what I was doing. Keep it simple, specific, and a little surprising, and target what the donor is thinking—from that postcard on, those were rules we followed and refined throughout the crazy roller-coaster ride the Dean Internet fund-raising campaign would become.

## How I Got to Burlington

I will only raise money taking the donor's point of view.

I am all about "protecting" the donor by making a case for giving that is transparent and truthful. That had been my philosophy throughout more than thirty years of nonprofit fund-raising, primarily in the small-dollar arena. Though I could reluctantly work the society niche, sending flowers on big donors' birthdays and such, that wasn't my comfort zone. I come from the masses, think like them, and respect their right to understand how and why their financial support is making a difference.

Also, I am as tenacious as they come. I will work doggedly to make a goal.

Tenacity came in handy when I made the leap into the political world. It all started when a fellow board member of a Philadelphia charity asked if I knew of a fund-raiser who could be finance director for an upcoming U.S. Senate primary campaign—that of Pennsylvania state senator Allyson Schwartz, who was running for the Democratic nomination in the 2000 cycle.

I stayed up all night thinking about this new opportunity. My family had been involved with Delaware politics as far back as I could remember. My mother would take me to the polls where she worked as a watcher. I would play around the voting machines. My brother was appointed Delaware's assistant secretary of state. I knew how to raise money—more than $300 million, mostly working with nonprofits. So I called back and said I knew of someone who was interested in Allyson's finance director position—me.

The challenge for me was how to raise money for political campaigns. I needed a model. Through a friend, I had met Ellen Malcolm, president of the powerful political action committee EMILY's List, which works to elect pro-choice Democratic women on the federal level. I heard they had an upcoming fund-raising training course. I called and asked if I could attend.

I was the oldest person in the class, which felt like a boot camp run by nuns—all geared toward shaping up naive idealists for the political big time. In three days and most of two nights, my team put together a mock campaign finance plan that won "best in show."

The two major tenets of the EMILY's List training are these: (1) Understand that there are four basic target groups in every campaign, starting with the easiest to attract—the candidate's friends and family—and continuing up to the last group "in" just before election day, those waiting to be as sure as possible the candidate is likely to win; (2) build a *detailed* spreadsheet for each target group, and a projection of how much they will give and when. The end result is a complete political finance campaign plan—very time-consuming, yet indispensable. During a campaign, the actual results substitute for the projected goal, so the plan changes frequently—daily during the final days before an election.

Drawing on knowledge I gained in the training and my own prior experience, I created a model for Allyson's campaign, raising a record amount for a Democratic primary candidate in Pennsylvania. Though she didn't win the primary (a temporary setback—she's now a U.S. congressperson), the fund-raising success helped me win the job of finance director for Chellie Pingree's campaign for U.S. Senate in Maine for 2002.

That's when I had my first brush with Internet fund-raising. Chellie's daughter, Hannah Pingree, was on staff, and had worked during the 2000 election cycle as a political producer at iVillage. I learned a lot from her. In addition to Chellie's daily fund-raising calls, Hannah's events, and my direct mail and telemarketing, we sent e-mail updates to our small group of online constituents, and raised some money that way. As one of the first major Senate campaigns to make it possible for donors to give via the candidate's website, it was only modestly successful. That's because credit card users hadn't yet reached a sufficient trust level about giving their numbers over the Internet.

From there, it was on to Burlington. Rick Ridder, campaign manager at the time, hired me in February 2003, on the recommendation of Stephanie Schriock, Dean's national finance director. I had met Dean when he came to a Pingree fund-raiser at Tom and Kate Chappell's home in Maine. (Not until Dean left and they'd given him a host "goodie" bag did he realize Tom was *the* Tom's of Maine guy. That was a detail his staff hadn't shared with him.)

I liked Howard Dean immediately. I wasn't sure he was presidential timber, but I liked his frankness and approachability. I also knew he had signed a Vermont bill allowing gay and lesbian couples civil union status. For me that was a good indication that Governor Dean was on the right side of my political spectrum. In the back of my mind, I thought perhaps my longtime partner and I could get "civil unionized" as well. (Several months later, we did just that—with Howard's signature on our c.u. certificate.)

From the beginning, I knew what I wanted the Internet to do: Give people the opportunity to get to know and care about Howard Dean and his political positions, and to support him financially. I remembered from reading Peter Drucker (known as the father of American management) that the business of business was to create and maintain a customer. I had already translated that to the nonprofit fund-raising world: The business of nonprofits was to create and maintain a constituency. Now I realized that the same model could be applied to a political campaign; the Internet offered a means of engaging a campaign constituency so that many of them would support it financially.

Ensconced in the Howard Dean Internet closet, Bobby and I were trying to make something work better than it ever had before—with barely a notion of what had preceded us. We struggled each day to invent stuff and make it look and feel like something that our online users had never seen but would attract their loyalty. It was a prescient, if humble, beginning to a campaign whose leaders would eventually be acclaimed for their groundbreaking use of the Internet.

## Secrets of the Republicans

I joined the Dean finance staff as deputy national finance director on February 2, 2003—hired, as I mentioned, by Stephanie Schriock, who'd met me when I worked on the Pingree campaign. As national finance director, Stephanie was the mastermind behind the campaign's record $50 million. She hasn't gotten enough recognition for that momentous accomplishment. She hired a scrappy staff of fund-raisers, built a coordinated productive team, integrated the work of raising money within the Internet phenomenon, managed us through the good times and the hard times, protected us from the vagaries of campaign pandemonium, and provided solid leadership on the campaign management team. All of the finance staff loved working with her—this amazingly talented, thirtysomething woman. Maybe that's why she didn't get the recognition she deserves—she's staggeringly successful, but she's a woman. That happens a lot in politics.

I was happy that Stephanie also hired Linnea Dyer as the deputy national finance director responsible for major gifts and events. I am terrible at special events. My job was to raise Dean money from direct mail, telemarketing, and, in the beginning, whatever possible through the Internet.

My primary responsibility at first was direct mail. I knew just whom to call: Katie Cook, a direct marketing consultant I'd worked with in the nonprofit sector.

But the call had to be clandestine. Though Katie is a Democrat, she was working as a partner in a well-known political direct marketing firm that had several conservative Republican political candidates or advocacy clients. I thought she could give me, on the sly, some advice that would get me successfully started in my work with Dean. Then, at breakfast, she told me that she had had a disagreement with her business partner and was now opening up her own direct marketing business, Direct Line Politics. Holy fund-raising! I knew we could make the sun shine even in the dark of Vermont—and even among Democrats. They were notoriously bad at direct-mail fund-raising, but with Katie's knowledge of successful Republican techniques I was sure we would be "golden." Nothing would make me happier than to raise lots of small-dollar donations for the Dean campaign.

The campaign hired Direct Line Politics as its direct-mail consultant, and we put together a direct-mail plan for raising more money than EMILY's List would have ever thought possible.

I am sure many staffers at EMILY's List still don't believe we raised $10 million for Dean for America at an overhead cost of less than 35 percent. As much as the EMILY's List political fund-raising model is essential to follow, their direct-mail section (it may be different now) was underwhelming at the time.

At first, with any new direct-mail effort, expenses will exceed revenue. The one-time cost of renting mailing lists is then balanced by reuse of lists that prove successful, and a practical direct-mail program can reduce expenses to 45 percent to 65 percent of gross revenue. The Dean campaign, however, did better than that: Our direct-mail campaign ended up with a 35 percent overhead price tag.

One way in which I tried to save money was to integrate direct-mail and Internet opportunities, providing direct-mail donors the option to make their gifts online. This would, I hoped, increase response rates and decrease the direct-mail expense ratio. (It costs only about $.07 to raise every dollar online, about 90 percent less than the cost of direct mail, according to a recent study in *Wired* magazine.)[1] We tracked online donations to specific direct-mail packages so that we knew what was working and what wasn't, and transferred 15 percent of our donor list to online; we were then able to drop those donors from the direct-mail solicitation list to save money. Had we had more time to test this transfer paradigm, I am confident we would have been able to convert much more than 15 percent to online donors.

In another experiment in cost efficiency, we took the longer direct-mail content and edited it down to a very short e-mail (always "above the fold" so viewers didn't have to scroll down the page to read the full text). My intention was to snail-mail to those constituents who responded to the mailings, and to e-mail those who responded online. We didn't really perfect that model, though; frankly, saving money became less of a priority as the campaign went on.

And here's one story that explains why. In August 2003 I dropped 250,000 prospecting pieces of direct mail. That usually means spending sleepless nights hoping that all the money will lead to good results. But a few days after the mailing, just before the mail was to arrive in homes, Joe Trippi, the new campaign manager, shocked me with the news that Howard Dean's picture was going to be on the cover of three—*three*—major national magazines over the next week. I'll never forget that moment. Talk about momentum—this was way mo' momentum than I could have ever expected. I was ecstatic.

The fund-raising results were great; we more than covered the expense. Which goes to show you that the surest way to raise a lot of money in a presidential campaign is to have a candidate people adore.

## Trippi's Big Idea

The Dean Internet phenomenon kicked into high gear when Joe Trippi was hired as campaign manager to replace Rick Ritter in April 2003. Trippi couldn't have been more different than Rick. Rick hired me and I could talk with him and he believed in me. Trippi talked to himself and extolled us to "'get it'—his way" on the Internet and beyond. Neither Howard nor Trippi ever understood direct mail, but Stephanie did and that was enough for me. Trippi's Internet scheme was right, but he was not a great manager of staff. Regardless of his shortcomings, Joe's vision grew to positively pervade the campaign. He saw the power of building an online community of individuals who believed in and would act locally in support of Howard Dean. He believed the staff could create opportunities for grassroots individuals to take our country back. Joe emblazoned in our minds—after many meetings of his saying, "Don't you get it yet"—the power of the ripple effect. He repeatedly talked about how a stone dropped in the water would move out to include more and more surface and include more and more people, and on and on. He anticipated the whole word-of-mouth/viral phenomenon that would later become the major currency of this Internet campaign.

It became all about grassroots organizing. We had to build a community of grassroots individuals, and let them lead us to more people like them. I had to try to understand and keep up with what was successful on the Internet, this new organic growth model, and turn it into donations. A wicked good idea, that ripple effect.

Thankfully, I was never in charge of the so-called Internet strategy (there was never a plan or anyone really in charge) but rather a colleague in its implementation. The campaign felt more out of control than most, as Trippi hired more and more staff—developers, more bloggers, a webmaster—without considering what their particular roles were. I just tried to keep up with what was going on, and keep the fund-raising e-mails productive.

I thought it was important to create some synergy between direct mail and the Internet fund-raising appeals. At first it was relatively easy for me to maintain a connection between direct-mail and e-mail content, but as more and more staff began to feel territorial about writing e-mails it got harder and harder for us to maintain what we knew was good fund-raising text.

Trippi brought on Zack Exley, who had worked at Moveon.org, to help us devise better methods of connecting the Dean campaign online action center with Meetup, a tool we had been using since February. He persuaded us to use Moveon.com's successful fund-raising e-mail format—paragraph, donation link, paragraph, donation link, and closing with a final link at the bottom. It worked well, and now it's an industry standard for good e-mails: short, with text that reads more like an advertisement than a letter.

Direct mail and e-mail are all about urgency in their appeal for funds. E-mails, however, must be short, and direct mail long. (The most productive fund-raising letter was seven—that's right, seven—pages long.) Online requires a direct line of attack, a quick read and reiteration of the need two or three times—usually in less than 100 words. The average bloke looks at an e-mail for 20 to 30 seconds and then decides what to do. Direct-mail donors love long, interesting stories. Online donors give an average of $100, and direct-mail donors give more like $25.

Although it's easy to find a list of direct-mail donors to rent, you'd best not "rent" online lists; recipients will invariably regard your e-missives as spam. I rented one e-mail list during the Dean campaign and we got so busted, I was thankful it was a small list. It was a damn scary moment. I was sure I had ruined a good thing. But as we realized throughout the campaign, Deaniacs were very forgiving.

## Only Connect

The exponential growth of the Dean e-mail list to more then 600,000 addresses presented major technical problems, and managing it for quick response was a challenge. Amazing people came up with solutions on the fly. From the fund-raising side, the system worked very well. We could move information to our e-mail list in timely fashion and connect solicitations with timely and specific campaign activities or expenses needing support—usually within twelve hours.

It is essential for many in the political or nonprofit fund-raising fields to understand that online giving has changed. I lived through a time when an institution or candidate could just ask for money for general purposes. I tell everyone who will listen now that the days of general institutional giving are over; online givers want to financially support specific actions.

The key is targeting the need with what the user values. Over time, that's possible to execute online. It's pay-as-you-go fund-raising; for example, we were amazed at how much we raised from online donors when we asked them to help us buy water and provide transportation for field volunteers walking and knocking on doors in New Hampshire.

I was interested in trying to connect direct-mail donations to what I thought our Internet community wanted. In addition to connecting direct-mail packages with the option to make credit card donations online, we asked online contributors to give monthly, using an auto-responder page they would see after making a onetime contribution. This was only modestly successful; it could be that this technique works best for online fund-raising efforts that last longer than most campaigns do.

We tried other ways to get people to donate online. Linnea Dyer asked us to create the option for those attending her events to respond through the website, with all donations tracked to particular events. We did that. Then Bobby Clark developed TeamRaiser® pages, on which people could set goals to raise money using their own e-mail lists. They could create their own content on personal pages within the website—most often telling friends and family why they supported Howard Dean and asking them to do the same. The pages could also include pictures. I think the cutest was a picture of a TeamRaiser's baby, with text about making sure this child lived in a good country without federal debt. The TeamRaiser pages were amazingly popular, giving the campaign's supporters a real sense of accomplishment. Although I don't know how much they raised (after the campaign ended, our technical team wiped our computers of all campaign data and content), I am sure it totaled several hundred thousand dollars.

It's important to recognize that most online activists don't usually give money. In the Dean campaign, only about 10 percent did, though more than half of them contributed two or three times.[2] One technique I devised, though, did turn activists into donors.

Near the end of the campaign hundreds of thousands of people were doing needed grassroots organizing on their own, with the campaign supplying the materials, direction, and messages but not much else. I wanted to devise a way to test whether we could make these non-donor activists donors. With the genius of our database developers, a file was created of superactive (more than one volunteer activity) Dean online constituents. In addition to contact information, the data included a detailed report of what actions each had taken. I sent the file to our telemarketing vendor, the Share Group. The script opened with a congratulatory message acknowledging the work the activists were doing or had done for the Dean campaign. Then, after a short discussion of the importance and value of that work, the telemarketers asked them to make a contribution to support the campaign expenses related to their accomplishments. The result: More than 30 percent of these activists became donors, averaging $100.

For me, the experiment proved that people are more likely to support activities they are engaged in and value. (I recently learned that Oxfam now uses this technique.) Another lesson for then and now: Online giving occurs only after people perceive value. Asking people for money before they perceive value is useless. Often, organizations create websites that are nothing more than "brochure-ware"; their sites don't provide an opportunity for two-way discussion and activism, and the fund-raising results are accordingly disappointing.

## Online/Offline

Happy marriages of online and offline continued to develop—chief among them the Dean fund-raising house parties (not to be confused with Meetups). These were the sole vision, creation, and management of staff member David Salie (now of Party2Win. com). The parties got off to a very slow start, but David was amazingly tenacious, ending up with 3,500 volunteer leaders scattered throughout all 50 states. Those leaders would in turn recruit and train local house party hosts in their state. "National House Party

Day" was held monthly, with Howard Dean calling in for a fifteen-minute conference call that reached every party across the country. There was usually someone important to introduce Howard—including Al and Tipper Gore.

The parties reflected the power of the campaign's get-local/self-organizing ethos, made possible using Internet technology and resources. For the fund-raising house parties, David created a downloadable instruction kit for hosts. He held conference calls before house party night with hosts to make sure that everything was done right, that parties were productive (raising money and recruiting volunteers) and meaningful for participants. Fund-raising house parties raised $2 million, with more than 80,000 participants. On one night in September 2003, David had more than 3,000 separate phone lines participating in a single conference call; we entered the call into consideration for a *Guinness* world record.

Another person on staff, Murshed Zaheed, contributed mightily to the integration of the Internet and finance operations. Murshed created, organized, and managed Forum for America. It was an information exchange of peer-to-peer groups focusing on fund-raising and organizing experiences. Murshed organized a network of 8,000 registered forum users, and expanded the use of this forum on various topics defined by users.

## Nicco, Trippi, The Bat

Joe Trippi was inarguably the Internet genius of the campaign. But he needed a team of people to take those ideas and make them work. (One of my favorite affirmations is "Sooner or later every good idea deteriorates into work.")

So clearly one of the best decisions Trippi made was to hire Nicco Mele, webmaster. He is an amazing human being and, I learned over time, one of the most creative, inventive web designers around. The maestro of the Dean Internet operation, he made most of the new ideas work online, as rapidly as possible turning them into user-friendly and workable functions.

June was sort of a tipping point for the campaign. National attention was coming our way, more and more people were on the Dean for America Internet list, and we were successfully raising money—people were becoming an enthusiastic engaged constituency.

It was also, finally, getting close to summer, and we had just moved out of the Internet closet into the light of day: an entire floor of an office building with lots of windows. (A floor above us was the local office of UBS, whose Republican bankers always looked with disdain at the sometimes grubby lefties with whom they had to share an elevator.) Though the weather was still not what you'd call warm, the sun was staying up longer each day. And it was baseball season, with the Red Sox not that far away.

So, in a seasonal celebration of our shift toward national victory, I had started running around the office (this was before it was populated by a cast of hundreds) swinging an imaginary bat. I was hitting "home runs" because the campaign was hitting home runs.

As creative comrades, Nicco and I were trying to come up with new ways to raise funds online. Since another FEC filing deadline was coming up at the end of June, we needed a big fund-raising goal—another way to spread the passion and capture the audaciousness our website was beginning to take on.

Obsessed with our ostensible home runs, Nicco and I came up with the idea of setting up a baseball playing field on the DFA homepage with a cartoon-like picture of Howard Dean at bat. I saw the bat as representing the power, as in our campaign slogan, "You've got the power." As people gave us more money—more "power"—and we progressed toward our goal, the cartoon picture would move around the bases. It was a little hokey, and perhaps too abstract, but Nicco and I thought it might work. It was at least fun and would get people's attention in a new way. It worked as we had planned. As people gave money, Howard moved toward home base and the donors gave him a "home run."

I wanted to add some kind of fund-raising thermometer—but instead of the traditional icon, I suggested we use the image of a vertical bat.

Nicco loved the idea; he designed it and made it workable in a matter of days. (I think the other major innovation that DFA brought to online politics was the speed with which things made it onto our website. I tell my clients now that a good website is like a daily newspaper, only better. If you're not keeping the site current, forget getting users to come back.)

Again and again, we would put up the bat as we set a new goal to raise online support—soon without the baseball field. When we made the goal, the top of the bat would explode. Several times we continued to raise money even *after* it exploded, just changing the to-date totals during the day by checking the website dashboard and giving the latest data to the web team.

We never imagined the bat would become an icon for the Dean campaign. Between online solicitations, we'd take the bat off the site, sometimes for several weeks. I remember Zephyr Teachout coming to my office telling me that blog posters were calling to "bring the bat back." I knew we had stumbled on a great inspiration.

Having worked in several political campaigns, however, I was also a little worried that opponents, or the Republicans when Dean was moving up the electable scale, or *someone* would put something out that implied that the candidate was "batty."

Which brings us to the so-called Dean scream.

Stephanie Schriock and I were watching a TV monitor after the big loss in the Iowa primary. I was standing in front of Stephanie closest to the monitor when we heard the "I have a scream speech," as it came to be called. I heard his increasingly manic yelling and turned to look at Stephanie. I said, "What was that?" She replied, "The end, I am afraid."

I felt so terrible for so many people, mostly Howard Dean and his vast network of supporters. We heard the replay so many times it became excruciating. As I understand it, Dean was given the wrong microphone as he was going on stage. He thought it was for the auditorium public address system. The crowd was wildly loud. He yelled in an effort to try to be heard. But the microphone was for TV broadcast—a tragic mistake by someone.

## After Dean: Testing the Innovations in Florida

The Dean campaign ended too soon, but the success of our Internet fund-raising efforts was a lasting achievement. I remember thinking how important it would be to replicate that success in a statewide effort; otherwise, I was sure people would say we'd been successful only because we had the numbers and the attention that came with a presidential run. I was sure that wasn't the case. And soon after the campaign, I got a chance to test my theory when I received a call from Deborah Reed, manager of Betty Castor's campaign for U.S. Senate in Florida in 2004. She had managed Chellie Pingree's campaign as well, and had hired me as Chellie's finance director. As Deborah's deputy campaign manager and with Betty's support for the Internet, it became possible for me to apply Dean lessons in Florida. I was fortunate to have Karin Roland as our webmaster. She had also worked on Chellie's campaign. Karen has since become the web manager for Moveon.org.

Even though Betty Castor didn't win the Senate seat, we managed to execute a robust Internet campaign. We launched the website in May—it was essentially operating for only six months. We raised $1.6 million online with an average contribution of $171 (almost double the Dean average gift), and during the last month before the election, the site averaged more than 18,000 views each day, most of them (as has been corroborated by Pew reports[3]) by likely independent voters deciding whom to vote for. We offered the Dean-style TeamRaiser option, and sustained giving raised almost 10 percent of the total. More than 50 percent of the 9,206 donations were repeat gifts. We didn't have a bat, but we did have Mount Kilimanjaro as our goal thermometer. Betty Castor climbed the fabled mountain when she was a teacher, during a trip to Africa with her students.

In the September 2004 edition of *Wired* magazine,[4] an article was published about the aftermath of the Dean Internet phenomenon. In a story about the Betty Castor Internet campaign, I was referred to as "the arbiter of the new hotness." Not bad for a guy in his sixties.

In 2006, I worked as an Internet adviser for Alex Sink in her campaign to become chief financial officer (CFO) of Florida. She was elected in 2006—in fact, she was the only Democrat running statewide who won her election.

The CFO is a new political position, created by Governor Jeb Bush and his Republican legislature in 2000, and combines the offices of comptroller, treasurer, insurance commissioner, consumer advocate, and fire marshal. The Internet played an important role in Alex's election. In addition to now-standard political action options and e-mail solicitations, the information on the site was a primary source for learning about the responsibilities of this new Florida cabinet position. The site also provided a way to highlight Alex's unique qualifications as former president of Florida's Bank of America. She is no stranger to politics; although she had never run for public office before this race, her husband, Bill McBride, ran against Jeb Bush in his first gubernatorial election.

One aspect of the Sink campaign I want to share with you is our experience with online advertising. Because it was a "down ballot" race with limited funds, and because most political campaigns have limited experience with online advertising, we weren't able to complete the full program I recommended. We did, however, learn some things. These portend that online political advertising will be very big in 2008—on the Internet and on mobile technology as well.

One month before the election it looked like there wouldn't be enough funding to cover the usual TV and cable TV media in the expensive Miami market. With that in mind, we decided to buy ads on both MiamiHerald.com and ElNuevoHerald.com. For about $3,000, the campaign was guaranteed 100,000 impressions with a banner ad over the last 30 days before the election. The ad included a click-through button to the campaign website. The results were better than expected: 1.34 percent clicked through on MiamiHerald.com, with more than 50 percent joining the campaign. Most shocking was the response on the Spanish-language site, ElNuevoHerald.com: The click-through rate was 2.4 percent. The *Miami Herald* publishes stats in which they compare their website viewers—for both English and Spanish sites—to prime-time TV viewers, cable and radio. Website views averaged almost double the penetration rates of TV views. I admit that TV ad watching is different from online banner ad impression, but at a cost of pennies per impression by comparison, and with an option to immediately learn more about the candidate from the campaign website, I believe that in future campaigns there will be a shift away from TV media buys to Internet advertising. There won't be a choice if a candidate wants to reach all of the potential voters.

In addition, we bought lots of Google key words for five months before the election. Spending almost $6,000, with an average cost of $2.94 per click-through, more than 2,000 people visited the Sink site from Google impressions. (We were not able to check the actual number of those signing up on the e-mail list.) For a "down ballot" race for an essentially unknown office, that was very successful. Although the Google click rate was small, there were more than 5.2 million impressions of the sponsor key word ads.

We weren't able to place one more ad I had recommended. For about $10,000 we could have had the Sink ad show up on 2 million MySpace pages of Florida women from the ages of 24 to 35—far less expensive than buying 5 million points on TV.

## Campaign Futures

Since the Dean campaign there have been many changes in interactive technology (now including mobile phones). There are many new applications and functionalities, providing new options for future campaigns.

TV and cable viewership is clearly shifting to the Internet and to mobile phone platforms. Not many media consultants seem to understand that. That's not too unexpected; their revenue model entails getting paid through TV ad buys—it's the only legitimate "kickback" allowed in politics. On the other hand, I am very sure Internet ad buyers are marking up their prices for their revenue models. However, as you can see above, the total dollars spent (at least until more ad demand is placed on interactive technology) add up to far less than the cost of TV and radio. Right now, the options present a business dilemma for media buyers, but I predict that in 2008, millions will be shifted to interactive technology—social networks, Internet sites, mobile platforms, and so forth.

Now there are communities a campaign can "attach" itself to through social networks—MySpace campaign pages, for example. The Sink campaign had a variety of groups or communities on Gather.com. YouTube is an additional way to get exposure. For example, a guy videotaped giving his bird, named Alex, a bath in his sink—get it, Alex Sink. It was wonderful, whimsical, and very helpful for name recognition—so Alex, the candidate, didn't mind.

Mobile technology is moving fast. In addition to the whole smart mob system for quickly creating a crowd (after the Madrid terrorist bombing in 2004, text-messaging was used to change the likely election results in two days), individuals can "join" a campaign's mobile network with a simple quick code input. The campaign can then communicate with alerts and so on. In 2008, state party voter files can be connected with mobile technology for persuasion, GOTV, and vote confirmation. This can be done using an already available political online tool, VivaDemocracy.com, that makes it possible for activists to "adopt" voters in their neighborhoods. I predict that TV ads will be available and forwarded via mobile phones—for those who have joined a campaign's mobile network.

## A Stressful Dream

To celebrate our accomplishments at the end of the campaign, the finance department administrative assistant, Jay Schroeder, took up a collection from each of us and had T-shirts made. They each had printed on them, "I raised $50 million for the Dean Campaign and all I got was this lousy T-shirt." That sums up the amazing work and the legacy, and yet how this massive endeavor seemed to disappear overnight—like a stressful dream.

Let's hope the lessons learned don't disappear, too. In the final episode of *The West Wing*, Martin Sheen's President Bartlet (a character that reminded some of Howard Dean) had the last word: "Tomorrow."

We'll have to wait until then.

## Notes

1. Joanna Pearlstein, "Click Here to Donate," *Wired* (February 2006).
2. This is from my experience at the Dean campaign and in the three political campaigns that followed.
3. Lee Rainie, Michael Cornfield, and John Horrigan, "The Internet and Campaign 2004," Pew Internet and American Life Project, March 6, 2005.
4. Samantha M. Shapiro, "The Dean Machine Marches On," *Wired* (September 2004), 140.

# 13

# A Web Activist Finds Dean

## Nicco Mele

*Nicco Mele, the Dean for America webmaster, came to the campaign with more political experience and more technical experience than many others. But his first mode of contact with the campaign—of his own accord running a Google ad to help Googlers find Dean's then-obscure website—was an archetypal example of the many spontaneous acts of support that came to the campaign from the outside. His discussion of the process of redesigning the website illustrates the often chaotic and creative character of the campaign, as well as some of the difficult structural questions, such as the tension between a polished design and one that looks "grassroots."*

## Introduction: From a Meetup to a Spontaneous Google Ad

I was in a fairly boring webmastering job when I first heard about Howard Dean. It was in March 2003, and a couple of my friends had invited me to come hear him speak at an event organized through a website called Meetup.com. I remember very distinctly sitting at my desk and visiting Meetup.com for the first time, before I even visited Dean's own website. I was intrigued. Then I did some web searching on Howard Dean; his website didn't come up, but a bunch of blog posts by his fans did. I'd never heard of the guy, but people sounded pretty excited about him.

So I went to the Meetup—in New York City, at the Essex Lounge—and there were so many people there you couldn't get into the bar. It was intense. The crowd was crackling with energy. Even though I didn't get to hear Dean speak, I went home kind of fired-up. I spent the next couple days reading about the guy, and got annoyed that it was so hard to find his website—instead of something straightforward and political like Dean2004.com, it was DeanForAmerica.com. A Google search didn't show his official website right away, so I bought a Google ad for him—when you searched for Howard Dean on Google, a little box popped up that said something like "DeanForAmerica.com, the official website of presidential candidate Howard Dean."

Then, having done my small part in my quiet way for the underdog, I went back to my boring job and forgot about Howard Dean.

Forgot about him until three weeks later, when Google put a massive charge on my credit card. When I first bought the Google ad, it was only costing me a couple of dollars a day because nobody was searching for Howard Dean. Then the thing started to pick up steam, and while I was going about my New York life, more and more people were searching Google for Howard Dean, finding my ad, and clicking on it. The daily charges were starting to be in the hundreds of dollars—sure as hell a little bit more than the $60 a month I thought I was getting into in the first place.

I called up the campaign. I looked up the phone number on the website, called, and asked to speak to whoever was in charge of the Internet. They put me through to Zephyr Teachout. I said the campaign should probably run the ads, as I couldn't afford it much longer. The first thing Zephyr said was, "I wondered who was running those ads!" and she went on to explain that the campaign didn't have the money to run the ads, and if I really wanted the ads to run, maybe I should figure out a way to raise money to run the ads through my own website, nicco.org.

Three weeks later I packed up my life and moved to Vermont to be the webmaster of the Dean campaign. I arrived in Burlington, Vermont, on May 3, 2003.

But here's the amazing thing about my story: It's not unique. Thousands of people heard about Howard Dean, and figured out some small thing they could do, on their own, of their own volition, without direction or instruction, to help Dean's campaign. I started by buying Google ads, but many more did other things: volunteering to organize and run the monthly Dean Meetup meetings, designing flyers and posters, and organizing their own fund-raising events. In my months at the campaign headquarters in Burlington, Vermont, I was constantly inspired by the innovation, energy, and motivation of the people around this country. Americans do care about their government, about their country, about their neighborhood, and about their politics. When a candidate came along in whom they believed, well—they'd figure out their own way to help him.

## Web Activist Experience before Dean

It's hard to say what drew me to Dean. A combination of factors—my own background in politics, the opportunity to just have some fun and try some new stuff, the sheer grassroots energy of the campaign—all swirled together and made the campaign seem like the perfect place for me. I had first gotten involved in computer work in high school, when I figured out that doing technical work on computers was infinitely more lucrative than waiting tables as a way to make some cash. When I got to college, I continued this line of work: Tech work was fun—and you got paid pretty well as far as college jobs went.

While I was in college, I also started to become politically active. While a freshman, I started doing volunteer tech work at a small nonprofit that worked with political refugees. They introduced me to their "regular techie," this amazing guy named Bill

Howells. Bill wanted to provide the best tech work possible to progressive nonprofit organizations at the most minimal cost. He had a small consulting company, Programming For Change, Inc. When you called the phone number, you got a message that said: "You've reached Programming for Change. We can't take your call right now, so leave a message. And don't forget: Subvert the dominant paradigm."

Bill gave me an enormous education in all things technical and political. He took all kinds of clients, from national nonprofits with large budgets like Common Cause to shoestring operations doing important work, like the Guatemalan Human Rights Commission. Bill was pretty picky about his clients; they had to have an authentic grassroots spirit, a populist intensity to them. Under Bill's direction, I worked at a wide variety of grassroots groups doing technical work throughout my college career.

Then I graduated from the College of William and Mary with a degree in government and the vague notion that I wanted to go into "politics." I didn't realize it at the time, but my understanding of politics was pretty different from what was happening in the political parties in Washington, D.C. Thanks to Bill Howells, I thought politics was about community organizing, about Saul Alinsky and Common Cause founder John Gardner.[1] I started interviewing for jobs in Washington, D.C., and realized that most of what was happening there was a far cry from the grassroots politics Bill had taught me.

While I was working for Bill, I had spent a good chunk of time at the offices of Common Cause. In fact, I remember helping them set up their first Internet connection through AOL. About the time I started job hunting, Common Cause was winding down their magazine and ramping up their web efforts. They hired me at Common Cause to help take their online organizing program, CauseNet, to the next level. I started as the first full-time webmaster of CommonCause.org and an "online organizer"—a newly created position. I was thrilled—I took the job, and plunged myself into the grassroots culture of Common Cause and the writing of John Gardner.

Common Cause was an incredible place to work in the late 1990s. John McCain was running for president, and campaign finance reform was at the front and center of several campaigns—from the presidential primaries to Hillary Clinton's Senate race. People around the country were angry about the influence of money in politics, and they were getting engaged about it. An elderly woman from New Hampshire named Granny D walked across the country and back to talk about money in politics. People seemed to be rising up to do something about it. To work at an organization that was about people power, that was founded out of the notion that the public interest needed to be organized, was a perfect learning ground for what was to come later in my career.

Just as the public was starting to get organized around campaign finance reform (galvanized in part by John McCain's presidential run), the Internet world was at the height of its dot-com intensity. I managed to get a good, strong taste of populist presidential campaigning and the new, emerging online world. These two worlds collided at the Shadow Conventions in the summer of 2000. Hastily organized by Arianna Huffington and a small group of other organizations, the Shadow Conventions were meant to be a grassroots convention mirroring the major political conventions—the

Republican Convention in Philadelphia and the Democratic Convention in Los Angeles—by talking about real issues and engaging real people in a way that the major party conventions weren't going to touch. The point was to prove that the conventions were mostly a show put on for major donors and the media—dramatically removed from the issues that matter to people's lives.

As it happened, Common Cause was one of the convening organizations of the Shadow Conventions—and I went on loan to the Shadow Conventions staff as webmaster and technical director. We put together an amazing website, utilizing an early "blog" technology (under the direction of Dave Winer) and cutting-edge web streaming with the help of RealImpact, the nonprofit services division of RealNetworks. It was a critical proving ground for me, putting my technical skills to real grassroots political purpose. It also seeded many of my ideas and experiences for the Dean campaign three years later.

At the same time, the Shadow Conventions made me deeply cynical about politics. The stunning juxtaposition of people talking about real issues (money in politics, drug policy, and the growing income gap in the United States) across the street from the major parties throwing lavish dinners for their major donors made me sick to my stomach. Then, after all that, we stumbled into a divided election that ended with *Gore v. Bush*. I came away from that election cycle with the profound sense that politics was broken in the United States. The system rewarded the worst kinds of candidates and virtually guaranteed that candidates who represented real change would never be allowed an honest chance. I gradually disengaged from my political work in D.C. and moved to New York City to pursue a completely different, nonpolitical career path.

## Discovering Dean

And two years later, that's where I was—in New York City, in a nonpolitical webmastering job, with a simmering political consciousness that was not put to bed so easily. It was a Saturday morning in late April, around 9:00 A.M., when the phone rang in the hall of my apartment in Queens. I picked it up and this garbled voice on the other end of the line said, "This is Joe Trippi. I don't have much time. How much money can you survive on and how soon can you move to Vermont?" I answered, "I don't need much money and I can be there in seven days." One week later I was in Burlington, Vermont, watching the television with Bobby Clark and Zephyr Teachout as Dean held his own in the first Democratic presidential primary debate in South Carolina.

Given my experience at Common Cause and on the Shadow Conventions, the Dean campaign offered me the perfect opportunity to practice the two things I love most: technology and politics. But it also taught me that something radical was happening with emerging technologies: People around the country were becoming more connected to each other than we'd ever seen before. One of my favorite stories happened at the height of the campaign in November 2004. It was Thanksgiving, and I had taken a much-needed break and driven down to New York City to visit my family before flying to Seattle to see my parents. Walking through Brooklyn to meet my brother, I noticed a flyer posted on a telephone pole advertising a Dean tabling event at the Brooklyn Farmer's Market. It invited Dean supporters to come and help get the word out. The flyer was well designed and caught the eye, and I marveled at the amazing work and energy people were pouring into the campaign. The next day I flew to Seattle, and walking around downtown Seattle I saw the exact same flyer—but this time advertising a Dean self-organized event in Seattle, not Brooklyn.

Now I was curious. I went online and discovered that a group on the West Coast—I think it was North Bay for Dean—had developed their own poster tool. It took the details of your event and inserted them into a pretty little flyer, complete with tear-offs for more info. Thousands of people around the country were using this tool to make flyers for their little local Dean events, and here I was, ostensibly in charge of the web operations for the entire campaign, and I had only just learned of its existence. It was a beautiful, amazing moment. Some folks in California had seen the need for a clever tool for poster making—and instead of waiting on the campaign to provide something, they went ahead and built it themselves, on their own, and then invited the nation to use it.

I've got so many memories from the Dean campaign, but many of them are personal stories—like the day I nearly had a complete breakdown at the campaign office, and Matt Gross took me to the lake to swim with his dogs (which probably saved my life, my sanity was so tenuous). Or the late night about two weeks after I arrived at the campaign when I realized that these people were *serious;* even though Dean was polling below Al Sharpton, they planned on winning.

It was a night that I will never forget. I remember looking around the room at everybody and thinking, "Boy, you folks are nuts," but over the course of the next few hours, hearing Joe Trippi talk about how we could do it, I, too, joined the ranks of the nuts and believed. We had recently moved from the tiny cramped offices in downtown Burlington to a larger, corporate office park space on the outskirts of town. It was the second week of May and everyone was starting to notice that the Internet was really beginning to bring in significant money on a daily basis. Suddenly everyone in the campaign seemed to have an opinion as to what to do online. These competing visions were frequently in conflict, so a grand meeting was called to sort out our "online strategy." I vaguely recollect it was on a Tuesday—which would have placed it on May 13, 2003. Ten or twelve people were there—most of the senior management of the campaign at the time: Joe Trippi, Bob Rogan, Stephanie Schriock, Tamara Pogue, Larry Biddle—and the fledgling Internet team: Zephyr Teachout, Bobby Clark, Michael Silberman, Matt Gross, Dave Kochbeck, and I. The meeting was called to begin at 10:00 P.M. I remember that I was sufficiently new to the campaign that the late hour of the meeting schedule was a shock to me. I also remember that the meeting started with a real air of animosity—everyone was tired, confused, and sure that they understood something special about the Internet that no one else understood.

The meeting went on for a while in the way that meetings do, kind of ambling around with everyone speaking their piece but no one listening and no real point to the thing. Then, somewhere around 11:30 P.M., Trippi stood up and started to bring together all the disparate pieces of everyone's vision. And he started to imagine, out loud, what the Internet might do for us, where the Internet might take us, and how we might use it to win this campaign. It was a big, beautiful, bold vision. And, as unlikely as it seemed at that stage in the game, I began to believe we could do this. We could come from nowhere—from the campaign dead last by every measure—to actually win. It was exhilarating to simply consider: We might be able to use the Internet to harness grassroots energy to raise enough money to be competitive.

I went into the meeting at 10:00 P.M. cranky and thinking about moving back to my old life in New York City. I left the meeting and the next morning called my landlord in New York to say that I was permanently moving to Vermont, so don't hold my old apartment for me. It was all or nothing. As Trippi said, sometimes you just have to jump off the top of the building.

## Designing the Website: Does Grassroots Have a Look?

One of my passions in life is design. Any kind of design, really—buying a new coffeemaker recently was torturous because I did not like the functional or the aesthetic design of any of them. But especially web design—it is one of the most challenging fields of design for a variety of reasons: It has strange constraints, where some things are impossible but others are boundlessly possible. Part of the reason for the strange constraints is how text-heavy most websites are. Function is king (in terms of useability) but function is meshed with aesthetics in unpredictable ways—the more candylike a button is, the more likely people are to click on it. I always think of Vitruvius—good design is reliable, useful, and an utter delight.

When I arrived in Burlington, DeanForAmerica.com was quickly outgrowing its $40-a-month hosting account and its layout and design. Bobby Clark had already made plans to grow the site to a content management and contact management system, and that transfer was in progress when I arrived. The design of the site was a web-standard three-column layout with a large, heavy top banner. The banner didn't reflect the campaign's logo, but it did have a large American flag backdrop with a head-and-shoulders photo of Dean. Unfortunately, the photo was somewhat unflattering and we took to calling it "Angry Dean."[2]

I distinctly recall my first design addition to the site—I added a little "Hot!" icon to give a recent press release more visual attention. The site's design was overall kind of bland—a simple white background with this heavy dark blue banner. The red and yellow "Hot!" icon with flames bursting out (created with the aid of Adobe Illustrator's built-in clip art) seemed to light up the page and call attention to the text it was promoting. It was such a hit that we used it until the final days of the campaign. In creating it, I consciously thought about the early days of Yahoo! when they would use little "new" and "cool" icons that looked kind of corny but made the text stand out.

I was proud of the Hot! icon, but things quickly spiraled out of control from there. We did a comprehensive redesign (and not just the design, but the back end) of the blog, renaming it BlogForAmerica.com. This had been started before I showed up at the campaign by a volunteer (and later critical staff member), Jim Brayton, and tech intern Marc Chadwick. By late June we had a redesign of the entire site in progress with the help of Jeff Stanger at NetCampaigns. But I want to step back and make a few overall observations of design on the Dean campaign.

I remember early on in the campaign, in May or June, slaving over the design of something—I can't remember what, but it was some button or header image or something—and when I presented it to Zephyr she was kind of nonplussed about it. She didn't have a specific criticism about it, but I could tell she didn't care for it. Seeking validation, I went to Trippi and asked him what he thought of it. He had a strong negative reaction, and told me it looked too polished—this was a grassroots campaign, and the visual representations of the campaign (especially on the web) needed to represent a certain rough intensity and avoid a corporate, polished look.

Prior to this particular design, everything I had designed for the campaign was lacking in polish—but not by choice. It was purely a function of limited time and resources and the need to get things out the door. So when I finally found time to design something and get it "finished" in my little design mind, it looked too boring and too institutional for the campaign that we were building.

I tried to take that design lesson to heart—especially when working with Jeff on the redesign of the website template. Jeff Stanger stuck with the basic three-column, top-banner layout, but changed it around. We got rid of "Angry Dean," added photos of supporters from rallies, shrank the size of the header, added some navigation to the header (especially to get to the blog, which was a stand-alone site), and, most interesting, chose black as the dominant color. Black was an intentional choice, and I came to think of it as so perfect (in that weird designer kind of way) that when I showed it to the campaign senior management and they universally had a bad reaction to black, I was shocked. In the end, Bob Rogan gave me the approval just to go ahead with it for the sake of expediency.

But black was a great color for the design. Every single other candidate was blue—out of red, white, and blue, blue was the best color for design. Blue isn't as loud as red, or as washed-out and bland as white. I wanted the campaign to be cutting-edge, to be challenging the establishment, to stand out among all the presidential campaign websites as being intense and active. In the end, a black background for the navigation column and the top header achieved that goal with remarkable effectiveness.

Anyone on the web team can tell you what a production the Dean websites were on a daily basis. Not only was there constant content production (write, write, write!) for the blog and the main site, but there was constant design—and I'm not even starting to talk about the monitoring of things like the Get Local event database, the Meetup Hosts feedback tool, the photo gallery, and the hundreds of other features that sprang up like large, colorful, yummy mushrooms in the dark forest that was the campaign. Virtually everything that went on the website needed some kind of iconography, and so my job comprised a significant amount of daily design time, making an icon for whatever was the new item of the day. Soon others, like Jim Brayton, Karl Frisch, and Allen Smith, joined me in the icon factory. It was one of the things I loved and hated most about the job. I loved it because it was constant, creative design on a real small level—which I just enjoy. And I hated it because there was never enough time to get something that looked really good—we always had to just get it out the door.

I think one of the reasons we developed an icon-centric design is that in the pressure-cooker, time-sensitive environment of the campaign, it's a hell of a lot easier to find an hour to design one little icon than to find six hours to do a much bigger design job. It also just so happens that I am personally much better at little icon design; I don't have as good an eye for larger design jobs.

The more I think about it and write about it, the more I wonder what other people—especially other designers—thought about the designs on the campaign. I think that much of the design work bore my aesthetic imprint in some way—bold colors, clear lines, and a sort of industrial/revolutionary feel from the 1940s. One of my favorite design books is *All American Ads of the 1940s* by Jim Heimann; I also love another book in the series from the 1950s. Through it all is a sense of unfinishedness, or of amateurishness. It's very hard to figure out if I'm being fair here; one is always in love with one's own designs and sees their influence everywhere. At the end of the day, my purpose in every design was to communicate the energy and intensity of the campaign, to generate excitement and enthusiasm.

The iconography of the campaign took a particular turn with the arrival in Burlington of Zack Exley, from Moveon.org. Moveon had offered its services to all the campaigns, and we took them up on it. Zack told me that you need to clearly identify what actions you wanted people to take—and he pointed to Moveon.org's standard action design, where there is 1-2-3, a way of prioritizing the organization's needs for its activists and inviting them to keep going—after you do the first one, you do the second one, and so on. We enthusiastically adopted the 1-2-3, and ever after, when we had a strong drive toward a series of actions, we implemented the 1-2-3. I think we all got sick of designing new ways of representing those three numbers, but we kept reinventing visual looks for them, hoping to this time find a more compelling visual button, something people wanted to click on.

One of the things—one of the many things!—that I'm sure people found frustrating about the Dean websites is how different tools had different layouts and different designs—frequently wildly different designs. Initially, this happened by accident—it was, again, a matter of time, of getting things out the door, and whoever was working on it just slapped something vaguely resembling navigation on the newest tool and live it went. However, as the different properties grew, and more and more tools were added to the mix, this became a serious problem. We actually had a complete redesign in the works that would have resolved many of the most frustrating navigational issues, but the campaign ended before we could implement all of the design changes we had lined up.

One of the funniest changes I remember making early on is with the Contribute button. When I first arrived on the campaign, there was this vaguely medical icon that said "Prescription For Change." You'd never have known it to look at it, but it

**CONTRIBUTE >**

was the link to the contribution page for the campaign. After consulting Stephanie and Larry, we changed it to a simple, single word: "Contribute." Interestingly enough, I remember some discussion among Matt, Zephyr, Stephanie, Larry, and me about whether it should be "donate," "give," or "contribute"—what was the best verb to use? Somehow we settled on "contribute"—I recall that it was in part because *contribute* is a much more inclusive verb—that is, both *donate* and *give* imply some distance, "you give us money and we'll do the work," while *contribute* is much more "this campaign is the sum of all of our efforts."

And soon thereafter came the bat. In my old New York life, I had been an avid minor league baseball fan, attending Brooklyn Cyclone games religiously all summer long. The hardest thing about being in Vermont—yes, harder than the winter—was being away from my beloved Cyclones. (Luckily enough, Burlington actually has a minor league team in the same league—Single A Short Season—as the Cyclones. Campaign life was unforgiving, but I managed to steal a few nights out to the ballpark.)

With the approaching end of June, the end of the second quarter for campaign fund-raising was also approaching. Larry Biddle had this notion for a baseball-themed fund-raising drive—he wanted me to design a bat as a thermometer to measure how much money was being raised. At the end of the first quarter, Larry had designed an online e-mail appeal around a standard thermometer image. But here it was Friday afternoon and I had promised Larry a thermometer before the close of business. I remember it was a beautiful June day, and I was desperate to get to the minor league baseball park for the Friday night game. It was just one of those nights, those clear, cool, early summer nights, when a baseball game—with the beer, the cotton candy, the hot dogs, the lights on the field—is just about as perfect as life gets. I was in a hurry and so I slapped together this baseball bat graphic, posted it on the site, and managed to only miss the first half of the game. I figure it must have been June 20, 2003. What's funny is to look back at all the fund-raising bats I designed and watch their evolution, from that initial hurried rough graphic to the later bats, which were carefully crafted on-message iconography.

Although the last few days of that June are a sleepless blur, I do remember how stunned we all were watching what was happening. Zephyr and Matt started keeping a running tally of the hourly totals on a whiteboard in their section, and at every half-hour mark we'd just stare, stunned, at the amount of money flowing into the campaign. About six weeks earlier we'd had a similar experience, as we had watched thousands of people comment on our website when the Democratic Leadership Council had slammed Howard Dean as a fringe lunatic. It was a humbling and amazing thing to be there and watch Americans around this country who cared about the leadership of the Democratic Party and of the nation start to take action and make themselves heard. I also remember that after the end of the fund-raising quarter, I went home and slept for eighteen straight hours. In the last three or four days of June, I had been

*Howard Dean's famous fund-raising bat from*
*DeanForAmerica.com, September 23, 2003*

manually updating the bat. Initially I was just updating it two or three times a day, but Trippi began irritably demanding more and more frequent updates, until the final day of the quarter we were updating every half hour. Thank God that a few weeks later a tech genius, Jascha Franklin-Hodge, joined our ranks and designed an automatic bat updater. By the end of the third quarter, the bat automatically updated itself without the need for human intervention.

For the end of the third quarter, Trippi set a goal of $15 million. That number was so astonishing that I began dreaming of gigantic number 5's chasing me, crushing me. Gradually I realized that my caffeine-addled brain had taken the golden number 5 from Charles Demuth's 1928 painting *The Figure 5 in Gold,* in the Metropolitan Museum of Art. You can see in the icons from the end of the third quarter the influence of Demuth's painting in the exact font of the number 5.

There are two design projects from the campaign that I just love. Of course, in each case the graphic design was my doing, so take it all with a grain of salt. The first was the Sleepless Summer Tour logo in late August. Trish Enright, the campaign's press secretary, thought of the name, and it was like a logo appeared to me out of the sky, and I turned around and in short order produced the tour's logo. Another favorite design book of mine is *The Art of Rock: Posters from Presley to Punk* by Paul D. Grushkin, and in making the Sleepless Summer Tour logo, I could see in my head all of those rock 'n' roll tour posters and T-shirts. Combine that with the intensity of campaign life, a

**PEOPLE-POWERED
H O W A R D !**

# SLEEPLESS SUMMER TOUR

## Rally for Gov. Howard Dean, Democrat for President!

### Seattle, WA
### Date and Location TBA
### *sign up at:* ***www.DeanForAmerica.com***

palpable sense of sleeplessness, and a blindingly hot summer, and the logo just tumbled from the Mac, driven by a higher sense of purpose. It seemed to communicate perfectly the intensity of the campaign and the whole point of the tour. It was also impossible to read—making it borderline useless. But I loved it.

The other design project I loved was *Common Sense*, a modern-day pamphlet and manifesto for change in this country that referenced the most powerful political writing our nation has seen throughout its history. Julie Norton had given me a photocopy of the original *Common Sense* and I tacked it up on the wall to look at as I worked on the layout of our modern-day version. It was intensely text-heavy, and a bizarre size, but we finally worked out what felt to me like an elegant, powerful product. We printed a whole ton of them, and then I discovered a couple of glaring typos. So much for the ten or twelve obsessive proofreadings we pushed it through. Literally fifteen or twenty people read it before it went to press, and nobody caught the typos. Ah, well—campaign life!

Unfortunately the pamphlet made its debut toward the end of the campaign, so it got a bit lost in the shuffle. But a lot of people in the grassroots loved it; I remember one person who wrote a note back saying she had sent it enclosed in all of her Christmas cards. It was not your normal piece of campaign literature, and that was part of what I loved about it—it was trying to reference the grand tradition of pamphleteering that figures so prominently in our history.

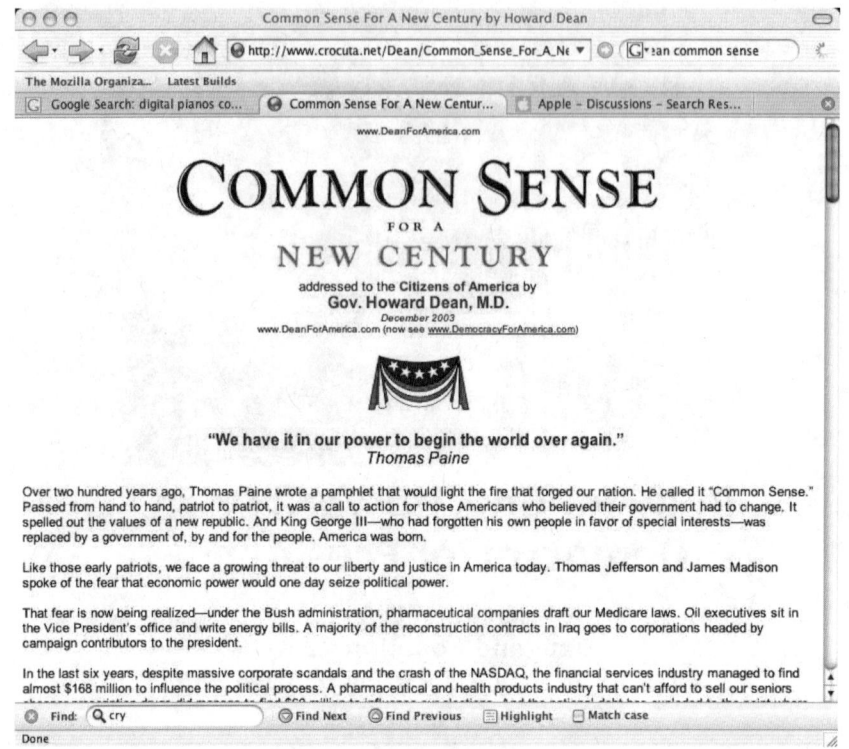

## Bring the Skills You've Got

Printing, through sites like lulu.com and cafepress.com, has changed dramatically, opening up so many new avenues for campaigns. As the cost drops and the wide availability of various technologies increases, design becomes a more and more important element. If everyone—even the most shoestring budget campaign—can have a website with a bunch of incredible tools, then how it looks and presents matters; it's what can distinguish a candidate.

At the end of the day, I'm an amateur designer who happened to be in the right place at the right time and was willing to bring my limited skill set to bear on the needs of the moment, even though the odds were stacked against us. "Why, sometimes I've believed as many as six impossible things before breakfast," says the queen in *Alice in Wonderland.* That's at the heart of the matter: Just about everything worth doing appears impossible. You bring the skills you've got and take to the impossible with all the vigor your ever-loving bones can muster, and who knows what might happen? Pack a sufficient dose of humor, a willingness to love and trust your neighbor, and go out there and subvert the dominant paradigm.

## Notes

1. Saul Alinsky, *Rules for Radicals,* 1st ed. (New York: Random House, 1971).
2. http://web.archive.org/web/20030320180711/http://www.deanforamerica.com (accessed March 20, 2003).

# 14

# E-Mail

## *Sign Your Own Name*

### *Kelly Nuxoll*

*Kelly Nuxoll, a freelance writer and the e-mail manager for the Dean campaign, nicely describes the feelings of helplessness and outrage in the face of the Bush administration's war in Iraq that motivated so many to join the campaign. Most of her chapter, however, is devoted to the structural dilemmas that the campaign faced around e-mail. E-mail remains the most basic and common form of Internet communication, and it constituted much of the fabric of the campaign. Nuxoll shows how the campaign struggled to maintain a personal, grassroots feel with the then-unusual principle of signing one's own name to e-mails. But how is this feel maintained in the context of an energetic, burgeoning national political effort involving hundreds of thousands of activists and several times that many e-mails? Was e-mail in this context simply a form of marketing, like bulk mail? Or could it be more interactive? To the extent that it is interactive, who decides how and when those interactions should take place? The Dean campaign maintained a remarkably creative tension between these competing ideas; as Nuxoll illustrates, maintaining a balance was not always effortless or clear-cut.*

*In describing her experiences, Nuxoll elegantly illustrates how these dilemmas were manifested and dealt with in the heat of the campaign. And because she transferred from the web team to the finance department, she also experienced the very different styles and approaches that characterized both parts. But this was, in retrospect, a taste of the future; as she puts it, "Even if we didn't have everything figured out yet, the old way of doing campaigns was beginning to creak and groan, getting ready to topple." No doubt these tensions will be experienced and experimented with in many campaigns in the future.*

### Introduction: Losing My Voice

In the summer of 2003 I was living in a convent in Connecticut. I didn't have any intention of becoming a nun; I just wanted to write my master's thesis. For four years I'd been working part-time on a degree in Creative Writing, and I couldn't seem to finish my book—it was as if I'd lost my voice. I hoped a month as a guest in a monastery, where I could reserve all my words for the page, would do the trick.

It didn't. A cloistered convent in the middle of nowhere turns out not to be a great place if you're already feeling stifled. The quiet was making me crazy. I missed the noise of Manhattan, the sense that I was where things were *happening*, although, since 9/11, New York had been losing some of its magic for me. The newspaper stoked fear so badly I cancelled my subscription. I grew nervous on subways and buses. I panted with rage whenever I heard Bush use the Twin Towers to turn American sympathy toward the war in Iraq, a war I believed was immoral and would only make us less safe. The worst part was, I felt like there was nothing I could do. I commiserated with friends and attended a few antiwar rallies, but the administration didn't respond even to global protests. I felt as voiceless politically as I was artistically.

Desperate for communication, I rigged an Internet connection from the convent's emergency rotary phone. In the afternoons I biked to the public library. I found that I could get a cell phone signal behind the barn and called my mother to find out what was happening in the world. Our conversations did not cheer me up. The war in Iraq blazed on, and there I was standing in a cow pasture.

"I have a job for you," my mother said several weeks into this routine. She was worried about me—whether it was my ranting or the fact that I'd apparently joined a nunnery, she sensed my despair. "Nicco Mele's running the Howard Dean campaign. His mother says they need writers."

Nicco and I had known each other since junior high; now, it seemed, Nicco was the webmaster for Dean. I called him immediately.

Yes, said Nicco. Things were taking off, and they were looking for people who could drop everything, move to Vermont, and work long hours for next to nothing.

"That's me!" I said.

I couldn't think of a more appealing offer. Although I knew hardly anything about Howard Dean—except that he was from Vermont and possibly gay—I wanted to be with anyone who was against Bush, and I wanted to be very, very loud about it.

## E-Mail: What's It For?

I moved to Burlington at the end of August, after the Sleepless Summer Tour. When Nicco introduced me at headquarters the campaign was no longer a fledgling start-up; it was a behemoth, with over 100 people crammed into cubicles or scurrying around the halls.

Nicco and Larry Biddle, the deputy finance director, hired me on the spot as the e-mail manager. The job struck me as perfect. I love e-mail—how efficient it is, how personal and funny and immediate. As e-mail manager, I assumed I would be writing pithy messages to our supporters and answering the volumes that poured in. It turned out that wasn't quite what was needed.

"We need to know how many messages we send out, who's receiving them, and what they're doing with them," said Larry. He leaned across his desk. "Listen, it's not rocket science. E-mail is basically a marketing tool."

"We're not a marketing campaign," said Nicco. He had taken me out to dinner to impress upon me the importance of writing with "a real human voice," one of the commandments of *The Cluetrain Manifesto*. "Dean for America e-mails come from real people and they're signed by real people," he said.

"We need to restrict the number of e-mails we send," said Matt Gross, one of the bloggers. He took my elbow and steered me toward a corner, where we could talk privately. "We have a lot of people who just send out an e-mail whenever they feel like it. Your job is to put a stop to that."

"But I thought that was the whole point," I said. "That people could take action on behalf of the campaign."

Matt grinned. "Now don't *you* start believing that. What we need is message discipline."

"I don't care how many e-mails it takes," said Tamara Pogue, the field director. "As long as it builds crowds. If that takes a thousand e-mails, so be it."

"One question," I said. "What exactly is a field director?"

Nicco introduced me to Zephyr Teachout. "How do you manage your e-mail?" she asked.

"What?"

"We're hiring you as the e-mail manager. I think that's a fair question. How do you manage your e-mail?"

"I pretty much put it in folders with people's names on them."

"Makes sense," she said. "You're hired!"

Great—but to do what? No one seemed to know. The only thing that seemed clear was that e-mail mattered to *everybody*: The finance department used it to invite supporters to fund-raisers, the field department to advertise events, the political department to inform voters about voting locations and elections, the web team to establish the message. Somehow, I would have to streamline e-mail with the rest of the campaign.

For the first few weeks, I sat with the web team—including Matt, Joe Rospars, and Zephyr, the bloggers; Nicco, the webmaster; Joe Drymala, the speechwriter; and Jascha Franklin-Hodge, Alan Smith, John Pettit, Karl Frisch, and Jim Brayton, who produced the video, photos, designs, and back-end functioning of the website. They occupied a quiet, dark corner. The shades were pulled over the windows and everyone sat mesmerized by whatever puzzle they were trying to solve on their computers. They wore headphones and talked to each other silently, over IM. Every now and then someone would send around a joke, and they all chuckled in unison.

Graciously, Joe Drymala pulled up a chair and counseled me on campaign style. Never say "our" campaign; say "your" campaign. Put the action you want readers to take in the first paragraph of the message, above the fold. Build the message around one idea; use two- or three-sentence paragraphs; include the same link at least three times. Use everyday language. Sign your own name.

All this was around the end of the third quarter. We were trying to raise as much money as we could so we'd look good in the standings among the other primary candidates; every day for the final ten days of the quarter the campaign was sending an e-mail to all its supporters, asking them to contribute. In the late afternoon, Trippi would roar out of his office like a bear in springtime, red-eyed and blinking, and dictate a message that was part messianic vision, part exhortation to send money. In Trippi's vision, the campaign didn't distinguish between big donors and small. We were all in this campaign together, and the antiwar activists who gave ten bucks would receive the same message as the LGBT-er who had maxed out at $2,000. (Not that Trippi didn't care about money: I had the impression that if he could have reached through the computer screen, grabbed supporters by their ankles, and shaken them until $2,000 fell out of their pockets, he would have.) According to Trippi, e-mail seemed to be a call to prayer, and everyone heard it five times a day whether they were inclined to answer or not.

The bloggers and speechwriters and I spent the evening hammering Trippi's soliloquy into an e-mail, took it tentatively to him for approval, and then around 2:00 A.M., sweet, bleary-eyed Jim Brayton fed it into Lyris List Manager, which distributed it to hundreds of thousands of inboxes through the night—about 400,000 people in August, and 650,000 when the campaign ended in February 2004. By morning, the ink on the fund-raising bat would have shot up another inch.

## E-Mail Overload

When the quarter ended, I moved from the web team to the finance department. In contrast to the web team, the finance department operated at about 10,000 decibels. The finance staff—Stephanie Schriock, the director, and Larry Biddle and Linnea Dyer, her deputies, plus about a dozen other people—were separated by cubicles, so when they needed to talk to each other, they usually just hollered. Since finance worked with donors around the country, it was one of the few departments that actually used landline telephones. They rang from six in the morning until midnight.

Unlike the web team, which reacted to the daily ebbs and flows of the campaign, finance had a pretty standardized system. They had an internal hierarchy and well-established procedures. One of those procedures was to send at least three, if not five, e-mails for each fund-raising event.

Bobby Clark, director of online fund-raising, showed me the format for fund-raising e-mails: a thick black html border and a central column announcing the date, time, and location of a fund-raising event. It was exactly the opposite of the style *The Cluetrain Manifesto* had recommended: html took forever to download, and the messages were impersonal. Finance e-mails were also endless, popping up like the brooms in *The Sorcerer's Apprentice*.

The finance department's strategy was based on the idea that e-mail, like direct mail, was most effective when it caught a reader's eye and appeared in the mailbox every couple days. In many ways, e-mail was a much cheaper version of the tool they were already using to raise offline donations for the campaign—and surpassing, to their credit, the web team's online fund-raising.

Which raises the fundamental, still-unanswered question about campaign e-mail, inherent in the uncertainty as to whether I would sit with finance or the web team: Is campaign e-mail a broadcast medium, or is it a means of two-way communication?

I settled into my new role, optimistically buying a wall calendar to keep track of messages. Soon, I wasn't sending just finance invitations, but e-mails from field and political—more states were developing campaigns, and voter registration deadlines were coming up. At the same time, the grassroots were sprouting everywhere, and supporters wrote me urgent messages about local events. Couldn't I just give them the e-mail addresses of Deaniacs in their area? they pleaded. I pitched the idea to the legal department: Absolutely not. For privacy reasons, campaigns are not allowed to reveal supporters' personal information. I told the grassroots I'd send messages on their behalf, but the compromise was clunky; the campaign was moving faster than the law, and we all chafed under the restrictions.

At the end of my first month, I abandoned the calendar and resorted to sticking fluorescent Post-it notes with hastily jotted subject lines around my computer monitor. In a week, my machine was dotted with so many bright squares it looked like it had broken out in pox. By November, Post-it notes jutted from the screen like radioactive waves: My computer was *exploding* with e-mail.

Many supporters were also overloaded. Around Thanksgiving, Nicco showed me an editorial cartoon—syndicated in newspapers all over the country—of a man at his computer. The text was something to the effect of "Did you get any e-mail?" "Yeah. Two Viagra ads, ten offers for penis enlargements, and a message from Howard Dean." I was way too sleep deprived to have a sense of humor about it. I didn't even catch the irony that, if I had been at a loss for words before, now I had way too many.

The model, obviously, was not sustainable. Accommodatingly, Nicco added two volunteers to my team: Mike McCaskey and Kathy Lyons. They are among the most competent and generous human beings I've ever known. Mike is a freelance writer, and Kathy worked for Amazon.com in Washington before she and her husband, Tony, the campaign's IT director, abruptly sold their beloved boat and beautiful home on Puget Sound to move to Vermont and work eighteen-hour days for Howard Dean.

With Mike and Kathy taking over some of the formatting, I could attend to some other aspects of e-mail: the piles of requests to be taken off the e-mail list, for instance. Whereas I despaired at the postcards, phone calls, and all-capital-letter e-mails demanding a reprieve from DFA e-mail, Larry was heartened. One of the adages of direct mail is that if people aren't complaining, they're not paying. For every one person who was pursuing a lawsuit against us, there were five who were responding to DFA e-mails with a big, fat check.

For me, though, it was a question of our campaign *ethos*: How could we preach the transforming power of technology to create community when we were violating one of the basic tenets of e-citizenship—to let people get out when they wanted? This was a presidential campaign, not Hotel California. Besides, every time we lost a reader, we lost valuable information. Why did she unsubscribe? What had changed, and how could we apply what we learned? I fantasized about a neat little script that would produce a survey every time someone clicked to unsubscribe.

Unfortunately, everyone fantasized about neat little scripts: The line to get to the campaign's programmers wound around the office. For the power they wielded, you would have thought Zack Rosen and Clay Johnson, barefoot and munching potato chips, were the ones running for president. They would have liked to have accommodated everyone, of course, but I found that getting on their priority list required more political maneuvering than I could manage. Had I to do it again, I would be more aggressive about forming coalitions with other mid-level staff to push some good ideas through. And, as a short-term step, I would learn to write my own code.

## "Thousands of Brief, Urgent Interactions among Passionate People": Handling the Deluge

My other gnawing concern was that we answered hardly any of the thousands of e-mails coming in. This task had been given to the correspondence department, composed entirely of volunteers and headed by Steve, who, on the rare occasions he was not at the office, raised llamas. Like Mike and Kathy, Steve had both expertise and patience; he organized a troop of about half a dozen volunteers in sorting and replying to a few hundred e-mails a day. But as happens with e-mail, each reply usually engendered another response, and when the campaign surged, so did traffic. The volunteers could not begin to keep up.

Kathy, who also carried the torch for the correspondence department, identified me as sympathetic to the cause. We went for a walk one day around the parking lot—campaign headquarters was in the bleakest possible setting, wedged between an exit ramp, a grocery store, and a low-income housing development—and agreed that incoming e-mails represented huge, untapped potential for the campaign. By investing the appropriate resources, we could not only monitor trends but build relationships and identify transformational leaders. Kathy and I were sure that Trippi would agree with our assessment of incoming e-mail's value, if only somebody with political clout could get to him.

Kathy lifted her head. Snow swirled around us and covered even the dismal landmarks in the landscape. "We're like the peasants in Russia before the revolution," she said. "Listen to us: 'If only the czar knew.'"

But the revolution was already beginning: Even if we didn't have everything figured out yet, the old way of doing campaigns was beginning to creak and groan, getting ready to topple. You could feel it as soon as you walked in the door. The office was in a constant state of upheaval; hardly anyone sat in his or her own cubicle but moved through the hallway, seeking collaboration with people in other departments. In fact, it was beginning to be unclear that departments were separate entities at all, since field and communications were running together thanks to Meetup; finance was increasingly part of field, courtesy of house parties; the policy people realized they could get their message out with the web pages, blog, e-mail, and forums; and scheduling knew a few things that impacted the grassroots, reached partly through Meetup and partly through the blog.

Granted, this created an impression of office chaos, but out of this dynamic I believe came some of the best parts of the campaign. DFA, both in headquarters and with its social software, created energy by fostering thousands of brief, urgent interactions among passionate people. Staff and volunteers connected quite literally, running into each other in the hall and exchanging ideas, information, gossip—each interaction was like an electrical shock, or, more accurately, like a hit of cocaine. One of the original investors of ICQ, the first instant-messenger program, found that exchanging an IM released dopamine in the brain; likewise, the kind of rapid-fire interactions in the office, heightened by the enormity of our enterprise and the thrill of being with bright, like-minded people, seemed to produce a chemical pleasure, so much so that when I finally left the office, usually at midnight with an elevator full of other workaholics, I felt high.

## The Details: Technology and Political Style

Trippi e-mails were different from state e-mails. Trippi e-mails, usually sent each night the last two weeks of a big fund-raising push, were crafted by the bloggers and speechwriters.

The bulk of the e-mail I managed was sent on behalf of the finance and field departments, with the occasional political department message thrown in. Their purpose was not to inspire but to direct: Hear Dean speak in the area, come to a fund-raising event, host a house party. A variety of people wrote them, some from state offices, some from around headquarters, some people like Donna Redwing, an LGBT activist who had a close contact inside the campaign.

The messages came to me in my own inbox, and I translated them into Convio, our content manager, which we also used for web pages and online fund-raising. Convio's WYSIWYG e-mail module reminded me of AppleWorks: a blunt tool, but it did the job. Most of the time, creating an e-mail was a cut-and-paste job, with a quick pass-through on Notepad to scrape any stray html tags. Sometimes, though, Convio would develop a mind of its own, and I'd spend forty-five minutes trying to move a margin or figure out why one word was three sizes larger than all the others. (I'd come to think of Convio in extremely personal terms: We were locked in an abusive relationship.)

Convio also offered a window to create messages for readers who wanted text-only e-mail, another manual formatting job. I shuffled margins and spacing, waited to load a preview, reshuffled. All in all, each message took about an hour to create.

As a compromise between Larry's marketing and Trippi's muezzin strategy, Bobby had organized supporters by state and congressional districts. When the message was ready, I queried the database to get at least an approximation of geography. Later,

Kenn Herman, the database manager, wrote a script that allowed us to target supporters by zip code.

The more established state offices, like New Hampshire, Washington, Texas, and Maine, had been sending out weekly digests announcing volunteer opportunities and pertinent updates for months. With Mike's help, I added another dozen states to the roster of weekly digest senders, each of which developed its own style and relationship with supporters.

The other important step was to open up the content manager to staff and volunteers (password: ihavethepower). Instead of spending time formatting and sending messages, having more people use the system allowed me to develop a style manual and come up with a communications strategy. Plus, my remote colleagues were delightful. Kevin, who worked in California, composed IM haiku. Cameron, who I later found out was a college student, created beautiful html and sent tips on how to scrape off Microsoft tags. One of the volunteers in Wisconsin turned out to be a lawyer who'd taken a year off to work for Dean; he patiently formatted messages and queried the database while sending me wry e-mail one-liners. The decentralized system did not limit the number of e-mails, but it relieved some of the bottleneck at headquarters, and it seemed more in keeping with the spirit of the campaign.

To ensure at least some measure of consistency, Kathy, Mike, and I compiled a DFA e-mail handbook. The guidelines, copied below, were derived from our own experience, contemporary thinking on e-mail, the wisdom of Nicco and Zephyr, and the advice of Moveon.org.

1. Use your own voice. Imagine you're writing an email to a colleague.
2. Start with a salutation.
3. Tell your readers immediately what action you want them to take.
4. Include a link in the first third of the message—above the fold.
5. Use 1, 2, or 3 sentence paragraphs.
6. Keep the message short. Brevity is the soul of writing on the web.
7. Include all the information readers need to take action immediately. If possible, include phone numbers as well as web pages.
8. Avoid "we need your help," "help us," or phrases that suggest the campaign is divided between any kind of "us" and "them." Dean for America is always "your campaign."
9. Humor is good.
10. Put your name on the message. Write your title, include a phone number, email and state url. Dean for America is made up of real people who are accessible.
11. Don't worry about patterning your language after Joe Trippi's—by sounding like yourself, you are actually representing the campaign's most important message: power belongs in the hands of the individual, not the government or corporations.

Future campaigns will no doubt figure out a way to streamline their e-mail. I suspect it will reflect an integrated campaign, in which technology is infused in fund-raising, field building, messaging, and get-out-the-vote goals. It may also take advantage of the grassroots' capacity to send messages to their own networks, since most people are used to e-mail as a more intimate, two-way communication medium anyway.

Whatever the solution, a campaign's e-mail will tacitly communicate the structure and mood of the organization. I realized this sometime in the dead of winter, when we were hurtling toward Iowa, and I found a printout of a message on my desk. It was from my brother in Ann Arbor, Michigan, in response to one of our mass mailings. He wrote, "I can't tell you how strange it is to receive spam from one's own sister. I admit I don't read all the e-mail from you guys, but it's nice to know there's always something happening at the Dean campaign."

He didn't know how right he was. No matter what time I turned the corner into the office parking lot, the lights on the third floor were on and at least a dozen cars were huddled around the front door. I knew one of my friends was upstairs updating the bat or writing a blog or reading the AP wire. The thought filled me with happiness and hope, even though it was three in the morning and I'd just eaten a donut for dinner.

# 15

# Participatory Political Culture

## *Everyone's a Kingpin If He or She Wants to Be*

### *Josh Koenig*

*Josh Koenig, a young web designer, artist, and entrepreneur, became involved in the Dean campaign because of the war. He was an early contributor to hack4dean/Deanspace, and worked for Music for America. In this chapter, he tells the story of finding the blogosphere, and then finding a space for antiestablishment politics within the establishment of a presidential campaign. He brings his own political vision to the story, and writes about how he sees technology as a critical player in a contemporary democratic society.*

Like many, my journey into the Dean for America campaign began with the war in Iraq. By late 2002 I'd completely abandoned television as a reliable source of information. I was disgusted by the crass emotional manipulation of the 9/11 anniversary, the blustering pundits, the disturbingly imperial swagger of newscasts hyping the potential fireworks of invasion. Pentagon stock footage, advanced weapons systems explained, visions of Paris in '42 ... the drums of war were everywhere, inevitable. My only solace lay online.

I was living in Brooklyn at the time, a recent art school graduate from New York University splitting time between experimental theater performances and making what living I could—in the midst of a broken bubble economy—from my skills on the web. Having experienced the WTC attacks and their effects in real time, the television coverage felt repetitive, plastic, and surreal. I looked to the web for data as an antidote to sensationalism, for the freshness of CNN.com, and the depth and variety of information available from international news sources.

During the run-up to war, I increasingly logged on to connect with other concerned citizens from around the world, to discuss the news rather than just passively consuming. My opposition had a personal character to it. Events that had happened to me, to "my city," were being used as part of a campaign of deception and manipulation, and this seemingly obvious graft was being ignored (when not actively perpetuated) by the institutional press.

I went online to try in my own way to counterbalance this, to contribute to an alternate, more truthful universe of information. I went, in short, to blog.

As things came to a head in early 2003, I threw myself into activism, helping to organize teach-ins, attending protests, blogging, e-mailing, and personally lobbying in any way I could think of to mobilize public opinion against the idea of invasion. On February 15 the largest coordinated global protest event in human history, coordinated largely through e-mail, went down. More than 15 million citizens representing every democracy around the world marched in concert against the war. I was with them on First Avenue in New York City, freezing my feet off and holding a boombox above my head to help out the sound system on stage, which was thirty-five blocks away and couldn't really be heard but was being broadcast via radio.

It was a high and heady moment, a peak for protest activism with all its merits and faults, and on that frigid afternoon I really thought that it would work, that all these people across the globe acting together would turn the tide. "He can't do it now," I thought. "How could he?"

That was before I learned we were seen by members of the political press as "dirty fucking hippies," or, in the president's somewhat kinder words, as a "focus group." In any case, beneath notice.

In hindsight it is clear that no mere street rally could possibly have altered Bush's long-ago-decided course of action. However, I still believe that the war could have been avoided if it had been opposed by institutional voices of power as well as by grassroots activists. Popular support was never strong before the invasion began, and that was without anyone who "mattered" taking a stand against the idea. However, naive trust in the leader (or perhaps a cynical and misguided political calculus) won out, and nobody with any serious profile in politics or the press took a stand.

Without institutional support all the marches and rallies in the world couldn't move popular opinion far enough to derail the Bush administration's campaign of propaganda. Thus, bombs over Baghdad.

The days after hostilities began were tense and strange. I felt disengaged, beaten. I stopped reading the news for a while, but eventually came back online, and to the blogs in particular. I needed camaraderie, to have a community in those dark days, watching this destruction unfold in our name. Knowing I was not alone, and believing that I, we, were right, I resolved not to drop out; but this begged the question of what it was I would do instead. Realizing that the tactics of protest were meaningless if the people at the top weren't listening, I resolved to focus my future activism on defeating George W. Bush in the 2004 election.

## "What I Wanna Know"

This decision led me into the strange and savage dogfight that is the presidential primary season, ten months out from Iowa. Reading and posting on the website antiwar.com—which served as an important clearinghouse for news and a hub for both left- and right-wing commentary opposed to invading Iraq—I had discovered a small one-man blog written by a struggling political consultant from Berkeley named Markos, the now-famous Daily Kos. I found that I agreed with his tenacious perspective and greatly enjoyed the cadre of eloquent comment-leaving readers who gathered there. I also enjoyed that the community was actively following the nuts and bolts of politics, primary season in particular. I soon became a regular under my Internet handle "Outlandish Josh."

My background in the theater and close observation of leading Democrats during the run-up to war left me with very little faith that any establishment Democrats—in particular the at-the-time "anointed one" John Kerry—had the necessary energy, insight, and integrity to defeat Bush. The dynamic that is generally summarized as "strong and wrong beats weak and right" was intuitively apparent to me at the time, looking at politicians on a performance level. They're on TV, so it might as well be a TV show. How good are they? I didn't think John Kerry or Dick Gephardt or Joe Lieberman was good enough to beat GWB.

Unsure how to proceed, I turned to the Daily Kos community, posting a comment explaining my dilemma, my hunger to work to change our leadership, and asking people to convince me who I should throw my support behind and why. Markos, who for this will always have my gratitude, responded with a link to C-SPAN's archive of the seminal "What I Wanna Know" speech that Governor Dean gave at the 2003 California Democratic Convention in Sacramento, suggesting I check out his campaign.

That link is a good example of how the Internet can bring things together for several reasons. First of all, it came from a trusted source. Markos was a nobody at the time like the rest of us—his website didn't have log-ins, let alone fame, just a regular pool of maybe 50 or 100 readers who liked to talk back intelligently—but he had earned my trust over the previous months. More importantly, he linked me to something really engaging: a highly watchable video of an impassioned speech by an energized and charismatic candidate.

The California Democratic Convention was just a few weeks before the "Shock and Awe" bombing campaign started, although by the time I got around to seeing Dean's speech, "Saving Private Jessica" was the dominant news of the day. It begins with the governor asking a simple question: "What I wanna know," he says, "what I wanna know … what I wanna *know*, is what in the world so many Democrats are doing supporting the president's unilateral intervention in Iraq?" At which point the crowd—and me in my underwear in my apartment in Brooklyn eating oatmeal—went wild.

It was an amazing performance, and especially courageous given the timing. Even now—I rewatched it in preparation for writing this—it still packs a wallop. Here was a candidate who was in my court on the issues but, more important, was *authentically and infectiously passionate* about them, using language strikingly similar to my own, language that I believed in, to get the message across.

In twenty minutes Dean lays out a compelling vision for a progressive America, one that prefers providing health care over launching unprovoked wars of aggression. But more than taking the right positions, he conveyed the sense in which this America-to-be was *right*, and how what was going on at the time was *wrong*, was an America governed through manipulation and fear, an America divided, led astray. In what amounts to a few short paragraphs of text, he gave voice to everyone like me who felt frustrated, enraged even, that the country itself had been hijacked. Finally, he had the audacity to proclaim that there was hope, that if we had the courage to stand up for what we believed in, to put our agenda up against theirs and speak the truth of our convictions, we could take it back.

"I want my country back!" It was a powerful call to action, especially for me, as I'd literally said these exact words in days and weeks previous. Here was someone who looked good and sounded great, who my theatrical sense said would thrill people if they got a chance to see him, and who seemed literally to be speaking my language. I was hooked. This was it! This would work! I was literally jumping up and down. I ran to get my roommate Frank (who would end up working the campaign through Iowa and New Hampshire and even as far as Wisconsin) and made him watch the whole thing with me again. We were newly minted Deaniacs.

## Blog for America

It was around that time that Blog for America was born and most of that core HQ staff, notably Zephyr Teachout, began contributing regularly. Over the next month of reading and writing online, I became convinced that Howard Dean was my ticket to ride. I wanted to use all my skills, my talents at writing, my Internet know-how, my ability to be persuasive. I wanted to be more than just a warm body stuffing envelopes. I sent in my résumé, and once again started blogging, raising funds, and e-mailing my circle of recent-grad friends with news and appeals, much as I'd done with my antiwar activism.

The more time I spent with the campaign, living vicariously through the talented writing of those bloggers in Burlington, the more I became convinced not only of the viability of Dean's candidacy, but also of the potential power in a participatory, peer-to-peer, Internet-driven Dean for America movement.

So much of mainstream life revolves around consumption, being a spectator, watching and buying and eating and watching. This was the Bush message right after 9/11: Say your prayers and don't stop shopping. For me and millions of others it was a remarkably unfulfilling call to action at a time when the need to connect, to get to work, to participate, seemed paramount.

As numerous academic and popular thinkers have documented, over the past several decades the trend in American social life has been toward an increasingly atomized society, isolated nuclear families composed of further isolated individuals. Our culture and our politics have been dominated by broadcast figures, Important People and Wise Men with cable programs and think tank fellowships and op-ed page slots. They speak, and the little people must listen. Membership organizations are impotent and ineffectual. Dialogue does not exist.

In contrast, the Net implies infinite potential space for expression and connection. It's an open place, and this creates a much more competitive marketplace of ideas, a place for discovery and discourse, but also a place that bends strongly toward truth. It is a medium founded with the explicit purpose of making links, and one in which it's astonishingly easy for those who want to publish themselves to find a global audience, providing they've got something to say.

This meant that in a Net-centric campaign, not only would the norm be connectivity and community, but there was room for all comers. Not only for people like me—a neo-bohemian ex-actor with a website full of cuss words and drug references—but for every other sort of potential supporter as well.

Culturally, I'm an outlier when it comes to politics; "off message," the veterans might say. For instance, even with all my involvement, I never managed to get a link to my personal site on the Blog for America front page. Eventually I learned this was because of a banner I had posted that proclaimed, "Pussy, it's what's for dinner." C'est la vie. I stand by my words.

However, in spite of all our cultural differences Dean supporters were able to discover meaningful common ground. The reasons we came together meant more than the variations that set us apart. We built a real grassroots network in ways that would never have been possible had we been dependent on consumer or broadcast channels—or on traditional coalition politics—to create a sense of identity.

The campaign we built was much more diverse and eccentric than the conventional wisdom appreciated. A popular media narrative held that the Dean campaign was a "Starbucks Ghetto," and it is true that there were a lot of yuppies on board, but that's true of every campaign. There were also plenty of freaks like me, not to mention the South Asian deli owners, retired police officers, young single mothers, full-bore student radicals, and many others I met along the way. This was a source of strength.

America is full of characters, freethinking individuals with the kinds of personalities that don't necessarily fit well into blunt institutional molds like high school or corporate bureaucracy. A lot of us also happen to be highly capable individuals: creative, hardworking, intelligent, and passionate. A campaign that lets these sorts of people connect as supporters can tap deep resources unavailable to those that enforce rigid "message discipline," that see their would-be citizen-enthusiasts as pawns.

The genius of making empowerment the core of Dean's candidacy, something that was explicitly made possible by the campaign's Internet-enabled character, is that it turned the whole operation into an incubator of new leadership rather than a place for conscripts to sign up and wait for their day to be called upon to act (or, more likely, to donate money). The grassroots movement growing around Dean's candidacy was decentralized, yet connected. It was in some ways elite, yet very heterogeneous, inclusive, and transparent. It was unabashedly idealistic, but also stubbornly pragmatic. It was a nationwide network of individuals grouping together in organic and ad hoc ways to reclaim responsibility for their country.

Openness, pluralism, participation, and interconnectedness had been part of the online culture I'd known for years, and they were definitely a part of the blogging ethic. I'd considered the political implications before as an idealistic student, but pessimistically never expected to see it happen, let alone applied directly to what I felt were the most pressing issues of the day. It was truly thrilling to see theories I believed in become practices I took part in, and to see this praxis generate results, actually *working*, outperforming the old ways and saving the day in one fell swoop.

It gave me great joy to realize that nobody cares what Judy Woodruff or Wolf Blitzer or even Bill O'Reilly thinks, if their friend or neighbor or buddy from high school is telling him or her what he or she believes and why. We'd just have to scale that kind of peer network out to reach a hundred million people, and the end result would be that we'd have literally taken the country back. Easy, see?

I was participating in a campaign that had as its means and objective the repudiation of the sickly symbiotic system of politics and what remained of the Fourth Estate. We sought to replace what was with a dynamic, network-centric, meritocratic, and above all transparent and fact-based ideal of democracy. It was a deeply American, deeply moral vision. We were *right,* just as candidate Dean was right in many statements that were deemed "gaffes" at the time. Sadly, as we would see, we were also fatally ahead of the curve.

## Deanspace

The fact that all this activity was being driven via the Internet made it all the more engaging for me personally, not just because I already had some vision for the inter-section of the Internet and democracy, but because I had skills and expertise online. I had something to offer. Campaign HQ never got back to me in response to my résumé and impassioned cover letter—I later discovered they were overwhelmed by the people who just started showing up at the office—but I kept on reading and writing, searching for an opportunity to do more than beat the drum and raise money to make a difference for my chosen cause. Sometime in May 2003 I discovered a website called hack4dean.com.

Hack4dean was the creation of Zack Rosen, a Pittsburgh native and computer science sophomore at the University of Illinois at Urbana/Champaign, home of the first web browser and a slew of other great technological breakthroughs. He and his college friend Neil Drumm set it up as a rallying point for Dean supporters like me with technical skills to self-organize.

We started off with a mailing list on which we debated potential projects, how and whether to engage with the official campaign, and other issues such as whether or not we should keep the word *hack* in our group title. For those of us in the Internet community the word has a positive connotation. To *hack* means to innovate quickly, to tinker, to invent. Benjamin Franklin was a hacker, as Lisa Rein (an avid mailing list contributor) pointed out at the time. However, our growing political awareness sug-gested that "hack4dean" might sound like a black-ops group to the common person, and as a consensus emerged about what we intended to do, a name change was effected.

After a month of formin', stormin', and normin', we were reborn as Deanspace, a volunteer community of web developers who took it upon themselves to create an Internet platform that the myriad "for Dean" groups (e.g., Pilots for Dean) could use to represent their communities of interest. Organized transparently and with regular meetings in open Internet chat rooms—one of the attendees for our inaugural meeting was an Edwards campaign staffer who was polite enough to leave when asked—we intentionally set out to create an open-source, decentralized network of sites rather than a hierarchical chain of command.

We can hardly claim to have developed much of the technology from scratch. A short survey of existing community-ware led us to the Drupal project, a great piece of open-source software described as "community plumbing" and developed by a cohort of volunteer programmers from around the world.[1] We based Deanspace on Drupal, and it worked. We added a few innovations—such as the ability for sites to share a calendar—as well as some Howard Dean themes and a lot of preconfiguration and how-to, and the package went on to power hundreds of Dean affinity websites, as well as official campaign state sites for Iowa, New Hampshire, and California.

The idea was that as the campaign season intensified, these communities could use technologies like RSS (one of the technology standards for sharing data that underpins the "Web 2.0" renaissance) to syndicate and aggregate one another's information about events, action alerts, important news, and so on. A nodal network would emerge. We were inspired by the revolutionary networked nature of the campaign and saw Deanspace as a way to further fuel those aspects. We believed that the same mathematical laws that have been shown to govern the growth of networks generally were working within the campaign, and that our platform would be an important part of continuing to drive that growth.

Ultimately Zack would go on to join Dean for America officially, living in Burlington through the winter. Neil and many others went to Iowa or other states to help out in the field. I envied their experience and cheered them on, but my involvement with Dean for America led me into a different, if not entirely unrelated, path.

## Music for America

In May 2003, around the same time that Deanspace started to really come together, I finally made it to my first Dean campaign Meetup in Manhattan. Honestly, I was a little underwhelmed. The crowd was a decade older than me on average, and there didn't seem to be much of a purpose other than to schmooze. However, there was a small knot of twentysomethings there, and they had somehow arranged for 1990s hip-hop pioneers Arrested Development to play a few songs for the crowd, including their version of Sly and the Family Stone's "Everyday People," which the twentysomethings' ringleader improbably introduced by noting how Sly's original had been used briefly by the McGovern campaign in 1972.

That speaker was Franz Hartl, and his cohorts were the founding members of Music for America. This group of friends—Dan Droller, Mike Connery, and Franz, and shortly thereafter Kevin Collinsworth and Rachel Postman—had taken it upon themselves to launch the cultural vanguard of the Dean for America movement. With no professional guidance (Franz was a second-year law student) they formed a political action committee (PAC), started organizing concerts, and launched a website aimed at the taste-making hipsters who populate downtown Manhattan and the trendy parts of Brooklyn.

Obviously we hit it off immediately, and Franz and I began meeting in the downstairs concourse of Grand Central Station, talking over the whole political scene and planning our next moves. It felt positively revolutionary, even if it was going down in a food court. We shared a vision of Dean for America as a movement campaign, for how networks in general and the Internet in particular could be brought into play in fresh and exciting ways.

We saw things in similar ways, and more than that we believed specifically in the promise of our generation, of the millennial population wave. We believed, still believe, that by creating a politically astute culture and practicing culturally savvy politics supercharged with the peer-to-peer methods we were pioneering, great advances could be made in our lifetimes.

Music for America was a direct response to these general beliefs and the specific circumstances of the Dean campaign. Naturally, I went to work using Deanspace to upgrade the organization's web presence. Other young leaders discovered the organization and began building chapters in several states. As the campaign in general took off and Dean moved from also-ran asterisk to dark horse contender to upset front-runner, the profile of all these activities continued to grow.

By the end of the summer, Music for America made the transition from shoestring volunteer PAC to fully funded 527 advocacy group, thanks to the vision and generous support of Andy and Deborah Rappaport, two leading figures bringing together new money and new ideas from Silicon Valley, progressive values, and establishment Democratic politics from D.C.

They understood what we were doing, and once we'd had a few conversations they asked, "If you could, would you do this full-time for the next year?" Of course we said yes. What was once an act of pure passion and civic duty had transformed into a real job with benefits. We even got to attend a fund-raiser as a group and meet the governor in person, which was ironic because starting up as a 527 meant we'd need to put the campaign itself at arm's length through the home stretch; any communication between ourselves and Dean campaign staff would have been a potential FEC violation.

Although we were no longer focused on the candidate, we continued to drive the kind of movement politics and organizing that defined the campaign. The national MFA operation consisted of building relationships with artists who would give up two or more of their complimentary tickets to their shows to volunteers, who were in turn recruited through our website. These volunteers would wear our stylish T-shirts, register voters, distribute high-quality "issue cards" explaining politics in our voice, and sign concertgoers up for a mailing list, which drew last night's spectators to the website, where they were converted into tomorrow's active participants.

We focused on small to midsized artists, whose shows would give volunteers a chance to make direct peer-to-peer contact with many if not all of the individual attendees, and we made good inroads with emerging artists, especially in the indie rock and underground hip-hop realms, whose DIY musical ethos had strong parallels to our organizational and campaign paradigm.

It was a successful experiment. We participated meaningfully with hundreds of artists, building a cadre of thousands of volunteers who reached millions of concertgoers. In part because of our work, my generation, the millennials, the generation native to the Internet, most naturally in tune with the movement, are increasingly recognized as an emerging power in progressive politics.

## Epilogue

Before I officially began my tenure with Music for America I made a pilgrimage to Burlington. It was early September and I was packing up my life in New York and preparing to move to Google's neck of the woods to start my new job. I'd just returned from the far-out Burning Man festival in the desert of Nevada—"spiritually cleansed" one colleague said; "a bit crispy" was how I put it—and I took time for a weeklong trip up to Vermont. I went with serial entrepreneur and longtime Deanspace adviser/booster Britt Blaser, one of the many amazing individuals above my station in life whom I probably would never have otherwise met. It was a great trip, coming at a high point for the campaign and at one of the most beautiful times to visit New England.

As Britt and I discovered, there was a very thin line between who was staff and who was a volunteer, mainly defined by tiny paychecks, business cards, and @deanforamerica. com e-mail addresses. Our first day we sat in on a meeting for a record-breaking conference call initiative—the most people on the horn for a political campaign at the time—and our idea for how to brand it was immediately picked up over and above the one they'd been working with internally. Naturally, we (the volunteers with the idea) were paired with a volunteer graphic designer somewhere in California creating something to promote it.

In the conventional corporate sense, turf did not exist in Burlington, only goals. What network scientists call "fitness," the utilitarian measure of how well something works, seemed to honestly be the driving criterion for the organization. It sounds Pollyannaish, but the truth is that most large organizations are too bureaucratic and inflexible to really deal with high-speed internal activity, let alone lots of success. It threatens too many fiefdoms. By contrast, the bullshit-to-purpose ratio at campaign HQ was unbelievably sweet, and the sunset views were awesome.

For a minute it seemed like we might be branching out from the mean, zero-sum trench warfare of traditional politics, like we could break the old muscle game, the turf wars, the whole 51 percent shuffle, everyone fighting over the same endorsements, the same TV show slots, the same pool of "likely voters." It felt like we really might just grow our way to victory, take the prize simply by doing the right thing and bringing enough folks on board.

Implicit in this vision was that if we went all the way, this is how a Dean administration would run as well. It represented a complete recapitulation of the Bush/Cheney gestalt—not just reversals on policy, but on the means and modes of governance too. We dreamed of building an inclusive and transparent movement that could not only win elections, but also support a true national consensus; of the reemergence of that classic standard of democracy, the public interest.

It was happening, and I believed—still believe—it would have kept happening if we'd made it past Iowa. But we didn't.

However, institutions still matter. Political machines matter. TV matters. And so do authentic (read: local) connections. For a day or two before the caucus, I made phone calls from my new home in California to help my friend and former roommate Frank check his count. He'd been with me at the beginning and had gone all the way to a small field office in Woodbine, Iowa, a small town just over the river from Omaha.

Reaching out across state lines to the names on the spreadsheet he e-mailed me, I was an enthusiastic voice on the phone, but still a stranger. They were kind to me, and I like to think that some of the earthy voices on the other end of the line went out to caucus, but the indigenous organizations—most notably Governor Vilsack's—that threw their support for Kerry were vastly more effective. After riding high in December, we slid to third, and then Matt Drudge picked up a ten-second sound bite from Dean's concession speech (aka "the scream") and created a media feeding frenzy. The campaign buckled. The front-loaded primary process allowed no time to recover, and in a week it was all over, a sad and brutal end to such an honest and idealistic endeavor.

However painful it was to lose like that, and to lose again in November after quite a second effort, few if any were permanently embittered. We're still at it. I'm still at it. The work continues. In and out of politics, business, technology, and culture, on the right and on the left, this network consciousness is growing.

What was once an airy-fairy belief that "everything is connected" is translating into pragmatic plans of action, entirely new operational models, ways of doing and being that engage more people as partners and participants. These aren't just feel-good traits: They help make these new models highly competitive, even advantageous, versus traditional methods.

And I feel it's important to say how much lasting good we accomplished in defeat. Howard Dean is now the Democratic Party chairman, decentralizing operations back out into the state parties and rebuilding Democratic infrastructure nationwide, and his fifty-state strategy helped drive a congressional realignment on par with 1994's "Republican revolution" in the 2006 election. Deanspace lives on as Civicspace, creating effective technology for public service and powering thousands of nonprofit, campaign, and community sites. Music for America continues to get volunteers into concerts for free, with a stable of artists running into the thousands. The worldwide open-source community continues to drive radical innovations, and Zack and I started our own company as a way to take part.

The Dean campaign was born out of a heightened moment in our history. It was unsuccessful in its primary objective, but looking back I think future generations will be glad that we were there, that our work heralded a new era. What is emerging now is not so much the oppositional, hard revolutionary process of one group's seizing power from another—the dynamic that caused our campaign to be buried in backlash—but something more inclusive, if a bit slower. There are still power struggles, as there always will be, but the ethos generally runs against zero-sum engagements, and the broader movement proceeds by osmosis.

Within the political establishment, the undeniable effectiveness of network tactics has earned them increasing respect, and a new wave of participants have connected to and strengthened preexisting party institutions and infrastructure. Sometimes it feels to me like our movement has been co-opted, with bloggers tied up in the national media narrative and secret meetings about the need to stop all the secret meetings; but this is a work very much in progress, and that progress is real. Transparency is up, and accountability too. Today's new kingpins are beholden to a much more empowered constituency, facing a much more competitive marketplace of ideas and action. In the face of record levels of inequality, we're seeding new fields of opportunity, widening the circle of participation. It's happening in the public and private sectors, in politics and in culture.

I'm looking forward to the end of pessimistic assessments about "the average American." We the people are smart, much smarter than most elite opinion makers ever give us credit for, and by and large we're tired of being marginalized, lectured, and funneled into catchall categories. New leaders and success stories emerge every day, but my guess is that most of us will never make the nightly news. Maybe we don't want to. Maybe we just want to be effective and respected, to lead a life of fun and purpose. Maybe if enough people do that, that's enough. Maybe that's really the point. I certainly don't feel a need to try to wear any kind of crown. As David Weinberger said, "Everyone will be famous to fifteen people."[2]

The twenty-first century presents enormous challenges, for the United States and for humanity as a whole: unsustainable levels of inequality, declining social mobility, global climate change, a looming energy crisis, and the inevitable—and now seemingly ignominious—end of America's role as the sole cops of the world. If we are to have any hope of proactively solving the problems we'll face, let alone holding it together in the instances where we can't, it's going to be critical to have a more connected, transparent, honest, engaged, *participatory* society: a body politic that is empowered, knowledgeable, and able to work together to get things done.

Luckily for us, that seems to be the world that's coming.

## Notes

1. http://drupal.org (accessed June 4, 2007).
2. David Weinberger, *Small Pieces Loosely Joined: A Unified Theory of the Web* (New York: Perseus Books, 2003), p. 104.

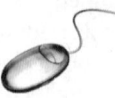

# 16

# An Organizer's View of the Internet Campaign

## Zack Exley

*Zack Exley was Moveon's organizing director when he took a brief leave of absence to work on the Dean campaign in spring 2003. By all accounts, his visit had a powerful impact on the campaign's Internet strategy, e-mail strategy, and use of organizing tools.*

*In this chapter, Exley explores the often cynical culture of political campaigns and the idealism that set the Dean campaign apart. He argues that one of the things that made the campaign unique was Joe Trippi's willingness to take risks, its cultural iconoclasm, and its focus on "the base," and that what made it successful were new, tech-savvy uses of old tricks of organizing and fund-raising. By the same token, he argues that its shortcomings lay in its inability to use the Internet as a field tool instead of as an "Internet tool."*

*Exley, the cofounder and president of the New Organizing Institute, coordinated online efforts for the British Labour Party's 2005 reelection campaign and was director of online organizing and communications at Kerry-Edwards 2004.*

I learned this terrifying fact in 2003 and 2004 (and not just from the Dean campaign): The world's richest and most powerful country chooses its leader through a competition of enterprises that are slapped together chaotically, are disastrously managed, and are not shaped or guided one bit by the men or women they are supposed to represent. These campaigns are driven by a ragtag fellowship of half-impoverished, half-crazy people whom a friend of mine refers to as "the carnies." The candidates just get pushed along haplessly, as if on the crest of a huge violent wave—not like surfers, but maybe like runaway surfboards. The winner is the first one to wash up on shore.

The typical carnies are not idealists. In general, they are climbers. But they have the redeeming quality of climbing not for money or power, but rather for good stories to tell each other at the bar on future campaigns. (However, they also have the unredeeming quality of climbing for—of all things—closeness to important politicians.) They live for the adrenaline rush of campaigns. These carnies, along with their spiritual soulmates—the bitter, cynical, burned-out journalists—are the people who determine the leader of our country.

Every four years, the cream of the carnie crop go to work for whichever candidate seems most likely to win. In early 2003, Kerry was the undisputed front-runner, and so they went to him. Carnies one rung down in the pecking order, or who had strong personal ties to particular politicians, went to Edwards, Lieberman, and Gephardt.

In early 2003, Leno and Letterman were still making jokes about "this little guy from Vermont." So Governor Dean's campaign kind of got the ragtaggest of the ragtag carnies. But this was why I loved the Dean campaign from the start: It was the hungry underdog campaign even before the governor became a grassroots hero. There was no arrogant swagger among the staff as there was at the top campaigns.

When the idea of Dean as a movement candidate began to percolate, suddenly other people besides carnies started showing up at the campaign headquarters. They were just getting into cars and driving to Burlington uninvited and more or less forcing themselves on the campaign.

These folks were the antithesis of the campaign carnie culture. They were not climbers (not yet anyway!) and they were not in politics just for cheap thrills. They just *really* wanted to take back their country.

When these movement-inspired people started showing up, the campaign didn't quite know what to do with them. Though they had no campaign experience, they were not wide-eyed and green college students. They had work experience and life experience. They were not obsessed with the press. They wanted to mobilize people. And they *actually* believed in the candidate! Several of them saw the Internet as a fantastic new organizing opportunity and threw themselves into the Internet department—or, rather, the Internet closet.

Months earlier, I had actually come close to crashing the Dean campaign myself. After the 2002 Democratic election losses, I was inspired by Dean when I saw him on TV saying, "We don't win if we don't fight." I had been playing around with political organizing on the web for a few years since leaving my post-college career as a union organizer. One project, a parody site called GWBush.com, had earned me the title "garbage man" from President Bush and given me a small base of activists to experiment with. For example, in 2000 I had organized flash-mob protests in more than 100 cities around the election crisis—an experience that convinced me that a huge change in political organizing was on the way. I called the headquarters and asked if I could help with Internet strategy. I was told, as it turns out by a high school volunteer, that it was all taken care of. But he said he'd pass my name along to someone.

No one called. And then, just days later, I wound up meeting Wes Boyd and Joan Blades from Moveon and soon signed on as organizing director and the newest addition to Moveon's then-five-person staff.

Moveon was an amazing apprenticeship that allowed me to stop playing around haphazardly and be part of a disciplined team that was making amazing things happen. The Moveon team was practicing and developing online organizing, communication, and fund-raising as art and discipline. Things I couldn't make possible with my pathetic programming skills were now easy thanks to Moveon's technology partner, a boutique company called We Also Walk Dogs. Things I had done with my "base" of 20,000 or so readers/customers/curious people were nothing compared to what was possible with Moveon's base at the time of 600,000—supporters who had joined Moveon through Internet petitions. Best of all was simply being able to learn management skills from Wes, who had been a very successful software entrepreneur through the 1980s and 1990s.

I met Joe Trippi in March 2003, after seeing him on a panel talking about "giving away control of the campaign to activists," using Meetup.com as an example. I told him about the way Moveon used homemade tools to allow activists to organize events at venues and times of their own choosing, and how using our own tools allowed activists to do more both on their own as well as hand in hand with the campaign. He asked me to come to Burlington as soon as possible.

When I first visited Burlington in early April 2003, the people I found in the Internet cave, all about to make history, were true idealists: Bobby Clark, Matt Gross, and Zephyr Teachout. (Very soon, they'd be joined by several others who shaped the Internet campaign too, but that was after my brief visit to the campaign.)

In early May, I took a two-week leave from my job as Moveon's organizing director to share ideas and experiences from Moveon with the campaign. Trippi asked me to come to work on the tools we'd discussed in March and to share best practices from Moveon. To avoid playing favorites before asking Moveon members whom they supported, I called other leading campaigns as well with an offer to share Moveon's experiences and tools. But none of the carnies called me back.

My stay began right as the campaign moved into its larger and final headquarters. I met Nicco Mele, who had just started at the campaign and who brought a fantastic energy to the department. The Meetups had become a press story, heightening the profile of the Internet department. And Trippi, who had personal experience with online communities, had become the new campaign manager. The Internet team came out of the closet and now sat right outside Trippi's office (the exact opposite office geography of other 2004 campaigns—and most 2008 campaigns too—which tended to put the Internet as far away from the manager's office as possible).

The process of presidential campaigning is chaotic and unhinged, but it produces campaign managers who are staid and risk-averse. Not Trippi. Why did the Dean campaign, through the Internet, spur an unprecedented movement? It's because Trippi was willing to take risks, to try things that were crazy. And not just ideas on the margin—he was willing to stake the entire campaign on a new crazy way of going about things, and did that several times.

But it wouldn't have accomplished anything if there had not been a method to his madness: Trippi, and the folks in the Internet department, cared about one thing above everything else. They cared about their base, their supporters: about making a sincere, powerful connection with them, mobilizing them, giving them the tools to connect with each other and grow the movement even in unpredictable ways. It wasn't something Trippi thought would be nice to do. It wasn't something he told his Internet department to go do. It was literally the only thing he thought about.

In those early days, Trippi spent just about all of his time behind his computer, staring at messages that members of the base were writing on blogs (even tiny, personal blogs), on discussion forums, and in e-mails coming into the campaign. These messages, and the sentiments behind them, were all he seemed to know existed. (Yes, of course, that single-minded obsession was a detriment to every other piece of the campaign, including even reliable execution of the Internet program. But the mistake was not the obsession with the base, but rather a lack of similar obsessions with other important pieces of the campaign.)

The Internet staff was just as driven. They had no idea what would best serve and mobilize the base—no one did back then, and we still hardly do. But every week they poured their hearts into eighteen-hour days of trying things out. Most of what they did—and most of what I recommended they do in the short time I was up there—was either wrong or executed too poorly to work because of staffing or technical limitations. But every now and then, they hit the nail on the head. Or, more often, something would hit *them* on the head—something that supporters were picking up and using themselves: Meetup, blogging, incredible responsiveness to the e-mail list. When they saw something taking off like that, they pounced and fed it with everything they had. This same obsession with the base is exactly what fuels Moveon's nonstop growth. I didn't know it yet, but this base obsession is the single hardest thing to re-create in other organizations and campaigns.

The story of constant trial, mostly error, is the story of every campaign. What made the Dean campaign different was that all that trial-and-error passion was poured into the goal of winning over and exciting the base. The tangible results were a massive number of people taking action of *some kind,* and an online fund-raising breakthrough that convinced the press that Dean would be the next nominee.

It is true that the campaign failed to achieve the great potential of using the Internet to turn all the excitement into actual votes in early primary states. Later, journalists and carnies cynically said, "All that Internet mania: It got them nothing!" But you can't blame the Internet team for failing to persuade and turn out voters in primary states. They achieved the impossible by creating a real grassroots movement around a presidential campaign. Not only did they give the Dean campaign all the money and bodies it needed to win (if they had been used better by the rest of the campaign), but they also laid the groundwork for the eventual Democratic nominee to raise more than $100 million online and for a huge chunk of his field operation. The Dean Internet team, for all its chaos, was the first *ever* to do anything like that. Is it really fair to have expected them to do more, including save parts of the campaign in which they had no say?

During the time I was in the office, I tried to focus the team on e-mail as a source of strength for the campaign. Often, Trippi would write something amazing, post it to the blog, and no one would think to send it to the list. There was this idea that people should be able to come check out the blog if they wanted to, and that we shouldn't bother them if they didn't visit on their own. Eventually, the good stuff started going out in e-mail form as well. And that meaningful communication was able to support some fund-raising. When a little bit of money started coming in, the campaign suddenly took e-mail seriously on an entirely different level.

Also, I worked with We Also Walk Dogs to install a meeting tool for the campaign.[1] That tool was not meant to take people away from Meetup, but simply to allow supporters to hold events at times and in venues of their choosing. Very quickly, more events were being planned with the Get Local meeting tool than with Meetup. com. However, Meetup was still very important because communities had grown up around the site, and the Dean numbers on Meetup were independently verifiable by journalists in a way that the numbers from the internal tool were not.

My two weeks in Burlington were incredibly exciting. Part of me really wanted to stay. At that time there was room for as many mad Internet scientists as wanted to play. But like all political campaigns, it was an emotional minefield of complex and demanding office politics. I wasn't ready to operate in that environment. Before Moveon, I had been working independently for three years. I had been making political satire sites, building tools, and throwing (cultural) bombs on my own with no account-ability, no boss, no coworkers, and, most importantly, *no meetings*. At Moveon, it was hard enough for me to just have a boss again and get along with my four coworkers on weekly conference calls. I knew I was not ready to plunge into the madness and drama of a campaign office.

Campaigns are won in critical moments, when things are executed either perfectly or in innovative, barrier-breaking ways. Because of the press orientation of campaigns, those moments are usually media moments. However, the moment the Dean campaign catapulted to front-runner status was not a press moment. It was a *movement* moment that took place on the Internet and that galvanized the Dean base in an incredibly dramatic turn. Other contributors have told the story of "the bat." So I'll go light on description and heavy on analysis.

At the end of the second FEC reporting quarter, the Dean campaign faced a pre-dicament that any other campaign, with its monomaniacal press focus, would not have been able to solve. Thanks largely to Stephanie Schriock, Larry Biddle, and others in finance, Dean was close behind the two big money leaders: Kerry and Edwards. The grapevine had those two at around five million. Dean was somewhere around four million. This was already fairly good news for Dean, but not good enough. He had little going for him at this stage of the campaign. The press was ready to write him off, and after the FEC numbers came out, the consensus would be that Dean had put up a surprisingly good little fight in the early primary, but then fizzled out. Senators Kerry and Edwards would be left to battle it out.

Around FEC deadlines, campaigns have always had one, and only one, course of action available to influence events: Get on the phone, talk to reporters, manage expectations for your number, and try to weave a story in the media about how your number, whatever it was, showed something good. One hard-and-fast rule was that you never revealed your number until it became public a couple of weeks after the FEC filing deadline. If you revealed your number, all the other campaigns could disparage it and manage expectations for their own numbers in relation to yours. Releasing your number right before the deadline would be suicide.

I think it was about a week before the deadline when Joe called me at home. This was about a month after my stay at the campaign. He described the predicament. I think he knew exactly what he had to do, but he just needed some assurance that it could actually work. I explained the power that Moveon found over and over in fund-raising to its e-mail list with a goal and a progress meter. If Dean could pull off the miracle of raising another $4 million for a total of $8 million, then he would instantly be the front-runner—and it would also be an incredibly exciting story for the media to focus on and pump up. The combination of mass e-mails to Dean's list and a progress bar, with a little help from the blogs, could do it.

I encouraged Joe to set the goal at $8 million, to put a progress bar on the website, and to send out repeated appeals to the base through e-mail as well as blogs (e-mail was always Joe's orphan child). I pushed him hard with the argument that the base would go all the way to $8 million. The reason it would work is that he would be giving the base a simple button to push to make the impossible happen: to make Dean the front-runner. The e-mail and blog posts would explain the opportunity. And the contribution page was the button to push to make it happen. The progress bar would show people when the goal was accomplished and spur them on to keep pressing that button and even getting their friends involved.

This was an obvious idea, and I'm sure others in the campaign were pushing it too. However, it took huge courage for Joe to make this unconventional move. Moveon does this kind of goal-setting campaign all the time. But there is little risk associated with failure there. In Joe's case, if the base did not come out in support strongly enough, then he might lose the campaign in one fell swoop. He must have been getting some pretty strong arguments against it from the inside.

The next morning there was a mass e-mail from Trippi in my inbox: He had done it. I was amazed. He announced where the campaign was financially (cautiously underreporting the actual number), explained where the other candidates probably were, and then he asked the base to make a miracle happen.

Trippi didn't set the goal at the full $8 million, but at some much more quickly achievable level. I thought this was a mistake; I thought he should have just gone all the way. I didn't think people would respond as strongly if they weren't guaranteed to put Dean far ahead of the pack and make him the front-runner. But I was wrong—people sunk their teeth right into Trippi's smaller goal, and then the campaign set a new goal right away, and another, and another—all the way to just about $8 million by the midnight deadline.

It's important to stop and make note of something interesting here. In this fantastic moment, Joe did not outsource these big decisions to "Internet people." He knew his base better than I did, and so he didn't take my advice about the $8 million goal. His understanding came partly from his obsession with reading all the supporter messages and watching everything they did (in the same way that press-obsessed campaign managers have eight TVs in front of them at all times). But Joe's superior intuition about the goal came also from his decades of experience as a campaigner. He wasn't treating the Internet as a mysterious realm where none of his experience applied, but rather as a new realm populated by the same old political activists he had always known. This is something no other campaign manager has ever done. (But I'm writing this before 2008 has fully gotten under way, so we'll see what happens there.)

Nicco and Larry's famous bat was the brilliant progress meter for this FEC deadline campaign. Simple touches of creativity like that were among the amazing things about the Dean campaign that I wished we could have replicated more at Moveon. Though the basic dynamic didn't rely on the fun progress bar, it nevertheless changed everything about the moment. And who knows, maybe the whole thing wouldn't have worked without that stroke of fun. It also took a disciplined campaign of repeated e-mail appeals from Burlington, sometimes three in a day, to keep the momentum going. And it took thousands of individuals on the blogs cheering the whole thing along every minute.

In the days running up to the deadline, excitement built among Dean supporters who could see with their own eyes, every minute of each day, this amazing impossibility becoming reality. The insurgent, the underdog, the progressive, the antiwar contrarian—was actually winning the "money primary." The grassroots, with their $25 contributions, were actually beating the large donor machines that were supporting the other candidates. Before our eyes, the Internet was proving itself as a tool that we could wield to actually beat the establishment *at their own game*. It seemed too good to be true, but the proof was right there in the bat.

People got so swept up in making this bit of history that they gave over and over, and they pulled in their friends and family.

The staff at the other campaigns were glued to their computer screens. I later heard that on that last day, all screens at the Kerry and other campaigns were set to the bat, with the staff just hitting Refresh, Refresh, Refresh, watching the total rise. The cream of the carnie crop, their swagger and arrogance stripping away, just couldn't believe or understand what was happening to them.

The excitement was so enticing that even Carol Moseley Braun's finance director donated, apparently forgetting that her name was going to appear in the FEC report in two weeks. (She was fired and went to work for the Dean campaign.)

When you think about it, that fund-raising episode was remarkably similar to the classic Jerry Lewis telethon. It had all the same elements: Viewers could track progress any time of the day; there were forces cheering everyone along with great enthusiasm; and the participants had a feeling of collective action as they worked together yet apart toward a common goal.

In other words: The Legend of the Bat is not the product of the minds of "Internet people" but of people who understood old-fashioned organizing and fund-raising techniques and who applied tried and tested wisdom to a new medium in an innovative way. Those running campaigns in the present would do well to remember that.

Unfortunately, grassroots activity was not driven as hard in the e-mails. Why? Not for lack of desire by the Internet team. But this terrible thing happens with all e-mail lists on campaigns: The staff is acutely and accurately aware of how much money the e-mail list is raising—simply because it all goes into a single number in a bank account that must be reported to the FEC down to the very cent. However, grassroots activity tends not to get reported back as tangibly—especially when the tools that drive it are not in-house. And therefore every time the campaign faces a choice between sending an e-mail driving fund-raising and one driving activism, fund-raising almost always wins out because you can see the result in real dollars, whereas you often have no way of knowing whether anyone is responding to an activism ask. The solution here is to make sure that the campaign is getting numeric feedback on how many activists are responding to e-mails by taking action, and how many voters they're reaching.

But another problem prevents greater use of the Internet for on-the-ground organizing. The online tools that would let activists do effective campaign work on their own are only beginning to be developed. On the Dean campaign, thousands of people were mobilized to go to Iowa as volunteers. But the tools to put them to work were slapped together with Scotch tape and Elmer's. A hastily constructed contribution page will still take contributions. But it's much more difficult to build a web tool to accept a contribution of time effectively. There was an incredible amount of exciting self-organizing on the part of Dean volunteers, but absent structure and tools from the campaign, much of that work—as exciting as it was—didn't turn out votes.

To really unlock the full power of the grassroots, the same spirit that led to the Dean bat needs to be applied to organizing tools: Experienced field organizers need to personally figure out how this new medium can serve them. As long as the task is outsourced to "Internet people," we're just going to get one new MySpace knockoff after another, no matter how many times they fail.

## Note

1. http://www.wawd.com.

# 17

# After New Hampshire

## Kelly Nuxoll

*Kelly Nuxoll wrote the first draft of this essay in March 2004.*

After New Hampshire, supporters sent flowers. "Don't give up," said the notes wedged in plastic stalks; or, "We're still with you." They were unbelievably depressing. Walking in the front door of the office was like walking into a funeral parlor. Everything smelled like roses. Down the hallways, the TVs were silent (who wanted to see poll numbers or listen to John Kerry, the new antiwar candidate?), and staffers sat in front of their computers with their earphones on. Their screens flashed video games, Google searches, résumés.

"My friends keep asking me what the office is like," said Doug Sloane, one of the field staffers. I ran into him at a coffee shop downtown on a Thursday morning. He was reading a book, and I was on my way to get my hair cut. "I tell them, the office is like seventy workaholics with nothing to do."

The fund-raisers certainly couldn't be making phone calls; the field staff had no resources for their states; schedulers were reluctant to plan ahead. Zephyr and Nicco put together a radio show, repurposing the field director's office as a sound studio, but even that effort—which had gone up with the kind of alacrity I had not seen in the office for weeks—seemed nostalgic. I tuned in to it one evening in bed, the room dark except for the green glow of the computer screen. It was like listening to a serial populated by old, beloved characters: Nicco, plowing ahead with a voice so deep and kind it seemed a parody of a radio deejay's; Zephyr's fast and lithe as a hummingbird. I grinned through almost the whole show, amused at the absurdity of hearing my friends' voices in the privacy of my bedroom, until the whole thing became too poignant and I had to shut it off.

The life had gone out of the office on the day after New Hampshire, when the governor had called us into the conference room and announced, without any preamble, "Here's the thing: We're out of money." Almost no one had reacted, even though the temperature in the conference room, already roasting with the heat of a hundred and fifty bodies, ratcheted up to a broil. The governor described the parameters of the problem—we had put everything in Iowa and New Hampshire, hoping to blow everyone else out of the race (it was a good strategy; it just happened to have worked for our opponent), and now we had almost nothing left. As he spoke, he let his hands dangle at his sides, not folding them defensively across his chest or shoving them in his pockets. Although we would be getting a new CEO, there would be no changes, he said, no staff cuts. As for paying us, well, he knew we had all made tremendous sacrifices to be there, and if we couldn't afford to volunteer our time, he understood and thanked us for all we'd done. He spoke quickly and precisely, as if he were squeezing off rounds. At the end of the announcement, Zephyr said, "Governor, I've worked for you for almost eight years, and I've never wanted you to be president more than at this moment." The room burst into applause.

Only later, after Trippi pushed into the middle of the throng and told us, red-eyed, that working for the campaign had been the greatest privilege of his life and we could come to him for anything, absolutely anything, did it dawn on me that changes had in fact been made, people had been cut, and by not paying us the governor had not been firing bullets but handing each of us a gun, leaving us to determine the time and method of our own suicide.

For a little while, there was a burst of enthusiasm. The Meetup guys, seized by a spirit of glasnost, tore down their cube walls and pushed their desks together so the entire north side of the office was at last as open and interactive as the web team had been. Zephyr called for a meeting of anyone who worked with the grassroots and was committed to addressing their needs; a dozen people showed up and made a to-do list so long we agreed to meet every day at 9:00 A.M. to tackle it, thereby not only responding to the grassroots' concerns but giving ourselves a reason to come in every morning. Roy Neel, the new CEO, flyered the halls with posters announcing all-staff meetings, during which he congratulated everyone on their efforts and described the latest strategy—which amounted to hanging in there until we either won or lost. But after March 2, and then March 4, and then March 7, morale crumbled, and the office restructuring, with its haphazard desks and palimpsests of meeting notices, looked less like a renaissance and more like a ruin.

Jim Moore, one of the web team advisers, drove up from Boston to check things out and declared himself impressed with Roy Neel. "He's not a bad guy," Jim said over dinner. It was the first time we'd left the office early enough to find a restaurant in Burlington that was still open.

"Apparently, he was very trusted on the Gore campaign. He was so trusted—" Jim took a big bite of salmon. "—Gore trusted him so much that he asked Roy to plan his father's *funeral*." Jim had hardly finished the word when he realized the implication of what he was saying: Roy Neel, hired to oversee Phase Two of the campaign, specialized in burials.

The wakes began the night Trippi left, at an Irish pub downtown. Staff stood around awkwardly, gripping pints of beer and staring at the person who would soon be leaving. It was strange to think of one of our own reuniting with the rest of the world, like the shuttle had just called and said it was on its way to the space station to pick him up. Where would he live, what would he do, who would he know? We asked him questions until the alcohol kicked in and curiosity dissipated. Outside the snow kept falling, but around the bar everyone seemed remarkably warm and beautiful, haloed in a shimmering, amber light.

The remaining staff began getting together even when no one was leaving. They cooked, went to the movies, did two-hour workouts at the gym. The weather turned balmy, up to 20 degrees. A few people went cross-country skiing. The night before the must-win Wisconsin primary I had dinner with my roommate, then I went into my bedroom, crawled under my desk, pulled out four months of unopened bills, and began to redeem my credit record. We had wanted to take back our country, but now, with the whole thing on the skids, the best we could do was take back our bodies, our families, our lives.

If some people had not been able to imagine a Howard Dean presidency, the True Believers had envisioned it so completely they could now no longer imagine it might not be true. When I called Patty-in-Vermont—who had not only posted regularly on the blog but run the listserv for Dean Leaders, canvassed in Iowa, and dragged her two young sons to every Dean event in the tristate area—to tell her that the governor was withdrawing, she said brightly, "I know. I'm already on my way to the Sheraton. But he's not really withdrawing, right? He's just suspending the campaign."

"No," I said. "He's withdrawing."

Patty was silent on the other end of the phone. "I have to go," she said finally. I could hear the sob in the back of her throat. "I think I need to cry."

The press loved the tears. They cruised around the ballroom after Dean's withdrawal speech and snapped photographs of supporters in meltdown. For many of them, our zeal had been the story of the Dean campaign. I'd seen the word "Deaniac" as early as spring 2003; apparently, Karl Rove used it after he had been walking through a Dean rally near the capitol, grabbed a sign, lifted it above his head, and hollered his lungs out along with the rest of the crowd, presumably gleeful at the prospect of running against a candidate who spoke for a lot of crazy people.

In the cover story of the *New York Times Magazine* on December 7, 2003, Samantha Shapiro created an impression of Dean supporters as lonely, lovelorn people who had found their way to the campaign like drunks staggering down the church stairs into an AA meeting and there finding community, purpose, and solace. Around the time the article came out, my boyfriend and I split up, and a few days later he sent me an e-mail saying, "The worst part is, unlike every other man in America whose girlfriend has broken up with him, I can't go work for the Dean campaign."

Even if the slant of some of their stories was skewed, for once the media was right—that supporters gave their hearts *should* be the story of the Dean campaign. Competing in an election you helped build feels very different from casting a ballot and hoping for the best; it's something else again when you work alongside a lot of other people, all of you grunting and sweating as you throw your shoulders against the wheel. I imagined the night of November 2 when Tom Brokaw telephoned the states for their election results, only when he said "Maine," I knew that Maine meant field directors Melanie and David, and "Virginia" meant my new friends Don and Jennifer and Julie, and "Washington" meant the team of Betty and Bill and Ellen and Laura and Christy, and in this daydream I didn't exhale, literally breathless while I waited to see what color the map would turn. But this is one of the risks of participatory democracy: People will start to care.

Back at the office, after Dean's withdrawal announcement, department heads passed around sign-out forms, and IT set up folding tables where we were to turn in our equipment. Staff and volunteers staggered around like zombies. When we ran into someone we'd even tangentially worked with, we hugged and then wordlessly walked on. Phones kept ringing with supporters who wanted to make sure everyone was okay. I looked at the map of the United States pinned behind my computer and mentally walked east to west, thinking of all the people around the country to whom I needed to break the news.

About 5:00 P.M., Nicco called a meeting of the web team. It's a testament to Nicco's generosity that he kept adding more and more names to the web team listserv until it encompassed people from every department; about twenty-two of us tromped into the large conference room. Nicco told us all how great we were, how we had promising careers ahead of us, that we should collect unemployment for a while and go on vacation somewhere sunny. He started to work out some logistics but Zephyr interrupted him. She had something to say, she said, but it might take a while.

"I have to stand on a chair." She bounced onto the seat like she'd been released from a spring. Her mouth was grinning—top and bottom teeth—but her eyes were wet. "Kenn." She looked at the ceiling and took a deep breath. "Kenn, you built the most beautiful database I've ever seen."

Around the table, we all nodded. It had been a spectacular database.

"Zack," Zephyr choked. "The code for Deanspace. I mean, you created Deanspace. Deanspace is the key to everything." She had to whisper the last part. Zack dropped his head in his hands.

Zephyr turned to the next person—then the next and the next, describing his or her contribution to the campaign. Everyone stayed until she had finished.

If you've ever thought you'd like to hear your own eulogy, I can't say I recommend it. The attention is uncomfortable, like your birthday only worse, and it's distressing to hear your whole contribution distilled to a few sentences, without any of the nuances that made you rage and celebrate while you were experiencing them; however, there is something satisfying about clearing away all the details and holding up only the essential part that remains. Then you can feel amazed and even a little gratified. You can look at it from a distance and think, hey, really, we did *that*?

# III
# Reflections

# 18

# From Media Politics to Networked Politics

## The Internet and the Political Process

### Araba Sey and Manuel Castells

#### The Internet and Democracy: Utopias and Dystopias

Never in history has democracy been more pervasive throughout the world. Yet, available evidence points to a growing, widespread crisis of legitimacy of governments, parliaments, political parties, and politicians in most countries, including the United States and Western Europe.[1] Because the Internet is seen as the ultimate technology of freedom, its diffusion among citizens has been hailed as a potential savior for the political ills of representation and participation. At the same time, critics have sounded an alert on the dangers of electronic democracy, not the least being the potential fragmentation of citizenship and the capture of public attention by elites and demagogues.[2]

A symbolic manifestation of both utopian and dystopian views is apparent in the work of one of the world's leading political theorists, Benjamin Barber. In 1984, in his pioneering essay "Strong Democracy," he foresaw the possibility of using new information and communication technologies to energize citizen information and political participation. Fourteen years later, having observed the actual practice of democracy under the new technological paradigm, Barber himself called attention to the deteriorating quality of public debate and democratic decision making in the biased space of the new media.[3] In principle, both of his arguments are plausible and not contradictory. The Internet can, indeed, be an appropriate platform for informed, interactive politics, stimulating political participation and opening up possible avenues for enlarging decision making beyond the closed doors of political institutions. On the other hand, any technology—and this is particularly true of the Internet—is shaped by its uses and its users. The actual influence of the Internet on politics, and on the quality of democracy, has to be established by observation, not proclaimed as fate.

This chapter investigates the emerging interaction among people, democracy, and the process of political representation in the new form of networked public space constituted by the Internet. By illustrating the democratic potential of a particular pattern of interplay among political organizations, political messages, technologies of freedom, and an electorate that wants to increase its autonomy, the Dean campaign provides a striking example of how genuine network politics can transform the political process. Although Dean ultimately lost the nomination, this does not negate the power of his campaign. Our focus is not on the effectiveness of the campaign in winning the election, but on its success in stimulating political engagement and creating a campaign that was exceptionally democratic at its core.

We already know a number of things about democracy in a networked society, most of which played out in Dean's campaign. First, we know that the Internet is a powerful tool of autonomous political expression outside the formal political system.[4] Thus, grassroots groups from all ideologies find in the Internet their medium of communication of choice, and social movements and collective action are greatly enhanced in their capacity to influence society and government by using computer networks.[5] Second, the well-crafted research conducted by Bruce Bimber[6] on the impact of the use of the Internet on political behavior shows that there is no significant effect of increasing political engagement in formal politics, such as voting, although there is a positive correlation with donations of money to political candidates. Bimber does show a positive association between use of the Internet and level of political participation, but this is explained by other variables, primarily education. Third, we know that there is a positive correlation between exposure to the media and political participation,[7] and that the use of the Internet for political information adds to this media effect instead of substituting for it.[8] Fourth, the futuristic schemes of e-democracy and Internet voting have been discarded, in America and elsewhere, by several blue-ribbon panels, which have shown the dubious constitutionality and blatant social discrimination implicit in the procedure.[9]

However, we know much less about the actual effect of the Internet on the transformation of the formal political process. Does the Internet play a role in changing the process of political campaigns, and in creating new forms of political debate, political choice, political representation, and political decision making? Bimber argues that the effects of the Internet are more significant on the structure of the process of representation than on individual behavior. The most important effect may be the fact that "the flow of information is central to political structure and political behavior. Not only is information a tool and resource used by political actors in a strategic or psychological sense, its characteristics and qualities help define political actors themselves."[10] In other words, by changing the direction and the content of the flow of information through the use of the Internet, the range of political actors is broadened, new avenues of collective mobilization may appear, and a different format of debate may take place, transforming the political scene that had been framed by the one-way communication systems of the mass media era. The accounts in this volume demonstrate that this is what the Dean campaign did, with dramatic results.

## Traditional Uses of the Internet in the Political Process

Well into the twenty-first century, the Internet is no longer an exotic political medium. Yet there has been little real change in the structure and conduct of formal politics. Most online political campaigns have focused more on the provision of the candidate's position on issues and less on other types of participation.[11] Even then, Internet users are often unable to find the kind of political information they want, such as comparative information, explanation of voting records, and campaign finance.[12] Available information may be superficial,[13] nonanalytical,[14] or not user-friendly.[15] For example, less than a third of UK political sites examined by Ward and colleagues[16] had interactive capabilities, and during the 2002 U.S. elections, Internet portals such as Yahoo!, AOL, and MSN provided more tools for analysis and interaction than campaign sites did.[17] Where politicians have tried to interact with Internet users, the openness of such forums is questionable.[18] Internet users, in turn, have been more energized by websites offering political humor than by those of official campaigns.[19] Studies of online political campaigns in the United States and the United Kingdom conclude that most campaigns use the Internet as an "electronic brochure."[20] Widespread acceptance of the Internet as a tool for political campaigns and programs has not translated into a more open and participatory political process.

## The Political Limits of Internet-Based Politics

Why has widespread acceptance of the Internet as a tool for political campaigns not translated into a more open and participatory political process? In the past, there has been a general distrust of public engagement in politics. Increasing use of direct political methods, such as protest politics, direct balloting, and opinion polling, has not erased concerns about the limits of direct democracy. It is not surprising, then, that politicians have been skeptical, apprehensive, and/or ambivalent about the democratic capabilities of the Internet, which could take direct politics to its extreme. Politicians recognize the usefulness of the Internet, but fear that involving the public that deeply in the political processes will consume too much time and erode representative democracy.

It is not unusual for old models of political communication to linger while politicians get used to emerging methods.[21] However, the successful use of the medium by a few politicians, as well as the incorporation of Internet components into most political campaign operations, suggests that there are other, deep-rooted reasons for the current patterns of use.

The questions of what Internet politics really is and how it works remain vexing ones for politicians. There is a great deal of uncertainty about which models of political communication are most effective on the web. For now, the dominant model is one that perceives Internet politics as dealing mainly with the acquisition of information and financial resources. This is in line with the dominant political paradigm (managerial model of state/citizen interaction), which prioritizes efficiency of internal organizational activities and linear provision of information to citizens, in contrast to models that prioritize consultation or participation.[22] Consultative and participative models of politics require some loosening of control over the political apparatus. "Control of the message in a campaign is as much an obsession as is money and candidates fear this loss of control," which is likely to happen in an open Internet campaign.[23] Not only can Internet users exchange information that may not be "on message," but both supporters and opponents also have the capacity (thanks to hypertext and other Internet capabilities) to produce new messages using campaign information without approval from the official campaign, what Foot and Schneider call "unilateral coproduction."[24] Furthermore, politicians anticipate "burdensome exchange among candidates, campaign staffs, and citizens, which would entail … losing the ability to remain ambiguous in policy positions."[25] This is where the problem lies—how to find a model of Internet politics that captures the strengths of the medium, while retaining control and organizational precision in the hands of politicians. Consequently, political institutions lean toward developing only those aspects of Internet campaigning that are less subject to unwanted manipulation and input from users.

In this context bureaucratic politics will tend to use the Internet as a billboard for one-way communication. Cynicism and individualism from disaffected individuals will translate into the use of the Internet to deride politicians and call for insurgent expressions of alternative political values. Alternatively, an active citizenry may find in the Internet a medium of communication to bypass the filters of mass media and party machines and to network itself, asserting its collective autonomy. Dean's campaign chose to tap into the latter community.

In sum, if the added value of the Internet is its interactivity and its potential for autonomous communication, a political system predicated on the control of messages and the gatekeeping of access to institutions of representation and governance is unlikely to use the medium to its fullest potential. On the other hand, the more a political process is based on the building of citizens' autonomy, the more the Internet may play a role as an enhancing medium of political mobilization and influence. This does not, however, inoculate the process from the tensions, uncertainties, and general messiness inherent in such an experiment, as the accounts in this volume clearly demonstrate.

## The Internet as a Medium of Political Autonomy

The Internet potentially offers two levels of autonomy to the online electorate. First, users can access more campaign information outside of the mass media. The percentage of the U.S. public getting information online because they consider that other media do not provide enough information increased from 29 percent in 2000 to 45 percent in 2002 (see Table 18.1). This suggests that people turn to the Internet for political information when they are dissatisfied with traditional media content. Analysis of U.S. election data also indicates that people who use the Internet for political purposes are more likely to be skeptical of media information, and may be more independent and self-reliant.[26] Second, the Internet enables users to communicate without interven-

Table 18.1 Internet Use for Political Purposes in the United States, 1998–2002

| Internet Use | 1998 (%) | 2000 (%) | 2002 (%) |
|---|---|---|---|
| For election news | | | |
|     Internet users | 15 | 33 | 22 |
|     General public | 6 | 18 | 13 |
| Reasons for going online for election news | | | |
|     Information more convenient | – | 56 | |
|     Not enough information from | – | 29 | 57 |
|         other media | 24 | 6 | 43 |
|     News sources reflect personal | | | 8 |
|         interests | | | |
| Research candidates' position on issues | – | 69 | 79 |
| Research candidates' voting record | 30 | 33 | 45 |
| Participate in online polls | 26 | 35 | 39 |
| Join discussion/chat groups | 13 | 8 | 10 |
| Contribute money to candidate | – | 5 | 5 |
| Visit political websites | – | 19 | 32 |

*Source*: Pew Research Center for the People and the Press, "Modest Increase in Internet Use for Campaign 2002," *Pew Internet and American Life Project* (2003), available at www.pewinternet.org.

tion by politicians, thus providing channels of action for people disenchanted with traditional politics but desiring some political activity.[27]

Although some critics have warned of the tendency for citizen participation to excessively quicken the political process,[28] evidence from various initiatives suggests that citizens can make careful choices under the right conditions. Experiments in some parts of Europe and Asia show that citizens can not only engage in policy discourse with politicians but also deliberate on complex issues and make difficult trade-offs.[29]

Internet politics, however, is not for everyone. The different types of political engagement that citizens want contribute to the shape of politics on- and offline. Some people prefer strong hierarchical links with the formal organizations of the political system.[30] Such people may not be interested in the more horizontal aspects of Internet politics. Conversely, people who want autonomous political activity may turn to the Internet because it facilitates autonomous participation. However, whether this will influence formal politics or foster alternative politics depends on the willingness of politicians to give citizens full access to the political infrastructure. Perhaps the most distinctive characteristic of the Dean campaign is that it was willing to do just that.[31]

In sum, it is not that the Internet makes people want autonomy. It is that people searching for autonomy turn to the Internet as their medium of choice. If the political system is based on subordination to the party structure, the Internet becomes simply a billboard to post messages and process requests. If citizens are either disaffected from politics or find themselves searching for autonomy within an unresponsive political system, then the Internet is used by political activists without directly aiming at the process of political representation. It is only under the conditions of an autonomous citizenship and an open, participatory, formal political channel that the Internet may innovate the practice of politics.

## The Dean Model of Internet Politics?

Dean's campaign capitalized on the three strengths of Internet communication—information dissemination, mobilization, and interactivity—using these singly and in combination, as described throughout this volume, to shape an effective strategy. The result was a powerful, low-cost, person-to-person recruitment force that brought thousands of zealous people to the Dean campaign. This was not simply an outcome of using the Internet: It grew out of a strategic convergence of an open campaign philosophy, political issues, political Internet users, and the Internet itself. That is, a segment of the electorate, who happen to be active Internet users, found Dean's message appealing; and, because the campaign was open to letting them participate in new ways, it found a loyal following that could communicate and organize itself using the Internet as a tool.

As a nontraditional but effective way to achieve speedy political visibility, use of the Internet was not unique to the Dean campaign. However, other candidates were generally unable to achieve similar results either because they used it in fairly traditional ways or because they did not demonstrate the same commitment to using the medium in a truly democratic manner. Wesley Clark, for example, used online mobilization and fund-raising tools similar to Dean's. However, in direct contrast to Dean's campaign, the Clark campaign gradually dismantled unofficial structures once the official campaign was in place. While Dean supporters were given free rein to participate in the campaign to the extent of involving them in critical decision making, such as whether or not to receive federal funding, this level of commitment to direct politics was not evident in competing campaigns.

## Notes

1. Manuel Castells, *The Power of Identity*, 2nd ed. (Oxford: Blackwell, 2004), ch. 6.

2. D. M. Anderson and M. Cornfield, eds., *The Civic Web: Online Politics and Democratic Values* (Lanham, MD: Rowman and Littlefield, 2003).

3. Benjamin Barber, "The New Telecommunications Technology: Endless Frontier or End of Democracy?" in Roger G. Noll and Monroe Price, eds., *Communications Cornucopia* (Washington, DC: Brookings Institution, 1998), pp. 72–98.

4. Barry Hague and Brian Loader, eds., *Digital Democracy: Discourse and Decision Making in the Information Age* (London: Routledge, 1999); P. Norris, *Digital Divide: Civic Engagement, Information Poverty, and the Internet Worldwide* (Cambridge: Cambridge University Press, 2001).

5. J. S. Juris, "Networked Social Movements: Global Movements for Global Justice," in M. Castells, ed., *The Network Society: A Cross-Cultural Perspective* (Northampton, MA: Edward Elgar, 2004), pp. 341–362.

6. Bruce Bimber, *Information and American Democracy: Technology in the Evolution of Political Power* (New York: Cambridge University Press, 2003).

7. Pippa Norris, *A Virtuous Circle: Political Communications in Postindustrial Societies* (Cambridge: Cambridge University Press, 2000).

8. Ibid.

9. California Internet Voting Task Force, *A Report on the Feasibility of Internet Voting* (Sacramento: Office of California Secretary of State, 2000); Internet Policy Institute, "Report of the National Workshop on Internet Voting: Issues and Research Agenda" (2001), available at http://news.findlaw.com/hdocs/docs/election2000/nsfe-voterprt.pdf (accessed June 1, 2007).

10. California Internet Voting Task Force, *A Report on the Feasibility of Internet Voting*, p. 231.

11. David M. Anderson, "Cautious Optimism about Online Politics and Citizenship," in Anderson and Cornfield, eds., *The Civic Web*, pp. 19–34; Deborah G. Johnson, "Reflections on Campaign Politics, the Internet, and Ethics," in Anderson and Cornfield, eds., *The Civic Web*, pp. 9–18; Peter Levine, "Online Campaigning and the Public Interest," in Anderson and Cornfield, eds., *The Civic Web*, pp. 47–62; Pew Internet and American Life Project and Institute for Politics, Democracy, and the Internet, "Untuned Keyboards: Online Campaigners, Citizens, and Portals in the 2002 Elections" (2003), available at www.pewinternet.org (accessed June 1, 2007); S. J. Ward, R. K. Gibson, and W. Lusoli, "Online Participation and Mobilization in Britain: Hype, Hope, and Reality," *Parliamentary Affairs* 56 (2003): 652–668; P. Norris, "Revolution, What Revolution? The Internet and U.S. Elections, 1992–2000," in E. C. Kamarck and J. S. Nye, Jr., eds., *Governance.com: Democracy in the Information Age* (Washington, DC: Brookings Institution, 2002), pp. 59–80.

12. Graeme Browning, *Electronic Democracy: Using the Internet to Transform American Politics*, 2nd ed. (Medford, NJ: CyberAge Books, 2001); Pew Internet and American Life Project et al., "Untuned Keyboards."

13. Levine, "Online Campaigning and the Public Interest," pp. 47–62.

14. D. R. Wolfensberger, "Congress and the Internet: Democracy's Uncertain Link," in L. D. Simon, J. Corrales, and D. R. Wolfensberger, eds., *Democracy and the Internet: Allies or Adversaries?* (Washington, DC: Woodrow Wilson Center Press, 2002), pp. 67–102.

15. S. Coleman, "Westminster in the Information Age," *Parliamentary Affairs* 52 (1999): 371–387.

16. Ward, Gibson, and Lusoli, "Online Participation and Mobilization in Britain."

17. Pew Internet and American Life Project et al., "Untuned Keyboards."

18. R. K. Gibson, S. J. Ward, and W. Lusoli, "The Internet and Political Campaigning: The New Medium Comes of Age," *Representation* 39, no. 3 (2003): 166–180, available at www.esri.salford.ac.uk (accessed October 31, 2003).

19. S. Coleman, "The 2001 Election Online and the Future of E-Politics," in S. Coleman, ed., *2001, Cyber Space Odyssey: The Internet in the UK Election* (2001), available at www.hansardsociety.org.uk (accessed October 31, 2003); Pew Internet and American Life Project et al., "Untuned Keyboards."

20. E. C. Kamarck, "Political Campaigning on the Internet: Business as Usual?" in Kamarck and Nye, eds., *Governance.com*, p. 89.

21. Kamarck, "Political Campaigning on the Internet"; J. E. Katz and R. E. Rice, *Social Consequences of Internet Use: Access, Involvement, and Interaction* (Cambridge, MA: Massachusetts Institute of Technology Press, 2002).

22. A. Chadwick and C. May, "Interaction between States and Citizens in the Age of the Internet: 'E-Government' in the United States, Britain, and the European Union," *Governance:*

*An International Journal of Policy, Administration and Institutions* 16, no. 2 (2003): 271–300; Coleman, "The 2001 Election Online and the Future of E-Politics."

23.  Kamarck, "Political Campaigning on the Internet," p. 98.

24.  K. A. Foot and S. M. Schneider, "Online Action in Campaign 2000: An Exploratory Analysis of the U.S. Political Websphere," *Journal of Broadcasting and Electronic Media* 46, no. 2 (2002): 222.

25.  J. Stromer-Galley, "Online Interaction and Why Candidates Avoid It," *Journal of Communication* 50, no. 4 (2000): 112.

26.  Bimber, *Information and American Democracy.*

27.  S. Coleman and N. Hall, "Spinning on the Web: E-Campaigning and Beyond," in S. Coleman ed., *2001: Cyber Space Odyssey: The Internet in the UK Election* (2001), www.hansardsociety.org.uk (accessed October 31, 2003).

28.  For example, Y. Levin, "Politics after the Internet," *Public Interest* 149 (Fall 2002): 80.

29.  Y. Ishikawa, "Calls for Deliberative Democracy in Japan," *Rhetoric and Politics* 5, no. 2 (2002): 331–345; "Power to the People (Political Effects of the Internet)," *Economist* 366 (January 25, 2003): 8303.

30.  R. K. Gibson and S. J. Ward, "Participation, Political Organisations, and the Impact of the Internet," ESRC end of award report L215252036. Salford: ESRI (2003), available at http://www.esri.salford.ac.uk/ESRCResearchproject/papers/IPOP_final_report.pdf (accessed June 1, 2007).

31.  For example, Michel, this volume, and Teachout, this volume.

# 19

# The Legacies of Dean's Internet Campaign

## *Zephyr Teachout and Thomas Streeter*

The Dean campaign enabled the nearly instantaneous development of a new political structure, with over 1,000 chapters nationwide. Most of those chapters had local structures and governance mechanisms. Thousands of people engaged in the campaign in a creative way, by developing a slogan, a song, a poster, or a new way of gathering signatures and sharing information. Dean raised more money online than any candidate had to that point, from hundreds of thousands of small donors who had not previously been major players in primary politics. While not the sole cause, Dean's use of the Internet was critical in catapulting him into a leading role in the presidential primary, such that forty-six out of fifty pundits quizzed in December 2003 predicted that he would be the nominee.[1] The campaign overthrew the common wisdom about fund-raising that had dominated American politics for at least a generation. The campaign also confirmed, as William Greider has put it, "the existence of an energetic, informed dissent within the husk of the Democratic Party."[2]

Although candidates had used the Internet before—to greater and lesser effect—it had never before played such a critical role in the ascent of a major-party candidate in a closely watched presidential race. While it was happening, there was a consensus among those in the blogosphere, those who were supporters of Dean attending Meetups, and those in the mainstream media that this was a historic moment in electoral campaigning. The language of paradigm changing and revolutionizing politics was deeply felt by those who witnessed the campaign and those who lived it. Many went much further and claimed this was a historic moment for the future of democracy. The Dean campaign was not only a watershed moment, it was experienced as a watershed moment while it was happening; the message of transformation was itself part of the transformation.

In a broader sense the Dean campaign embodied a moment of prolific creativity in forms of political action, in a context where campaigning had become a formulaic affair. Many innovations have since become routine, such as Internet fund-raising via Moveon-styled e-mails, house parties, and the use of e-mail and web-based techniques to build databases of supporters. Others are still more talked about than imitated, such as the decentralization of the campaign and its openness to spontaneous action and decision making from the outside. Some of the innovations are less recognized, such as the shift from organizing college students to the broader focus on youth represented by Generation Dean, the efforts to use cell phones as well as the Internet, or the efforts to make social action a part of the campaign through Dean Corps. Most importantly, there is now a new generation of activists on the American political scene, who learned from both the successes and failures of the Dean campaign, and who are eager to experiment further.

Although the nature of the campaign's legacy is not yet entirely clear, in this chapter we lay out some things that we know were changed by the campaign, and suggest some struggles that we predict will be fought over the next dozens of years because of the impact of the Internet and the particular way it entered campaign life in 2003. We argue that there is a tension in the future of the Internet's role in electoral politics, contained even in the hopes of those who believe that the Internet is fundamentally democratizing: a tension between purely strategic uses—to win an election by any means—and uses of the Internet aimed at cultivating a more democratic society.

## The Direct Legacy: A New Generation of Activists

In coming years, Dean-inspired politicians will have substantial political power in the United States. The historical legacy of the campaign is often spoken about in indirect terms: It showed what was possible; it opened the doors to technology. But the direct legacy of those who were involved is also a critical part of the story. A nontrivial number of the people who commented on blogs, attended events, and suggested strategies were fundamentally reoriented by these experiences. The campaign was open to genuine voice, distributed political authority, and strategic ideas from the edges, so that people experienced being taken seriously and having impact.

Hundreds of thousands of people who had never previously been engaged in politics became authors and found a political voice and political authority. Pam Paul, Aldon Hynes, and Josh Koenig are both extraordinary and representative: Before 2003, they had not imagined themselves as political actors and political strategists, but their interaction with the campaign led them to understand themselves and their role in American electoral politics differently. Even Amanda Michel, Michael Silberman, Nicco Mele, and Bobby Clark—who, though political novices, entered as paid campaign professionals—were transformed by their experiences, and speak about democracy in a language that is unlikely to have come from any of them five or six years ago.

The direct legacy of the 650,000 people who were on the Dean e-mail list, the over 1,000 people who led local Meetups, the over 1,000 people who managed listservs on local and constituency topics, and the people who collectively organized over 3,000 events a month for several months in late 2003 should not be underestimated.

More than 100 communities created their own postcampaign political organizations—or active chapters of national groups—that comment on policy, send out press releases, endorse candidates, and perform public service. Many of these are incorporated nonprofits with strong structure and funding. Latinos for Texas, for example—a Texas group with thousands of members and over 25 events a year—is managed by Mario Champion, a technology educator who involved himself in politics because of the Dean campaign.[3] Ben Stanfield, the founder of the Draft Obama website, which organized thousands of people to attend events in New Hampshire, Maryland, and around the country in an effort to jump-start Obama's grassroots efforts, became politically active through Dean Meetups.

The strategic habits of the Dean campaign will also be felt directly, as Internet staffers become Internet directors and strategists; as of this writing, members of the Dean Internet team were running parts of the Internet operations for Edwards and Obama. Dozens of Dean alumni are regular and powerful voices on major blogs. As Jerome Armstrong points out in his chapter, the early, unofficial Dean blog was something of a farm team for major liberal bloggers, including Ezra Klein, Matt Singer, Annatopia, and himself.[4]

Thirty-five hundred out-of-state Dean supporters drove, flew, or bussed to Iowa to knock on doors in the Iowa caucuses. The 3,500 people who comprised the storm may have been disappointed that the "Dean Storm" did not end up tipping the Iowa voters to favor Dean, but that experience reoriented them to their own sense of themselves as political actors. Many have remained involved in political life, and many have grown into leadership roles. The Dean campaign created a new generation of individuals who think of themselves seriously as active citizens.

A month after the campaign ended, 110 Dean alumni had committed to running for local or federal office—that number is probably now in the 1,000-candidate range. After Dean dropped out of the race, he repeatedly exhorted people to run for office, and his campaign resources were put into an organization, Democracy for America, that is dedicated to training and supporting people who run for office at any level. In 20 years, hundreds of these Dean-inspired candidates will be in leadership in state houses, and dozens in Congress. These new politicians are politically diverse, but they tend to share an opposition to the Iraq War, a belief in public health care, and a political experience in which innovation is deeply tied to political meaning. That blending, in the imagination, of politics with innovation and edge-based creativity will doubtless affect American political life in the future in ways we do not now know.

These directly inspired people will also tend to bring with them particular ideas about technology and the role of technology in politics. There was an overrepresentation—compared to the population at large—of people in the Dean campaign who brought with them some technical ability, and this blending is likely to pop up in odd places. Mario Champion is not unique—a significant number of Dean leaders have some technological expertise, comfort with technology, or belief in technology that they will bring with them as they enter public life. The next generation of Dean-inspired candidates will use the Internet for numerous purposes, including agenda setting, problem identifying, and problem solving. Dean alumnus Andrew Raseij ran for New York City public advocate and created a tool enabling anyone to send in a picture of a pothole to be aggregated on a map on his website as an example of open involvement in government via the Internet.

The direct legacy will also show itself in the particular democratic faith shown by Dean supporters. Although the language of "bottom-up" politics has long been alive in progressive community organizing circles, the experience of all-volunteer offline organizing will continue to be a reference point for anyone who experienced Dean Meetups. For some, it is already a memory that invokes the hassles of democratic life (how difficult volunteers can be; how talkers take over meetings). But for many, it will be a memory of competence—how relative strangers worked together to plan functioning events and make decisions. By the most conservative estimates, over 200,000 people attended at least one volunteer-run meeting, and 50,000 people went to at least three Meetups. Each of those 50,000 people actively engaged in an entirely volunteer-run local organization, and tens of thousands of them played some leadership role—as a volunteer press assistant for the Louisville group, or on the outreach committee of Red River Valley for Dean. They experienced the headaches of loud venues and long-winded volunteers, and they experienced largely effective groups who received local press coverage, organized local outreach and evaluated the results, signed people up to vote, and ran community service events without any paid campaign presence. They heard strangers speaking clearly with their own political voices, and discussed political ideas beyond horse-race strategy and first impressions. They heard points of view and methods of analysis that they disagreed with and couldn't understand, and ideas that they thought were profound—and all these interactions improved their own political thinking. In short, they learned that people are capable, at least in some circumstances, of governing themselves.

In this way, the campaign reenergized the belief in the viability—and desirability—of democratic decentralized politics in a serious way, where groups of citizens play a central role as actors, not consumers. Although all the writers of this volume may have considered democratic theory previously, the fact of the campaign forced them to engage in democratic practice and turned many of them into believers in the possibility of competent, citizen-run government.

## Technological Innovations

Some tools and tactics derived from Joe Trippi's Internet strategy are now considered essential to all serious presidential campaigns, and all unveil technological innovations with fanfare. The basic tool suite of the Dean campaign is now almost essential to any presidential campaign. Most campaigns have variations of staff-driven blogs, on which staff regularly update readers, encourage supporters, and ask for feedback. Not only did the Dean campaign spawn candidate blogs, but the particular model used by the Dean campaign, where staffers—not the candidate—provide the primary voice, has become the standard.

Fund-raising house parties, which were innovated largely by David Salie, were imitated and developed by George Bush and John Kerry in the 2004 general election, each of whom planned massive, national, simultaneous house parties in which people raised lower-dollar funds with their friends and shared a phone call or video link with the candidate. In the 2008 election, house parties were already being used in early 2007 by a few candidates for fund-raising, and will presumably be used by all eventually. The TeamRaiser tool described by Bobby Clark in his chapter is also now popular; this tool allows individuals to be credited for money they raise from their friends by tracking online fund-raising efforts on a designated web page. (A supporter sends out an e-mail fund-raising solicitation with an embedded code, so if the person donates in direct response to that solicitation, the code allows him or her to be credited.)

Versions of Get Local, the public event-planning tool described in Exley's and Teachout's chapters, are being used in most of the 2008 presidential campaigns. The Get Local tool enables any supporter to plan an event on the candidates' site, and allows other supporters to easily find events by zip code. Many campaigns now have versions of the social networking Deanlink also described in Teachout's chapter, and almost all campaigns encourage supporters to join their candidates' group on social networking tools such as Facebook and MySpace. The e-mail group–forming capacity of Yahoo! that the Dean campaign depended upon is now being integrated into at least a few candidate sites.

All of these tools, especially used together, can be seen as structural tools that change the role of a supporter in a campaign. They allow a supporter to plan events, make suggestions laterally to other supporters, and raise money, receiving credit for it.

Nonstructural tools, such as the capacity to make a personalized, downloadable poster, are also popular with many campaigns. Curiously, the semi-failures of Dean's effort—Dean TV and Wireless for Dean—appear to be at the heart of the 2008 presidential candidates' new efforts at innovation. All are extensively using YouTube to share their own messages and experimenting, some more gingerly than others, with encouraging their supporters to create their own videos.

One of the most successful innovations of the Dean campaign was the development and use of a massive e-mail list, patterned upon the e-mail list built by Moveon.org. All the 2008 presidential candidates are focused intensively on e-mail list building, and, while attempting to carve their own way, many are using the same e-mail structure developed by Moveon and imitated by the Dean campaign: paragraph, link, paragraph, link, with a clear ask and a personal signature.

The indirect legacy is also revealed in a new culture of innovation in campaigns. Joe Trippi trained the Dean staff to be constantly looking for electoral applications for technological innovations in the non-electoral sphere; the post-Dean campaign generation of political staffs are trained to be constantly alert to new tools and ideas. Alongside YouTube, wikis and online games are also surely going to be a part of most or all new campaigns.

## Interactivity and Rhetoric

The technology, bringing profound changes in the ways in which ideas and stories are shared, created a new set of rhetorical and personal contexts in which people experienced political thought and speech. Although we cannot possibly discuss all the effects, a few of these changes are worth mentioning—most importantly, the effect of political learning happening in a place that was both privately accessible and intensely interactive.

Much of the information about Dean was embedded in or around interactive forums: Dean's California speech was found by Josh Koenig on the Daily Kos blog, and links to Dean policy positions were often found on forums like Democratic Underground. Once the Dean campaign started using a blog with comments, even the directly shared broadcast information was a click away from a page with a rich, ongoing debate. As the campaign grew, nearly all its functions included some form of interaction. Even if casual readers decided not to speak, their speech was constantly being invited. As anyone who has sat in a classroom and in front of a television knows, there is an enormous difference between listening somewhere where one might speak and somewhere where it is impossible or forbidden. Whereas the second invites a dispassionate analysis of what is being said, the first context often invites thinking about what one might say. It implicitly invites people to play a role in public thought.

Furthermore, much of the political speech that occurred in the early days of the Dean campaign was neither public nor private—it was on a listserv that anyone could join, or a blog that anyone could read, but it was unlikely to be read by many people. Prior to this, most political speech had been either intensely private (with friends or family at dinner) or intensely public (the speech of a lawmaker asking for attention). This liminal speech was new to both the lawmakers and the citizens, demanding a certain level of attention so as to avoid embarrassment, but not the same kind of attention that attends large public events. This kind of political speech was in embryo in 2003, with few people bringing conventions to what was appropriate and inappropriate. Yet since 2003, certain norms and cultural habits (mostly from nonpolitical blogs and forums) have been established, and millions of people are now comfortable with this kind of conversation. Candidates, once constitutionally terrified of semipublic speech on their behalf, let alone on their websites, now cautiously welcome it, following the lead of the Dean campaign.

Furthermore, one of Dean's most important legacies will come from his (and Joe Trippi's) innovation in rhetorical structure. "You have the power"—the phrase itself and the way it was expressed throughout the campaign in myriad ways—was a significant break from the rhetorical structure of past presidential campaigns. It was a new mode of address and a new kind of discourse, combined with a new method of sharing and developing messages to powerful effect. The message structure of "this is about your power" instead of "this is what is good about me" had in 2007 already been imitated by all the serious candidates for the 2008 presidential race (with varying degrees of effectiveness and sincerity).

Finally, the Dean campaign changed the attitude of presidential campaigns toward technological innovation, and toward innovation in general. Although certain orthodoxies were already developing in 2007, for the next few presidential cycles, we can expect an active openness toward innovation, pressed both by campaign managers and candidates and by the press, which will be looking to campaigns to ask them about ways in which they are innovating. Editors will be regularly asking reporters to write about innovation in online campaigning—an assignment that was presumably fairly rare even in the early 2000s, in the middle of the Internet stock bubble.

This is not a trivial change. An attitude of innovation itself can enable all kinds of changes, not merely technological ones. It can change who is promoted politically, and can end up having an affect on attitudes toward the core of politics. It creates an opportunity for people to say and do things outside the orthodoxy, using technological innovation as the justification for introducing new ideas, not just new tools.

## The Effect of List Building on Electoral Culture

The innovations in list building that came from a fusion of Joe Trippi's field background and the lessons of Zack Exley and Eli Pariser of Moveon have already been absorbed and turned into orthodoxies inside progressive and conservative politics. But this is just a beginning. List building will become an increasingly large part of all political campaigns. The best evidence of this may be that Harold Ickes—a very mainstream, powerful, democratic operative—shifted his lifework from media consulting to building major databases.[5]

There are fairly important structural consequences that will flow from the serious adoption of list building as a central part of the electoral enterprise. A focus on list building will, over time, gradually change the basic structure of fund-raising. The skills that have long been important in fund-raisers—the ability to cultivate the super-rich for bundling[6]—will gradually give way to the ability to build high-yield donor lists using e-mail, text-messaging, automatic bank withdrawals, and community creation.

The change will happen more slowly than is rational. (As of this writing, the early evidence showed that 2008 candidates had not significantly changed the way in which they raised money, although they were list building on the side. They still dedicated most of their fund-raising resources to big donors.) It will be more like the long, slow decline of the dominance of the big three American broadcast networks in the face of multichannel television, spread out over decades. It will be slow for a number of reasons. For one, the super-rich are richer than ever, and that much concentrated money will find ways to assert its power, subtly and unsubtly, for many years to come. But also the culture of high-donor fund-raisers is very entrenched in Washington and serves the fund-raisers, who have long been considered the most important people to woo (and who therefore get the biggest campaign salaries). The habits of cultivating them will die hard. The people who are used to needing them will be risk-averse and scared of losing their dependency on a known funding source, and the fund-raisers themselves will be incapable of seeing that their value is diminishing relative to the small-donor, online fund-raisers.

Finally, there is a culture of campaigning that has its own inertia. Candidates undoubtedly take some unspoken comfort in the relative simplicity that major fund-raisers provide—they smoothly outline issues that are important and unimportant, and become human contacts for working out the difficult work of fund-raising. The major donors tend to be highly intelligent, articulate people who largely support the major issues proffered by the candidates. They are, because of their wealth, seen as colleagues more than anything—people who have themselves taken risks and are willing to bet on those risks, and they tend to be neither slavish nor complaining in their interactions, but treat candidates as equals.

The candidates unconsciously translate their attitude into an understanding of large donors as colleagues, and end up using them to bounce ideas off of. Therefore, the general worldview of major donors starts to infuse the worldview of candidates. The donors also have a major effect on second-tier policies. If a candidate has a great interest in three or four issues, and the public has a great interest in the fifth issue, the sixth issue will be quietly owned by sets of donors. You see this now in the Net neutrality debate—most politicians do not consider it an important plank of their platform, do not care about it, and do not believe their constituency cares, so they will quickly support a platform that they might not otherwise support, because they do not have time to fully consider it. So fund-raisers use it as a way to get to donors who recognize their pull in these arenas.

The three-headed monster of fund-raisers, political staff, and communications staff, then, will remain comfortable for all involved, and since in few cases will that comfort be challenged, it will outlast its usefulness.

However, in the long run, we will start to see the ascendance of the list builder over the bundler fund-raiser and, fast on its heels, a real effect on policy issues. If the list builder starts to take over the position of trusted fund-raiser, the metrics from list growth will then start to take the position of major donors (to some degree—the first role of colleague will probably stay with fund-raisers). The list, then, will answer questions six to ten in policy initiatives—instead of the major donor. It seems likely that there will be, over the next decade, a major decline in the importance of trial lawyers and Hollywood donors—both of these depend upon the relative value of a small number of high-level donors over a large number of low-level donors. Even the most cynical use of the Internet, then, could very well shape our foreign policy and copyright directly and radically.

## Uncertain Futures: Will Politics Become More Open?

But what about the less cynical users, the hope that the Internet might empower a more open, more small *d* democratic process? On this we are hopeful, though more hopeful than certain, and it will happen only if one adopts a fairly practical definition of more democracy as simply substantially more citizen involvement in and power over the political system (not as utopia achieved).[7]

The Internet has been part of the resurgence of political involvement more broadly in the twenty-first century.[8] One question for the future is whether that involvement will become increasingly rationalized—consistent, strategically driven—or whether a federalist model like that which emerged, through an almost accidental convergence of personality and technology because of the Dean Meetups, will continue to develop.[9] Although there is no doubt that candidates will be eager to experiment with decentralized action, it remains to be seen whether they will be willing to work with any meaningful degree of decentralized power, and whether candidates who refuse to use decentralized power will be punished for their lack of democratic sensibility. Much of this will be driven by cultural choices that we collectively make, that are impossible to control and nearly impossible to exhort.

Here it is important to distinguish between distributed work and decentralized power. Distributed work will clearly be central to future electoral politics. Candidates will experiment with more complicated Internet-enabled phone-banking matching systems, door-knocking systems, and donor-incentive systems. However, distributed work is not necessarily work in which the *power* is decentralized. The fact that I can send a suggestion to Coke.com or participate in a contest about their next marketing effort does not meaningfully transform my lack of power in the organization into a fact of power. Likewise, the fact that a citizen might sign a petition or engage in a massive distributed literature-dropping effort may show great ingenuity on the part of the designer of that system, and involve new technologies, and enable people to be part of the political process—without giving any person involved any meaningful political power or meaningful way to have strategic input or make creative decisions.

The particular, data-driven capacities of the Internet allow for two opposing tendencies to flourish. On the one hand, the Internet provides many opportunities for creativity, dissidence within a group, and collaboration that were never previously available—and with them, new opportunities for learning the habit of responsibility taking. Data in the hands of many lead to creativity and mashups[10] and unexpected outcomes and iterative strategies—strategies that are constantly being adjusted based on constant feedback. On the other hand, more and more precise data allow for managing experiences very closely, through iterative surveys of experience. The appeal of the perfect political experience draws people from across the political and technological spectrums. The strong political tendency of the past half century is toward the completely mediated experience—shown most humorously in G.W. Bush's "town hall" speeches to people who have been handpicked for their affection for the president.

If we know that 15 percent of people will have bad experiences at local events held around the country, should we not do everything we can to study and perfect these experiences? Or should we instead think of our job as providing an opportunity, and the local groups' job as studying and perfecting the experience? This tension shows up in one reason given for several online groups' reluctance to hold regular events without vetted organizers—they want to ensure that people have productive, enjoyable political experiences, and have concluded that most people do not like unstructured experiences with a high risk of unproductive conversation. Although the Dean campaign regularly confronted similar concerns and attempted to provide support that limited the unproductive Meetups, the chapters in this volume show that staffers tended to think about their task less as ensuring a positive political experience and more as providing people a structure in which they could accrete and exercise power. In the worldview expressed in this approach, bad experiences, unexpected difficulties, and unproductive meetings are all inevitable parts of a democratic society—and a campaign's responsibility is not to avoid these, but to provide venues for local power creation.[11]

Candidates interested in decentralized power may not be the most innovative in the development of new, flashy technologies, but focus more on enabling sophisticated involvement by supporters. For example, instead of using e-mail lists to ask the standard questions, such as "What do you think are the most important issues?" which allow for a pro forma kind of feedback, they will actively recruit supporters to engage in massive research programs on issues.[12]

Those of us who think it crucial to expand democratic involvement in decision making have a dual obligation—to win elections and to cultivate democratic culture and institutions. Sometimes these two goals will doubtless seem coterminous, as they did so dramatically during the height of the Dean campaign. But at other times, they will seem separate. The only thing we can say for certain is that, in the future, this tension will persist. We see no other option than to proceed, with the best mixture of hope and wisdom we can muster, and with an eye on both goals.

## Notes

1. *National Journal,* Democratic Insider's Poll, December 13, 2003. Every week, fifty insiders were asked to rank Democratic presidential candidates. For at least twelve weeks, Dean consistently came in first.

2. William Greider, "Dean's Rough Ride," *Nation* (March 8, 2004).

3. "Politically, Mario was moved to organize and educate by Howard Dean. Dean's courageous honesty about the political process and the deep appeal and power of Progressive Values to improve society meant traveling to Iowa twice, New Mexico, Dallas, Houston, and all over Austin as a grassroots activist," available at http://www.latinosfortexas.com/about.php (accessed June 1, 2007).

4. See chapter 4 of this volume.

5. "Democrat's Data-Mining Stirs an Intraparty Battle," *Washington Post,* March 7, 2006, available at http://www.washingtonpost.com/wp-dyn/content/article/2006/03/07/AR2006030701860.html (accessed June 1, 2007).

6. Bundling is when donations from many individuals are collected by one person and presented to the recipient, therefore maximizing the influence of the individual doing the presenting.

7. There is a tendency among some to speak of grassroots democracy as if it would automatically mean the end of racism or corporate domination of the economy. In fact, more grassroots power in politics, at least over the short and medium terms, would probably mean an increase in some kinds of things we do not like; conservative evangelical Christians, for example, would likely take full advantage of any opening of the political system.

8. Lee Rainie and John Horrigan, "Election 2006 Online," Pew Internet and American Life Project, available at http://www.pewinternet.org/PPF/r/199/report_display.asp (accessed June 1, 2007).

9. A tension also exists between the Internet's capacity to enable us to speak as citizens and its tendency to enable us to speak like strategists. In the first chapter, we discussed the tendency of pundits to express their worldview as "cold hard facts," equating the world they would like to see with the strategy they think candidates should adopt. That language is increasingly used by people blogging or commenting on blogs—the primary political discussion is about strategy, not substance.

10. A *mashup* is a website or application that combines content from more than one source—for example, many people like to combine address lists with Google maps to display addresses in a Google maps mashup.

11. Crudely put, you could say this is about power devolution versus productivity, but actually these visions are quite close. (Those who prefer the monthly meeting model often base their argument upon the faith that many people will trade certainty for the possibility of the unexpected—and those who prefer the planned, structured meeting model will argue that power is more likely to devolve over the long run when people have positive experiences.) The tension between these two emphases is ongoing, and will persist in the presidential campaigns of the future. This tension is related to, but not exactly the same as, the core tension between the responsibility to win campaigns and the responsibility to build civic society.

12. This tension assumes that the campaigns' attitudes matter. It may be, as many hope, that 2008 is the year election strategy slips out of the hands of candidates and their consultants; creative supporters will independently make the best media and start to build the best organizing structures for their candidates.

# Index

# MEDIA and POWER

## David L. Paletz, Series Editor
### Duke University

Paradigm Publishers is proud to announce a new book series that publishes work uniting media studies with studies of power.

In keeping with Paradigm's mission, the series is innovative and original. It features books that challenge, even transcend, conventional disciplinary boundaries, construing both media and power in the broadest possible terms. At the same time, books in the series are designed to fit into several different types of college courses: in political science, public policy, communication, journalism, media, history, film, sociology, anthropology, and cultural studies.

Intended for the scholarly, text, and trade markets, the series should attract authors and inspire and provoke readers. Series editor David L. Paletz is Professor of Political Science and Director of the Film/Video/Digital Program at Duke University, and editor of *Political Communication*. He is known for his research on media and power and his encouragement of original work from others.

## Titles in the Series

*Creative Destruction: Modern Media and the End of the Citizen*, Andrew Calabrese

*The Age of Oprah: The Making of a Cultural Icon for the Neoliberal Era*, Janice Peck

*Art/Museums: International Relations Where You Least Expect It*, Christine Sylvester

*Mousepads, Shoe Leather and Hope: Lessons from the Howard Dean Campaign for the Future of Internet Politics*, Zephyr Teachout and Thomas Streeter, et al.

# About the Editors and Contributors

**Zephyr Teachout** is Visiting Assistant Professor of Law at Duke Law School, where she is researching law and political corruption. She was the Director of Online Organizing for Howard Dean's campaign, the National Director of the Sunlight Foundation, the Executive Director of the Fair Trial Initiative, and a consultant for several new media companies. In 2005–2006 she was a Fellow at the Harvard Law School Berkman Center for Internet and Society. She received her law degree summa cum laude from Duke Law School and holds a master's degree in political science from Duke University and a bachelor's degree in English from Yale University.

**Thomas Streeter** is Associate Professor at the University of Vermont, where he teaches about and studies the Internet and media. His *Selling the Air* (University of Chicago Press 1996) won the McGannon Award for Social and Ethical Relevance in Communication Policy Research. Other publications include "The Moment of Wired" (*Critical Inquiry*) and "The Romantic Self and the Politics of Internet Commercialization" (*Cultural Studies*). He has taught at the University of Wisconsin and the University of Southern California, and in 2000–2001 was a member of the School of Social Science at the Institute for Advanced Study in Princeton, New Jersey.

**Howard Dean** is Chair of the Democratic National Committee in Washington, D.C.

**Jerome Armstrong** is a political consultant and contributor to MyDD and other political blogs.

**Bobby Clark** is progressive Internet strategist and Deputy Director of ProgressNowAction and ProgressNow.org in Colorado.

**Aldon Hynes** is a campaign technology and social media consultant in Connecticut.

**Mathew Gross** currently provides online strategic guidance to a number of nonprofits and political campaigns in South Carolina.

**Michael Silberman** is Cofounder and President of EchoDitto, an Internet strategy and online community building consultancy.

**Pam Paul** is a student and a progressive activist working at the state, county, and precinct levels of the Oklahoma Democratic Party.

**Amanda Michel** is Director of the Off the Bus project, a new media collaboration between the *Huffington Post* and NewAssignment.Net and lives in New York.

**Larry Biddle** is principal of PlanningWorks, helping citizen-sector organizations develop interactive technology strategies.

**Nicco Mele** is Cofounder and Chair of EchoDitto, an Internet strategy and online community building consultancy.

**Kelly Nuxoll** is a freelance writer and an advocate for civic education.

**Josh Koenig** is a founding partner in Chapter Three LLC, a consulting firm in San Francisco.

**Zack Exley** is Cofounder and President of the New Organizing Institute and a vice president at OMP, a Washington, D.C.-based communications and fundraising firm.

**Araba Sey** is a doctoral candidate at the Annenberg School for Communication, University of Southern California.

**Manuel Castells** holds the Wallis Annenberg Chair in Communication Technology and Society at the University of Southern Califormia.